FAITH
to FAITH

Chawkat
Moucarry

FAITH
to FAITH
Christianity & Islam
in dialogue

ivp

Inter-Varsity Press

INTER-VARSITY PRESS
38 De Montfort Street, Leicester LE1 7GP, England
Email: ivp@uccf.org.uk
World Wide Web: www.ivpbooks.com

First published 2001

British Library Cataloguing in Publication Data
A catalogue record for this book is available from the British Library.

ISBN 0–85111–899–2

Set in Garamond
Typeset by Avocet Typeset, Brill, Aylesbury, Bucks
Printed and bound in Great Britain by Creative Print and Design
(Wales), Ebbw Vale

Inter-Varsity Press is the book-publishing division of the Universities and Colleges Christian Fellowship (formerly the Inter-Varsity Fellowship), a student movement linking Christian Unions in universities and colleges throughout Great Britain, and a member movement of the International Fellowship of Evangelical Students. For more information about local and national activities write to UCCF, 38 De Montfort Street, Leicester LE1 7GP, email us at email@uccf.org.uk, or visit the UCCF website at www.uccf.org.uk.

Contents

I dedicate this book to my good friends
Jamil Chabouh
and
Hassan Janbakli

Acknowledgments

I am most grateful to my friend and former student Richard Margetts for his invaluable contribution to the editing of this book. The whole manuscript came under his sharp scrutiny. His pertinent questions made me clarify my thoughts at several points. He made a number of incisive comments that have greatly helped to improve the original typescript.

My heartfelt thanks go to Mrs Sheila Brown for her assistance at a time when my English was not so fluent. My appreciation is also due to Mrs Christine King for her help in reading the manuscript and correcting my English at a later stage.

I would also like to express my gratitude to the staff and students of All Nations Christian College. Over the last few years, Martin Brown, Bernie Mascher and others, who have a keen interest in Christian–Muslim dialogue, have given me an ongoing opportunity to reflect afresh on the issues I deal with in this book.

Finally, it would be unfair not to mention my wife, Hanne-Lis, and our four children. In writing this book, as in everything else, I am much indebted to their loving support.

All Nations Christian College   *Chawkat Moucarry*

Abbreviations

Qur'anic references

Quotations from the Qur'an are based on 'Abdullah Yusuf 'Ali, *The Holy Qur'an: Translation and Commentary*, and Kenneth Cragg, *Readings in the Qur'an*, but the final translation is often my own. References appear in parenthesis with sura (chapter) and verse numbers: for example, (4:147) refers to sura 4 verse 147. Note that in some suras (e.g. sura 5) the verse numbering differs slightly in different translations.

Hadith references

References to the Hadith are based on the original text, which is in Arabic. In the case of Bukhari, Muslim, Abu Dawud and Ibn Majah, they include the English translation (e.g. Bukhari, *ṣawm* 13:III, p. 75, no. 137 [1780] refers to the compilation of the Hadith made by Bukhari, *Ṣaḥīḥ*, the book about fasting, *ṣawm*, ch. 13). In the Arabic–English edition of Bukhari's compilation, this hadith is found in volume 3, page 75, number 137. The figure in square brackets [1780] is the number of the hadith according to the CD version of the *Encyclopaedia of the Hadith* (see bibliography). Note that the chapters in this encyclopaedia are classified with a numbering system that occasionally varies from the usual one. The compilation done by Muslim has a different numbering system altogether.

Biblical references

Quotations from the Bible are taken from the New International Version (NIV) unless indicated otherwise. 'GNB' indicates the Good News Bible. References appear in parenthesis with book, chapter and verse: for example, (Rom. 6:23) refers to Romans chapter 6 verse 23.

Old Testament books

Gen.	Genesis	Song	Song of Songs
Exod.	Exodus	Is.	Isaiah
Lev.	Leviticus	Jer.	Jeremiah
Num.	Numbers	Lam.	Lamentations
Deut.	Deuteronomy	Ezek.	Ezekiel
Josh.	Joshua	Dan.	Daniel
Judg.	Judges	Hos.	Hosea
Ruth	Ruth	Joel	Joel
1, 2 Sam.	1, 2 Samuel	Amos	Amos
1, 2 Kgs.	1, 2 Kings	Obad.	Obadiah
1, 2 Chr.	1, 2 Chronicles	Jonah	Jonah
Ezra	Ezra	Mic.	Micah
Neh.	Nehemiah	Nah.	Nahum
Est.	Esther	Hab.	Habakkuk
Job	Job	Zeph.	Zephaniah
Ps(s).	Psalm(s)	Hag.	Haggai
Prov.	Proverb(s)	Zech.	Zechariah
Eccles.	Ecclesiastes	Mal.	Malachi

New Testament books

Matt.	Matthew	1, 2 Thess.	1, 2 Thessalonians
Mark	Mark	1, 2 Tim.	1, 2 Timothy
Luke	Luke	Titus	Titus
John	John	Philem.	Philemon
Acts	Acts	Heb.	Hebrews
Rom.	Romans	Jas.	James
1, 2 Cor.	1, 2 Corinthians	1, 2 Pet.	1, 2 Peter
Gal.	Galatians	1, 2, 3 John	1, 2, 3 John
Eph.	Ephesians	Jude	Jude
Phil.	Philippians	Rev.	Revelation
Col.	Colossians		

Dates

When dates appear on their own, they refer to the Christian calendar (AD or CE). When dates appear after the name of a Muslim scholar, both the Islamic (AH) and Christian (AD) dates are given and refer to the year of his death: for example, Razi (606/1209). The Islamic calendar begins in AD 622, the date of the *hijrah* 'migration', when Muhammad left the city of Mecca for Medina.

Transliteration of Arabic words

ا	*a*	ض	*ḍ*
ب	*b*	ط	*ṭ*
ت	*t*	ظ	*ẓ*
ث	*th*	ع	'
ج	*j*	غ	*gh*
ح	*ḥ*	ف	*f*
خ	*kh*	ق	*q*
د	*d*	ك	*k*
ذ	*dh*	ل	*l*
ر	*r*	م	*m*
ز	*z*	ن	*n*
س	*s*	ـه	*h*
ش	*sh*	و	*w*
ص	*ṣ*	ي	*y*
		ء	'

This simplified system does not take into account the difference between short and long vowels. However, the reader familiar with Arabic will easily identify the Arabic words. Those words that have become part of English (e.g. Hadith) have kept their usual spelling. The Prophet's name is spelt 'Muhammad', whereas the slightly different spelling 'Muḥammad' is used for other Muslims who have the same name (e.g. Muḥammad 'Abduh).

Introduction:
From mutual ignorance
to genuine dialogue

This book attempts to examine the claims of Christianity and Islam. Such cross-examination has always been my preoccupation, both in Syria, my home country, and abroad. As a Christian living in a predominantly Muslim society I wanted to know more about Islam, the *other* religion; and as an Arab I felt the need to know more about the *other* Arabs. Neither my 'Arab-ness' nor my Christian faith was in question; what I was seeking, I suppose, was to build bridges between the Christian and Muslim communities.

Although Christians and Muslims have been living together for hundreds of years, they have always had a ghetto mentality, especially with regard to their faiths. Mutual ignorance, some would argue, was the price of trouble-free coexistence, and for Christians, perhaps, the price of survival. This compromise proved quite unacceptable to the teenager I was at that time. The first real opportunity to challenge it came when I moved to high school. When I asked the Islamic education teacher if I could attend his class he was puzzled at my request: Christians and Muslims had separate classes for religious education. Having checked that I really meant what I said, he agreed. Through open, sometimes heated, but friendly discussions, I realized that Muslims are equally keen to know more about Christianity. These discussions were not confined to the classroom. Gradually, a number of my Muslim peers became close friends. Some had never been to a Christian home before and they too were pleased to invite a Christian to their home for the first time.

Leaving my home country and coming to Europe (first to France and then to Britain) did not diminish my commitment to Christian–Muslim relations. This commitment, I must add, stems from my understanding of the Christian faith. Because of my Arab and Christian background I found myself in a privileged position. I had no problem in identifying with people, especially Muslims, who, like me, do not live in their own country. At the same time, I was an active member of the Christian community. However, it is not very comfortable to be in a situation where one does not really feel at home on either side. I suspect that this perception is mutual. Thus some Christians, I am quite sure, will find my approach to Islam too conciliatory, possibly compromising and coloured too much by my Arab origins. Far from denying the influence of my background on my thinking, I take this as a balancing factor: my Christian reflection is not purely academic; it is rooted in my human experience with Muslims. The Muslim reader would be right to point out that, being written by a Christian, this study is not entirely neutral or impartial. But the question is: does absolute impartiality exist anyway? Christians and Muslims, indeed people of any faith, can hardly be completely neutral when dealing with faith issues. Those involved in inter-religious dialogue do, however, need to be respectful, and willing to learn and to be challenged; they should be fair when dealing with the teaching of other religions.

A right attitude

The Qur'an teaches Muslims the importance of fairness when dealing with non-Muslims. They should call people to God 'with wisdom and good exhortation' (16:125). This approach especially applies to Muslims when they debate with 'the People of the Book', that is, Jews and Christians. Muslims stand on the same ground as Jews and Christians, says the Qur'an, for we all believe in the same God:

> Do not argue with the People of the Book but *in the best possible way*, except in the case of those among them who have been unjust.
> Say: "We believe in what has been sent down to us and sent down to you. Our God and your God is One, and we are surrendered to Him [lit. 'we are Muslims to Him']". (29:46; cf. 3:64; my emphasis)

Thus the Qur'an urges Muslims to have a right attitude in debating with Jews and Christians; otherwise they should refrain. This attitude is referred to with the words *bi-llati hiya aḥsan*, 'in the best possible way', a very general expression. It includes having good relationships with people, and dealing courteously and gently with them. It also means adopting a right approach: recognizing that, prior to God's revelation to Muslims via the Prophet Muhammad, God had revealed himself to Jews and Christians in the Bible. As a result of these revelations, Jews, Christians and Muslims believe in God who is one and the same God. Thus we have in the above Qur'anic text a pressing call to Muslims to engage in a genuine and truthful debate with Jews and Christians. The only note of caution relates to those who in one way or another have acted wrongly towards Muslims. It is doubtful whether debating with hostile people could be helpful or fruitful. Having said that, the Qur'an does not completely rule out the possibility of turning an enemy into a friend by adopting a positive attitude towards him or her: '[The results of] goodness and wrongdoing are not the same. Repel [evil] *in the best possible way*. As a result your enemy will become like a close friend' (41:34; my emphasis).

The teaching of Jesus contains no specific recommendations on debating with people of other faiths. However, what Jesus says about how to relate to people in general has special relevance: 'So in everything, do to others what you would have them do to you, for this sums up the Law and the Prophets' (Matt. 7:12). This command implies that Christians should have a fair attitude to Islam and Muslims. In practical terms, it means not comparing the ideals of Christianity with the reality of Islam, radical Muslims with moderate Christians, or mainstream Christianity with Islamic sects. This is not as easy as it sounds. In order to minimize the risks of an unfair comparison between Christianity and Islam I have deliberately based my study of these religions on their respective Scriptures, rather than on the often disappointing reality of the Christian and Muslim communities. Scriptures, however, need interpreting and have been interpreted in more than one way. I have tried to present the teaching of the Bible as it has been understood by mainstream Christians, more specifically evangelical Christians. Similarly, I have tried to present the Qur'anic message as it is understood by Muslims themselves, more specifically Sunni Muslims.[1]

I have relied heavily on Razi's exegesis of the Qur'an for two main reasons. First, Razi (606/1209) is a prestigious representative of the Muslim community whose authority in Qur'anic exegesis is unanimously acknowledged. Second, Razi's *al-Tafsir al-kabir*, 'The Great Commentary', is an outstanding, comprehensive and stimulating commentary on the Qur'an.[2] Many times I have noticed that contemporary Muslim writers draw largely on this commentary, often without giving credit to the author. It is a commentary characterized by erudition, intellectual rigour and spiritual insight. Many of the issues Razi had to consider eight hundred years ago are the same as those we need to consider today.

Sunni Islam is based on both the Qur'an and the Hadith (i.e. the teaching and the life of the Prophet), which is why I have extensively used the Hadith, the Prophetic Tradition, whose importance is often underestimated in Western approaches to Islam.

The Qur'anic call is for Muslims to avoid antagonistic debate with Christians. But this does not mean that Muslims should refrain from criticizing Christian beliefs and practices, or from calling Christians to accept the message brought by the Prophet Muhammad. Quite the opposite: Islam is a missionary religion and Islamic mission, *da'wah*, includes Jews and Christians just as much as anybody else (cf. 3:20). The missionary dimension of Islam is based on its claim that the Qur'an is God's revelation for everyone (25:1; 38:87) and that Muhammad is the last Prophet (33:40), sent by God not just to Arabs but to all peoples (21:107). Muhammad's mission marked a new era in which Islam is announced as the only religion acceptable to God (3:19, 85). Therefore, it is not so much the principle of mission that is at stake as the way of carrying it out. Muslims are God's witnesses (2:143; 22:78; 33:45): it is part of their mission to debate with Jews and Christians, and they should do it 'in the best possible way'. Seen from this perspective, it is quite legitimate for Muslims to do their best to persuade Jews and Christians with the hope that they will convert to Islam. The Qur'an, however, emphatically states that it is God who converts people by revealing the truth to them (cf. 7:43; 13:31; 28:56). Therefore, no-one should be forced to convert to Islam: 'Let there be no compulsion in religion' (2:256). This should be especially true with regard to Jews and Christians, who have a special status in Islam as two monotheistic communities, each based on divine revelation.

Christianity makes claims that are equivalent to Islamic claims regarding the fullness of God's revelation, its universal destination and the unique role of Jesus Christ. Jesus Christ is God's final messenger and the one who brought God's revelation to completion (Matt. 21:33–39; Heb. 1:1–2). The gospel is the 'good news' about God's love for the whole world (John 3:16); therefore everyone should hear its message. Christians have been appointed by Jesus as his witnesses and commissioned to share the good news with every nation (Matt. 28:19–20; Acts 1:8). Jesus claimed to be *the* way to God (John 14:6), and is proclaimed as the only

Saviour of humankind (Acts 4:12). Thus Christians find themselves in a position parallel to that of Muslims: debating with Muslims is part of their mission. Anyone who has deep convictions, whether religious or secular, will try to substantiate their convictions and persuade others. Christian–Muslim dialogue is no exception. The distinctive characteristic of Christian apologetics is the way it is carried out. Christians are urged to present their case eagerly and humbly: 'Always be prepared to give an answer to everyone who asks you to give the reason for the hope that you have. But do this with gentleness and respect ...' (1 Pet. 3:15).

A genuine dialogue

While sharing a common faith in one God, Christians and Muslims have come to share the responsibility of discrediting that faith in the eyes of the world at large. The conflicts in which the two communities have faced each other are many. They have contributed to the growing scepticism of many people regarding the relevance, and indeed the usefulness, of any religion. It is also true that debates between Christians and Muslims have often turned into polemics in which one side tries to ridicule, attack and even defeat the other. For these reasons many have come to believe that Christians and Muslims should no longer engage in theological debates. Instead they should opt for mere dialogue. In Western countries, many promoters of Christian–Muslim dialogue, especially Christians, perceive this dialogue as an attempt to exchange information without any effort to argue for a position. One cannot but share their desire to encourage Christians and Muslims to know each other better and to have new relationships based on trust and mutual appreciation of their respective traditions. This is not, however, what genuine dialogue is all about. Is it possible for Christians and Muslims, who truly believe in the claims of their respective Scriptures, to rule out any apologetics in their dialogue? While conversion is neither the immediate nor the only aim of dialogue, it must, nevertheless, be accepted as a possible outcome. On what grounds could one exclude the possibility that new information might lead to the adoption of a new position and possibly to conversion? Would that not amount to denying a basic human right? Is there no fundamental difference between Christianity and Islam on which it would be worth taking up a position? Or do we presume that Christians and Muslims will never be able to engage in a genuine and respectful debate?

It is sometimes argued that for Christians and Muslims to be tolerant they must disown the very concept of conversion. My understanding of tolerance, which I consider a prerequisite in Christian–Muslim relationships, is different. To be tolerant is neither to deny nor to minimize the theological differences between Christianity and Islam. Christians and Muslims will be genuinely tolerant only when they have accepted the idea that debate, or dialogue, may lead to conversions either to Christianity or to Islam. True tolerance is to accept the other, not by ignoring the distance between us, but by measuring that distance accurately and by recognizing that whoever wants to cross over has the right and freedom to do so.

I am wholeheartedly committed to Christian–Muslim dialogue. Dialogue and mission are not to be seen as opposing concepts, but quite the reverse. Mission carried out without a dialogical approach is irrelevant, patronizing, and perhaps harmful; dialogue without a missionary perspective is an academic exercise, likely to be superficial and complacent. Missionary dialogue is a meaningful process that is highly educational. People learn to reconcile things that are too often dissociated: faith with humility, truth with love, religion with freedom, belief in life after death with commitment to life before death. I would like to see many people involved in Christian–Muslim dialogue at all levels, and not just at the institutional level.[3]

Christian–Muslim dialogue goes back to the time of Muhammad. The Prophet was involved in theological debates with Christians. In 630, for example, a Christian delegation from Najran (south of Arabia) came to Medina and had important discussions with him about the coexistence of the Christian community alongside the Muslim community.

This book is about comparing the Christian faith and the Muslim faith. Central to these faiths is God's revelation to us in the form of the Scriptures. In Part 1 we shall look at the Bible and the Qur'an and, in particular, assess the Bible's reliability. In Part 2 we shall focus on God and humanity, on the way we relate to God, taking a closer look at the meaning of salvation and the kingdom of God.

The Christian understanding of God is demonstrated in Jesus Christ, his death and his resurrection. These two events, which are denied by Islamic tradition, show the uniqueness of Jesus Christ and his message. Our focus in Part 3 will be to investigate further these different perspectives on Jesus. The Islamic teaching on God and humanity is illustrated in the mission of the Prophet Muhammad. The Qur'anic evidence for Muhammad's prophethood challenges everyone, including Christians, and calls us to give a suitable response. That is what we shall attempt to do in Part 4.

Since Islam and Christianity are two monotheistic faiths based on written divine revelation, debates between Christians and Muslims naturally relate to the role of the Scriptures, the attributes of God, and the condition of human beings, as well as to Jesus and Muhammad. Theology, however, is not the only decisive factor in shaping Christian–Muslim relationships. History also has had its part to play. Conflicts between 'Christian' and 'Muslim' nations have had, and continue to have, a negative impact. The Crusades and colonialism have contributed to undermining relationships between Christians and Muslims. As a result, a genuine dialogue has become more difficult. As an Arab Christian I am aware of how much Christian–Muslim relationships are conditioned by the wider historical context. This is why I felt I could not bring this book to a close without addressing two contemporary issues in Part 5, namely the conflict in the Middle East and the Muslim population in Western Europe.

The question interfaith dialogue implicitly poses is this: is it possible to reconcile firmness of conviction with openness to alternative views? I would like to think that for most Christians and Muslims the answer is yes. Dialogue is a good way of testing how open we are, in our minds and our hearts, to people of other faiths. It requires our commitment to both truth and love. Thus dialogue between Christians and Muslims is a serious business. Its primary concern is the truth about God, ourselves, our fellow human beings and the world in which we live. Political correctness, ignorance or theological relativism may lead to a superficial agreement between us. A confrontational debate, on the other hand, may run the risk of causing antagonism, which would hinder the search for truth. Only love, demonstrated through genuinely peaceful relationships, can create the necessary conditions for the truth to emerge and for mutual understanding to develop.

My prayer is that, as a result of this kind of dialogue, both Christian and Muslim communities will enjoy better relationships with one another. We shall get rid of our prejudice and mutual ignorance, and shall gain a better understanding of each other's faith as well as our own faith. Above all, we may find that God is speaking to us, and that he has something to say to us: we shall gain a better understanding of who he is.

Christians and Muslims must therefore engage in friendly relationships if we want to live according to the teaching of our respective Scriptures. It is also part of our calling to challenge each other about faith issues and to do it peacefully and truthfully. This is not an easy task: our beliefs will come under scrutiny; our ability to relate to each other as fellow human beings and as God-fearing people will also be tested. In short, engaging in dialogue means being prepared to put Christianity and Islam on trial. Will Christians and Muslims rise to this challenge? Will we be able to speak the truth in love (Eph. 4:15)? Will we honour God by fulfilling our mission 'in the best possible way'? This book endeavours to respond to this challenge. May God in his mercy forgive its shortcomings and use it as he pleases.

Notes

[1] I have consulted and often used two translations of the Qur'an: 'A. Yusuf 'Ali, *The Holy Qur'an: Translation and Commentary*, and Kenneth Cragg, *Readings in the Qur'an*. However, the final translation is my own. In many cases, it has been influenced by Razi's exegesis.

[2] The modern editions of this Commentary come in sixteen volumes and thirty-two parts. In the references to this work, the first figure is the volume number, and the second is the part: e.g. 'Razi, VI:11, pp. 78–83', refers to volume 6, part 1, on pp. 78–83.

[3] A survey of Christian–Muslim relationships is found in J.-M. Gaudeul, *Encounters and Clashes: Islam and Christianity in History*: vol. 1, *Survey*; vol. 2: *Texts*. For an overview of Christian–Muslim dialogue over the last decades, see A. Siddiqui, *Christian–Muslim Dialogue in the Twentieth Century*. Christian views of Islam and Muslim perceptions of Christianity are documented in K. Zebiri, *Muslims and Christians Face to Face*.

Part 1
The Scriptures

1

The Bible and the Qur'an

Christians and Muslims claim that they have received divine revelation and that this revelation is contained in Holy Scripture: the Bible or the Qur'an. Consequently one might think that the Bible occupies the same position in Christianity as the Qur'an in Islam. But it is not as simple as that! The Bible does not have the same significance for Christians as the Qur'an does for Muslims. There are certainly striking similarities between the two books, but there are also important differences.

The differences help to explain both the problems Christians face when they read the Qur'an and the problems Muslims face when they read the Bible. While some are easily discouraged and stop reading, others swiftly conclude that these differences indicate the mediocrity of one book as against the other. But both the Bible and the Qur'an deserve far more consideration than that. For centuries they have sustained the faith of millions of men and women. Although in reading them we do not necessarily have to assent in advance to what they say, we do need to try as sincerely as possible to understand their specific character and content.

We shall attempt to do this by looking at four different aspects of revelation: the *nature* of the revelation (what is revealed), the *method* of the revelation (how it came about), the *transmission* of the revelation (how it was passed on), and the *message* of the revelation (what it is all about).

The nature of revelation

Christians and Muslims believe in a Creator God who is sovereign and transcendent (radically different and separate from his creation). He created humankind and established us as his representatives on earth. He sent prophets so that we might know his word and learn his will.

In Islam God's revelation is found first of all in his creation. Nature contains many signs, *ayat*, that point to the Creator (2:164; 3:190; 10:5–6):

> Truly, in the alternation of the night and the day,
> and in all that God has created, in the heavens and the earth,
> are Signs for those who fear Him. (10:6)

The Qur'an teaches that God's verbal revelation is written on a heavenly template, *al-lawh al-mahfuz*, that represents his word (85:22). This original template, known as the 'Mother of the Book' (3:7; 13:39; 43:4), has been made known to humankind at various times. So God's supreme revelation has been revealed in a Book or a Scripture, *kitab*.

According to the Qur'an, there are four separate collections of such revelations in book form:

1. *The Torah* (*tawrat*) –revealed through Moses (3:93; 6:154), which is 'light and guidance for humankind', *nur wa huda* (6:91).
2. *The Psalms* (*zabur*) – revealed through David (4:163; 17:55; 21:105).
2. *The Gospel* (*injil*) – revealed through Jesus, in which there is also light and guidance and which confirms the Torah (5:46).[1]
3. *The Qur'an* – revealed through Muhammad, which is 'guidance and mercy', *huda wa rahma* (6:157). The message of the Qur'an is said to confirm, *yusaddiqu*, the Torah and the Gospel (2:91; 3:3, 81; 4:47), and explain, *yufassilu*, these former Scriptures (6:114; 10:37; 12:111), but its authority is greater, *muhaymin*, than theirs (5:48). The Islamic Scripture is seen as God's word destined for everyone (38:87; 68:52; 81:27).

The Qur'an is primarily the revelation of God's will, something that can be understood by human minds. It guides us in what we should believe and how to live in obedience and submission to God.

> It is not fitting for a man that God should speak to him except by inspiration, or from behind a veil, or by the sending of a Messenger

to reveal, with God's permission, what God wills: for He is Most High, Most Wise.

And thus have We, by Our command, sent inspiration to you: You did not know before what was Revelation, and what was Faith;

But We have made the Qur'an a Light, with which We guide such of Our servants as we will. (42:51–52)

The Islamic Scripture does not reveal who God is, lest his transcendence be negated. As one Muslim scholar has put it, 'You may not have complete transcendence and self-revelation at the same time.'[2]

This is quite different from the way Christians think about their Scriptures. The Bible not only claims to reveal God's will, his laws and commands; it claims to be God's *self*-disclosure – the revelation of God himself. This is not, of course, something we can fully comprehend with our minds, for God is infinite and we are sinful. His thoughts are higher than our thoughts and his ways higher than our ways: 'As the heavens are higher than the earth …' (Is. 55:9). Yet God wants to reveal himself to us through his word so that we can know him and relate to him.

As well as containing God's word spoken by his messengers, the biblical revelation contains many accounts of God's action in human history. The words explain the actions, and the actions confirm the truth of the words. In the days of Moses the climax of God's revelation was Israel's liberation from Egypt and the giving of the Law. The Torah is the written account of how God revealed himself through the history of Israel. The Creator God reveals himself in the Torah as the Saviour of his people:

'I, even I, am the LORD,
   and apart from me there is no saviour.
I have revealed and saved and proclaimed –
   I, and not some foreign god among you.
You are my witnesses,' declares the LORD, 'that I am God.'
(Is. 43:11–12)

I will give them a heart to know me, that I am the LORD. They will be my people, and I will be their God, for they will return to me with all their heart. (Jer. 24:7)

For Christians, God's revelation reached its climax two thousand years ago in the person of Jesus Christ.[3] Jesus is God's supreme revelation, God's Word made flesh (John 1:1, 10, 14). The gospel is the message of good news Jesus proclaimed in his words and actions. He is the fulfilment of God's revelation as the Saviour who came to redeem his human creatures. The Scriptures therefore point to who God is and how he has revealed himself in Jesus Christ.

Like Muslims, Jews and Christians are referred to in the Qur'an as 'the People of the Book'. This is an apt expression since each holds to the authority of their Holy Scriptures. Christians, however, see themselves as being much more than this. They define their identity primarily in relation to Jesus Christ – the eternal Word of God revealed as a man. Jesus therefore occupies a place in Christianity in a sense similar to that of the Qur'an in Islam. The role of the Bible is to make Jesus known just as Jesus has made God known. In Islam, by contrast, Muhammad is no more than God's Prophet whose mission was to transmit the Qur'an, the supreme word of God. Muslims are by definition those who abide by Qur'anic law, following the Prophet's example.

We shall consider these concepts in more detail throughout the book, but at this stage it is important to recognize that the Qur'an and the Bible are different because the nature of the revelation they contain is not the same.

The method of revelation

Christians and Muslims differ in regard to the method by which God revealed his word. This difference is seen largely in the extent to which human beings are understood to have been involved. Muslims are often surprised when they first look at the Bible, for its structure and literary style are not necessarily what they would have expected.

The books of the Bible

The word *Bible* is of Greek origin and simply means 'book'. This book is in fact a collection of sixty-six books divided into two major sections – the Old Testament, written before Jesus Christ, and the New Testament, written in the first century after Jesus Christ.[4]

The Old Testament is the Bible of the Jewish people, their Holy Scriptures. It consists of thirty-nine books:

- *The Pentateuch* ('five books'): Genesis, Exodus, Leviticus, Numbers and Deuteronomy – often called the books of Moses. In Genesis we find the account of creation and follow the lives of Adam, Noah,

Abraham, Ishmael, Isaac, Jacob and Joseph. In Exodus we read of God's rescuing the Israelites from slavery in Egypt, and giving the Law through Moses.

- *The historical books*: Joshua, Judges, Samuel, Kings and Chronicles. These narrate the history of the people of Israel, from the early days when they were ruled by judges, through the years of King David and Solomon, the division into the kingdoms of Israel and Judah, until the time God finally brought judgment through the Assyrian and Babylonian armies. Other historical books, Ezra and Nehemiah, describe the return of some of the Jews from exile.

- *The Psalms and Wisdom literature*: Psalms, Proverbs, Ecclesiastes, Job and Song of Solomon. The Psalms are a collection of individual and community songs of thanksgiving, praise and lament, some of which were written by King David.

- *The prophetic books*. These contain the messages God's prophets preached, calling people back to God and looking forward to the future. The longest of these books are Isaiah, Jeremiah, Ezekiel and Daniel; and the shortest include Hosea, Amos and Malachi.

The Old Testament Scriptures are often called the Torah, meaning 'instructions', or 'the Law' (Luke 16:17). The word 'Law' is understood in its widest sense, as referring to the whole of the Scriptures and not merely those sections that have to do with law. At the time of Jesus the Bible was also called 'the Law and the Prophets' (Matt. 5:17; 7:12; 11:13). In this expression 'the Law' referred specifically to the first five books of the Bible (Luke 16:19; 24:27) and 'the Prophets' referred to the prophetic books. Yet another expression used to refer to the Holy Scriptures is 'the Law of Moses, the Prophets and the Psalms' (Luke 24:44). Again, the word 'Psalms' is used in a wider sense, referring not only to the book of Psalms but to various writings and, in particular, the wisdom literature.

So the Old Testament is a collection of writings associated not only with Moses and David but with many other prophets: about thirty authors in all. Its composition took place over eight centuries from the time of Moses, through to David and Solomon, up to Malachi, who lived four centuries before Jesus Christ.

The message of the New Testament of the Bible is known as the gospel, a word, as we have seen, meaning 'good news'. In the singular ('the gospel') it refers to the message of Jesus Christ, while the plural ('the Gospels') refers to the four books that tell the story of Jesus. Thus the gospel of Jesus Christ is recounted in the four Gospels, but equally in the rest of the New Testament writings (see note 1).

The New Testament consists of twenty-seven books:

- *The Gospels*: Matthew, Mark, Luke and John.
- *Acts*: the second volume of Luke's record, which begins by announcing the mission Jesus gave his apostles before ascending to heaven: to take the gospel to all the peoples on earth. It goes on to tell how the gospel was announced from Jerusalem all the way to Rome, how men and women accepted the message, and how the Christian church grew rapidly despite persecution.
- *The Epistles, or Letters*, written mostly by Jesus' apostles, notably Paul, Peter and John. They were mainly addressed to churches or church leaders to give them a deeper understanding of the gospel and its practical consequences.
- *Revelation*, written by John. It recounts a vision given by Jesus to one of his disciples. It stresses that the gospel is destined to meet strong opposition as it advances. It also warns God's people of the sufferings that await them, while encouraging them to keep their hope alive. They are to draw strength from the promise that Jesus will return. By contrast with his first coming, Jesus' glorious second coming will fully establish the kingdom of God, a kingdom of peace and righteousness.

The books of the New Testament were written by approximately ten authors, all of whom lived during the first century of the Christian era. All of them were Jewish, with the probable exception of Luke.

The writers of the Bible

Christians believe that God inspired the writers of the Bible, who were often unaware of it at the time. Some of these writers, such as Moses or the apostle Paul, are famous, while others remain anonymous. All, however, were instruments of the Holy Spirit, who caused them, while fully respecting their individuality and using their own faculties, to write down God's word. God did not dictate to them: they participated fully in the formulation of the revealed message, and their writings are marked by their distinctive personalities.

The biblical writers also took into account the culture of those they were addressing and accordingly adapted the form of the message they were transmitting. For instance, even though the gospel proclaimed by Jesus Christ consists of a unique message, it is written in four versions, the four Gospels. Thus the gospel of Jesus Christ may be read in Matthew's Gospel as well as in that of Mark, Luke or John. Moreover, Jesus spoke with his disciples in Aramaic, the language spoken by Jews living in Palestine at that time. The four Gospels, however, were written in Greek, because they were addressed to different ethnic groups that used Greek as a lingua franca.

The term *inspiration* refers to the way God led people by his Spirit to write down his word, taking into account their historic context and the context of those for whom their writings were intended. 'Above all, you must understand that no prophecy of Scripture came about by the prophet's own interpretation. For prophecy never had its origin in the will of man, but men spoke from God as they were carried along by the Holy Spirit' (2 Pet. 1:20–21). Consequently the Bible is at the same time *the Word of God*, which guarantees its trustworthiness, and *the word of men*, which underlines its humanness. On the one hand, the human authorship of the Scriptures means that we can study the Bible the way we study other books. We can make use of all the available resources of human knowledge to help us to understand it better. We can look at the text from all possible angles without trying to force any one interpretation on to it. We take into account what kind of text it is (whether it is historical, poetic, prophetic, narrative, legislative, apocalyptic or wisdom literature), and thus decide how we should go about interpreting it. The divine authorship of the Scriptures, on the other hand, means that we must also approach the Bible with due humility, as we seek to understand and obey the word of God.

> All Scripture is God-breathed [or 'given by inspiration of God'] and is useful for teaching, rebuking, correcting and training in righteousness. (2 Tim. 3:16)

> For everything that was written in the past was written to teach us, so that through endurance and the encouragement of the Scriptures we might have hope. (Rom. 15:4)

Muhammad receives God's revelation

According to the Hadith,[5] God's revelation to Muhammad came about in more than one form. It was sometimes quite a painful experience:

Sometimes it is like the ringing of a bell; this form of inspiration is the hardest of all and then this state passes off after I have grasped what is inspired. At times, the angel Gabriel was the agent of revelation: 'Sometimes the Angel comes in the form of a man and talks to me and I grasp whatever he says.'

'A'icha, Muhammad's wife, noticed that it was usually a very intense experience: 'Verily I saw the Prophet being inspired divinely on a very cold day and noticed the sweat dropping from his forehead (as the inspiration was over).'[6]

When the angel Gabriel appeared to Muhammad the first time it was an unexpected and frightening encounter. Muhammad was about forty years old and married to Khadija. He was meditating in a cave near Mecca, his home town:

The commencement of the divine inspiration to God's Apostle was in the form of good dreams which came true like bright day, and then the love of seclusion was bestowed upon him. He used to go in seclusion in the cave of Hira' where he used to worship continuously for many days before he desired to see his family. He used to take with him the journey food for the stay and then come back to Khadija to take his food likewise again till suddenly the truth descended upon him while he was in the cave of Hira'. The angel came to him and asked him to read (*iqra'*).

The Prophet replied, 'I do not know how to read.'

The Prophet added, 'The angel caught me and pressed me so hard that I could not bear it any more. He then released me and again asked me to read and I replied, "I do not know how to read."

Thereupon he caught me again and pressed me a second time till I could not bear it any more. He then released me and again asked me to read but again I replied, "I do not know how to read."

'Thereupon he caught me for the third time and pressed me, and then released me and said, "Read in the name of your Lord, who has created (all that exists), has created man from a clod. Read! And your Lord is the most generous."' (96:1–3)

Then God's Apostle returned with the inspiration and with his heart beating severely. Then he went to Khadija b. Khuwaylid and said, 'Cover me! Cover me!' They covered him till his fear was over and after that he told her everything that had happened and said, 'I fear that something may happen to me.'

Khadija replied, 'Never! By God, God will never disgrace you. You keep good relations with your kith and kin, help the poor and the destitute, serve your guests generously and assist the deserving ones who are afflicted by calamity.'

Khadija then accompanied him to her cousin Waraqa b. Nawfal b. Asad b. 'Abdul 'Uzza, who, during the Pre-Islamic period, became a Christian and used to write the Hebrew Book. He would write from the Gospel in Hebrew as much as God wished him to write. He was an old man and had lost his eyesight. Khadija said to Waraqa, 'Listen to the story of our nephew, O my cousin!'

Waraqa asked, 'O my nephew! What have you seen?'

God's Apostle described what he had seen. Waraqa said, 'This is the same one who keeps the secrets whom God had sent to Moses. I wish I were young and could live up to the time when your people would turn you out.'

God's Apostle asked, 'Will they drive me out?'

Waraqa replied in the affirmative and said, 'Anyone who came with something similar to what you have brought was treated with hostility; and if I should remain alive till the day when you will be turned out then I would support you strongly.' But after a few days Waraqa died and the divine inspiration was also paused for a while.

(A few years later) while I was walking, all of a sudden I heard a voice from the sky. I looked up and saw the same angel who had visited me at the cave of Ḥira', sitting on a chair between the sky and the earth. I got afraid of him and came back home and said, 'Wrap me (in blankets).' And God revealed the following Holy Verses (of the Qur'an):

'O you [i.e. Muhammad]! Wrapped up in garments! Arise and warn (the people against God's punishments)' ... up to 'and desert the idols'. (74:1–5)

After this the revelation started coming strongly, frequently and regularly.[7]

Gabriel's command to Muhammad was *iqra*'. The verb *qara'a* usually means 'to read', whereas in a religious context, as here, it means 'to proclaim' or 'to recite' the word of God. The word *qur'ān* comes from the same root and thus means the ritual recitation of the sacred text. By extension the word has come to refer to the text itself.

In his astonishment Muhammad refused to receive the message the
angel had been ordered to give him. Three times he replied, '*ma ana bi-
qari*', an expression that means either 'I cannot read' or 'I am not going
to recite'. Traditionally Muslims have opted for the first interpretation, 'I
do not know how to read', referring to Muhammad's alleged illiteracy.
However, as far as we know Gabriel did not present Muhammad with a
written document, and he would surely have known if Muhammad was
illiterate. Moreover, when pressed by the heavenly messenger, Muhammad did eventually consent to recite the words he had heard. Yet the
hadith makes it clear that Muhammad's first encounter with Gabriel
was quite dreadful, which is why he first refused to yield to him.
He opposed the angel's injunction as long as he could by saying, 'I will
not recite.' But he ended up being overcome and forced to recite this
first revelation, which has been recorded in sura 96. This interpretation may surprise many Muslims, and some will certainly reject it.
It does, however, have its advocates among contemporary Muslim
scholars.[8]

The Prophet's role was to learn the message by heart and to preach it
to his fellow citizens in Mecca. It was communicated to him word for
word. He was not to intervene in the shaping of the message, but was to
learn and recite precisely the words he heard. The fact that the Qur'an
was dictated to Muhammad in this way means that the Islamic Scripture
is God's word and God's word alone. This is why the Qur'anic text is
usually in the first person plural, this being the plural of divine majesty.
Thus recitation, *qira'a*, indicates the way Muhammad received and
transmitted God's word. This represents the Prophet's only contribution
to the process by which God revealed his word, a process referred to in
the Qur'an by the verbs *anzala* and *nazzala*, meaning literally 'to send
down' and 'to bring down'. Since Muhammad was an Arab, the Qur'an
was revealed to him in Arabic.

Muhammad received his first revelation in AD 610. The inhabitants of
Mecca were not at all enthusiastic about the preaching of the Qur'an.
Although he was not openly persecuted, the Prophet met with
opposition and his message was rejected. In 622 he had to leave his native
town and took refuge with his companions in *Yathrib*, which later
became Medina (from *Medinat al-rasul*, 'the city of the Apostle'). This
journey, known as the *hijrah*, marks the beginning of the Islamic era, and
from this time the Muslim community developed quickly. Divine
revelations continued until the death of the Prophet in 632.

The Qur'an

The Qur'an is a collection of all the revelations given to Muhammad. It contains 114 chapters known as *suras*. These are classified more or less in descending order of length. The shortest suras are placed last in the Qur'an, although chronologically they may have been the first.

The opening chapter, *al-Fatiha* ('the exordium'), being a short sura, is an exception to this rule. Described in the Hadith as the greatest sura in the Qur'an,[9] it is placed first because of its importance. It is a prayer often recited by Muslims, who consider it to be a summary of the whole Qur'anic message. Like all suras, except the ninth, it begins with the invocation known as the *basmala*: 'In the name of God, Most Gracious, Most Merciful', *bismi-llah al-rahman al-rahim*:

> In the name of God, Most Gracious, Most Merciful.
> Praise be to God, the Cherisher and Sustainer of the Worlds;
> Most Gracious, Most Merciful;
> Master of the Day of Judgment.
> Thee do we worship, and Thine aid we seek.
> Show us the straight way,
> The way of those on whom Thou hast bestowed Thy Grace,
> those whose portion is not wrath, and who go not astray. (1:1–7)

Further differences

The biblical and Qur'anic revelations differ from each other in their historic perspective and in the number of recipients:

- *The historical perspective.* The Qur'an lacks the historical perspective of the Bible. In the latter the revelation was given over more than one thousand years; in the former over twenty-three years. Consequently we do not find in the Qur'an prophecies that are fulfilled during the period of its revelation.[10]
- *The recipients.* In contrast to the Qur'an, which was given to one man, the biblical revelation was entrusted to many people. This may explain why the Qur'an has greater literary unity than the Bible. However, since the human authors of the Bible are many, the concordant message of their writings is all the more remarkable.

The transmission of the revelation

The Qur'an was given in plain language (15:1; 27:1; 36:69), but the Prophet did not meet with much success when he began preaching in Mecca. Most of his hearers simply did not want to know. They did not believe in the divine origin of the Qur'an, and so in order to persuade them, Muhammad challenged them to produce ten suras (11:13), or even a single sura (2:23; 10:38), of a literary quality equal to that of the Qur'an:

> And if you are in doubt as to what We have revealed
> From time to time to Our servant,
> Then produce a Sura like it;
> And call your witnesses of helpers (if there are any) besides God,
> If your doubts are true. (2:23)

What is generally called the 'Qur'anic miracle', *i'jaz al-Qur'an*, consists in recognizing that the Qur'an has superhuman literary perfection. This is said to prove its divine character (cf. 2:1; 10:37; 17:88; 52:34).

> This Qur'an is not such as can be produced by other than God;
> On the contrary it is a confirmation of revelations that went
>   before it,
> And a fuller explanation of the Book – wherein there is no
>   doubt –
> From the Lord of the Worlds. (10:37)

This literary miracle is especially convincing evidence for Muslims since they consider Muhammad to have been illiterate.[11]

The language of the Qur'an

Inasmuch as the Qur'an was revealed in Arabic and its literary quality forms a major proof of its divine character, it follows that the Arabic of the Qur'an is an integral part of the word of God. Indeed, the Qur'an presents itself as an *Arabic Qur'an* (20:113; 39:28; 42:7):

> We have sent it down as an Arabic Qur'an,
> In order that you may learn wisdom. (12:2)

A revelation from God, Most Gracious, Most Merciful,
A Book, where the verses are explained in detail;
A Qur'an in Arabic, for people who understand. (41:2–3)

The logical consequence is that for Muslims the Qur'an as the word of
God is not translatable into any other language. For centuries there was
no question of translating it. Today, however, a number of translations
are available; some have even been endorsed by the highest Islamic
authorities. But these translations are not considered to be the word of
God. At best they represent a paraphrase or commentary on the Holy
Book. Thus the full title of the English translation of the Qur'an by 'A.
Yusuf 'Ali is *The Meaning of the Holy Qur'an.*

The essential unity between the letter and message of the Qur'an raises
the question of the universal character of Islam. The Qur'an claims that
Muhammad is a Prophet sent to all humanity (21:107) and that Islam is
the religion for all people (3:19, 85). But is it possible to reconcile this
claim with the fact that the Qur'an is the word of God only in Arabic
and that only Arabic-speaking Muslims can have direct access to God's
word? Is there not a real danger of Arabic language and culture becoming
supreme among all Muslim peoples? If God is close to those who call
upon him, as the Qur'an declares (2:186; 50:16), how is it that his word
will never be available except in Arabic?

It is true that it is not absolutely necessary to be able to read the
Qur'an or to be able to recite it in order to be a Muslim. It is only
necessary to subscribe to the confession of faith ('I declare that there
is no god but God and that Muhammad is His Apostle') and to carry
out the legal obligations: prayer, almsgiving, fasting and pilgrimage.
Nevertheless, if God is the God of all people, whatever our country or
language, would we not expect him to want to speak to us using our own
language?

The compilation of the Qur'an

Among the first generation of Muslims, memorization played a vital part
in the preservation and spread of the Qur'an. Some parts were also
recorded on materials such as bone and camel hide. The deciding factor
in prompting the religious authorities to have the whole Qur'an written
and collected in a book was the fact that many of those who had learned
it by heart were dying in battle. It was feared that their deaths would
result in the loss of some of the divine revelation.

According to the Hadith, the first attempt to compile the Qur'anic suras was made during the reign of the first caliph (632–634) on the suggestion of 'Umar (who was to become the second caliph). Zayd b. Thabit, who had been the Prophet's scribe, gives us an account of what happened:

> Abu Bakr al-Ṣiddiq sent for me when the people of Yamama had been killed. I went to him and found 'Umar b. al-Khaṭṭab sitting with him. Abu Bakr then said to me, ''Umar has come to me and said, "Casualties were heavy among the Qurra' of the Qur'an (i.e. those who knew the Qur'an by heart) on the day of the battle of Yamama, and I am afraid that more heavy casualties may take place among the Qurra' on other battlefields, whereby a large part of the Qur'an may be lost. Therefore I suggest you (Abu Bakr) order that the Qur'an be collected" …'
>
> Then Abu Bakr said (to me), 'You are a wise young man and we do not have any suspicion about you, and you used to write the Divine Inspiration for God's Apostle. So you should search for (the fragmentary scripts) of the Qur'an and collect it (in one book) …'
>
> So I started looking for the Qur'an and collecting it from (what was written on) palm-leaf stalks, thin white stones and also from the men who knew it by heart … Then the complete manuscripts of the Qur'an remained with Abu Bakr till he died, then with 'Umar till the end of his life, and then with Ḥafṣa, the daughter of 'Umar.[12]

The second stage in the compilation of the Qur'an took place during the reign of 'Uthman, the third caliph (644–656). Apart from the compilation of the Qur'an that Ḥafṣa had in Medina, there were four other collections in circulation: in Kufa (Iraq), Bassora (Baṣra; Iraq), Damascus (Syria) and Ḥoms (Syria). A commission was therefore made responsible for establishing the definitive text of the Qur'an. It was based on Ḥafṣa's compilation, and because discrepancies were found between the versions of the Qur'an the commission had to decide which one was authentic and conformed to the Prophet's own version. 'Uthman then ordered that all other versions of the text be destroyed so as to preserve the unity of the Muslim community:

> Ḥudhayfa b. al-Yaman came to 'Uthman at the time when the people of Syria and the people of Iraq were waging war to conquer

Armenia and Azerbaijan. Ḥudhayfa was afraid of their differences in the recitation of the Qur'an, so he said to 'Uthman, 'O the chief of the Believers! Save this nation before they differ about the Book as the Jews and the Christians did before.'

So 'Uthman sent a message to Ḥafṣa saying, 'Send us the manuscripts of the Qur'an so that we may compile the Qur'anic materials in perfect copies and return the manuscripts to you.'

Ḥafṣa sent it to 'Uthman. 'Uthman then ordered Zayd b. Thabit, 'Abdullah b. al-Zubayr, Sa'id b. al-'Aṣ and 'Abdurraḥman b. Ḥarith b. Hisham to rewrite the manuscripts in perfect copies ... They did so, and when they had written many copies, 'Uthman returned the original manuscripts to Ḥafṣa. 'Uthman sent to every Muslim province one copy of what they had copied, and ordered that all the other Qur'anic materials, whether written in fragmentary manuscripts or whole copies, be burnt.[13]

'Uthman's decision did not please all Muslims. The Shi'i Muslims in particular believed that their teachings were more clearly supported by the Kufa collection attributed to Ibn Mas'ud (one of the Prophet's companions) than by the official compilation of 'Uthman. This played an important part in his assassination by Shi'i Muslims.

The original text of the official compilation has not survived and our earliest fragments of the Qur'an date from the second century of the Islamic era. This text is the only one on which our editions of the Qur'an are based, yet it contains a number of variant readings. In the year AH 322 (AD 923) the number of such readings was officially limited to seven, because of a hadith attributed to the Prophet and reported by Ibn 'Abbas: 'Gabriel recited the Qur'an to me in one way. Then I requested him (to read it in another way), and continued asking him to recite it in other ways till he ultimately recited it in seven different ways.'[14]

Transmitting the text of the Bible

In contrast to the Arabic of the Qur'an, the biblical languages (Hebrew and Aramaic in the Old Testament, and Greek in the New) are not sacred in themselves, but are only means of communicating the divine revelation. In the first centuries of the Christian era, the Gospels were translated into many languages, such as Syriac, Coptic, Ethiopian, Armenian and Latin. The Latin version of the Bible, known as the Vulgate, prevailed throughout the Middle Ages in western Europe, where Latin

was widely used. Martin Luther (1483–1546) first translated the New
Testament into German to make God's word accessible to the people,
who hardly understood Latin. Translations of the Bible into other
European languages soon followed. Today the number of languages in
which there is at least one book of the Bible is over two thousand! This
exceptional effort in Bible translation surely would never have been
attempted without the conviction that the Bible is still the word of God
even when translated. For is not a loving God able and willing to reveal
his word in such a way that it is readable in any human language?

Unlike the Qur'an, the divine character of the Bible is not manifested
through its literary quality; rather, it is God's actions that accredit his
word. God chose Moses to be his messenger and later confirmed this by
liberating the Hebrews from their slavery in Egypt. The same is true of
Jesus. The gospel he preached is inseparable not only from his miracles
but above all from his death and resurrection. The resurrection of Jesus,
a fact without parallel in history, demonstrates the unique character of
his person and authenticates the extraordinary claims he made about
himself.

The Gospels probably date from the second half of the first century
AD, although they drew heavily from source material compiled earlier.
Christian writings from the first half of the second century quote freely
from them. From the beginning of the second half of the second century
the authority of the Gospels, which was increasingly being accepted,
superseded the authority given to other similar writings. From the end of
the second century the Gospels were accepted as part of the canon of
Scripture.[15]

We no longer possess the original manuscripts of the Bible, but the
study of the biblical manuscripts we do have confirms the Bible's
authenticity. In 1947 a large number of manuscripts were found in the
caves of Qumran, near the Dead Sea. They date at the latest from the first
century AD. Among them is the entire text of Isaiah and fragments of all
the other books of the Old Testament, except Esther. Until this discovery
was made, the oldest manuscripts of the Old Testament dated from the
tenth century AD. Here was a unique and unexpected opportunity to
check, over a period of a thousand years, the accuracy of their transmission. All the experts who examined the texts (not all of them
Christians) judged that the copying was done with remarkable accuracy.
The textual variations found, though relatively numerous, were not of
such a kind as to call into question the integrity of the Old Testament
texts. The comparison of these manuscripts therefore testifies to the

conscientiousness of the scribes who copied and transmitted the text of the Torah from generation to generation.

The same is true of the New Testament manuscripts. The oldest Gospel fragments date from the middle of the second century AD, and there are hundreds of later manuscripts. The large number in existence, far from being a handicap, enables us to assess their quality. Despite many variants of minor importance, they testify to the perennial truth of the gospel as it was preached by Jesus and handed down by his disciples.

This brief survey of the history of the transmission of the Bible and of the Qur'an indicates that the text of the Bible is at least as reliable as that of the Qur'an.

The message of the revelation

The *reliability* of the revelation depends on its divine origin and its faithful transmission. But what about the *message* of the revelation that has shaped the faith and lives of so many Christians and Muslims? We shall take a brief look at the teaching of the Bible and of the Qur'an before exploring their message in depth in other chapters.

The Qur'anic revelation is essentially a law given in a book to show us the will of God and the way we should follow. From an Islamic perspective humans are seen as weak and ignorant creatures. We break the divine commandments and so, in order to stop us straying, we need a law to redirect us on to the straight path.

The biblical revelation also contains a law summarized in the Ten Commandments, but the whole history of Israel shows us that people confronted with this law are incapable of obeying it. Our problem is not so much that we do not know God's will, but that we do not *want* to obey it or *are not able* to do so. We need more than a light to direct us. That is why, having sent many prophets, God sent Jesus to be our Saviour, and gave the Holy Spirit to help us to live according to his standards.

Islam too promises divine help to the Muslim. This help is given in the form of teaching that regulates all aspects of religious, family, social, economic and political life. From this teaching, available in the Qur'an and the Hadith, Muslims learn to live according to the will of God. Qur'anic education encourages Muslims to do good works and thus to be prepared for the Day of Judgment. Muslims can hope for salvation by their good works, but this salvation will be revealed only on the last day. The life of the Prophet was a particularly powerful illustration of the

Qur'anic message, since he was simultaneously a prophet, political leader, social reformer and military leader. He is held up as an example to all Muslims, in whose favour he will intercede at the last judgment.

Unlike Muhammad, Jesus did not seek to establish God's kingdom on earth in all its power. Why not? Because evil is written into the hearts of men and women. This means that the kingdom cannot be established by reform of the structures of the world, or even simply by religious education. Now it can be established only as people respond freely to the message of the gospel. There will come a day when Jesus will fully establish God's kingdom on earth – the day he returns in glory. Until then God is giving everyone the opportunity to believe in Jesus Christ so that they may be saved. Those who believe in him as their Saviour commit themselves to furthering his kingdom in society.

From the perspective of the Qur'an, the final purpose of revelation is to bring people to Islam, so that we may submit to the Creator and adore him. Humans are seen as the servants of God and, conscious of the innumerable blessings we receive, we are to show our gratitude by living in complete submission to the will of our master. The question is: can we truly submit to God and worship him without being radically transformed in our innermost beings?

Serving God is certainly one of the great privileges we have as human beings. But the greatest of these privileges from the viewpoint of the gospel is that human beings, created in the image of our Maker, are called to enter into a new relationship with him. Only humans, of all living creatures, have this unique calling. For us God is more than a master. He is, if we respond to his call, our Father. What a blessing for us, his creatures, to be able to enjoy such intimate fellowship with our Creator, and what a joy to be called his children! This relationship, to which the gospel invites us, does not imply any merging of God's nature with ours. God remains who he is, as do we, without any mingling of his divinity and our humanity.

Notes

[1] The word *Gospel* (in Arabic, *injil*) is the translation of the Greek word *euangelion*, meaning 'good news'. The Arabic equivalent would be *bishara*. In this book the word 'Gospel' is used with two distinct meanings. First, in the Qur'anic context it means 'the Scripture' of the Christian community. In a Christian sense it refers to one of the four written Gospels (Matthew, Mark, Luke, John). Secondly, 'gospel' refers

exclusively to the message preached by Jesus and his disciples.

[2] I. Faruqi et al., *Christian Mission and Islamic Da'wa*, p. 48.

[3] The title 'Christ' comes from the Greek word *Christos*. It is the equivalent of 'Messiah' in Hebrew and *al-Masih* in Arabic. As we shall see again in chapter 14, it is a title for Jesus found in both the Bible and the Qur'an.

[4] In addition to these sixty-six books, some editions of the Bible include other books, which occur in the Greek translation of the Old Testament (the Septuagint or LXX): Judith, Tobit, 1 and 2 Maccabees, Wisdom, Ecclesiasticus, Baruch, the Epistle of Jeremiah, and the Greek versions of the books of Esther and Daniel. These additional books are known as the *deutero-canonical* or *apocryphal* books. They appear today in translations of the Bible used by the Roman Catholic Church.

[5] A more detailed introduction to the Hadith will be found in chapter 3.

[6] Bukhari, *bad' al-wahy* 2:I, p. 2, no. 2 [2].

[7] Ibid., 3:I, p. 2, no. 3 [3].

[8] Cf. M. Shahrur, *al-Kitab wa-l-Qur'an: Qira'a mu'asira*, pp. 139–143.

[9] Bukhari, *fada'il al-Qur'an* 9:VI, p. 489, no. 528 [4622].

[10] The only exception in this respect would be the 'prophecy' found in Qur'an 30:1–4 about the victory and the defeat of the Byzantine army. However, the prophetic character of this text is very doubtful owing to uncertainty over the vocalization of v. 2 and the dating of vv. 1–4.

[11] We shall consider the subject of Muhammad's illiteracy in more detail in chapter 18.

[12] Bukhari, *fada'il al-Qur'an* 3:VI, p. 477, no. 509 [4603].

[13] Ibid., p. 478, no. 510 [4604].

[14] Ibid., 5:VI, p. 481, no. 513 [4607]; *tawhid* 53:IX, p. 479, no. 640 [6995].

[15] The *canon*, in Christian terminology, is the list of those books stamped with divine authority, which therefore constitute the Holy Scriptures.

2

Have the Scriptures been falsified?

Those involved in dialogue between Muslims and Christians know that sooner or later one question is bound to arise: the question of the authenticity of the Judaeo-Christian Scriptures. It is the source of many arguments. Although not always the first question to be asked, in the final analysis most arguments boil down to this.

The Qur'anic claim about Muhammad

The Qur'an asserts that the Torah and the Gospel had predicted the coming of the *ummi* Prophet, 'the unlettered (or Gentile) Prophet', (that is, Muhammad). In sura 7, God declares, 'I shall ordain mercy for … those who follow the Apostle, the unlettered Prophet, whom they find mentioned in their own (Scriptures), in the Torah and the Gospel (7:157).

Abraham and Jesus are said to have pointed to Muhammad. With his son Ishmael, Abraham laid down the foundation of the temple in Mecca, praying to God that he might send their offspring an Apostle from among them:

> Our Lord! Send among our people after us an Apostle of their own kin, who will recite to them Your revelations, teach them the Book and the wisdom and purge them from evil. For You are ever powerful and wise. (2:129)

Muhammad is seen as God's answer to Abraham's prayer.

According to the Qur'an, Jesus foretold the coming of a prophet called *Ahmad*, a name similar to *Muhammad* and understood by Muslims as another name given to their Prophet:[1] 'People of Israel! I am the Apostle of God to you, confirming the truth of the Torah which you have already and giving you glad word of an Apostle who will come after me, whose name is Ahmad' (61:6). It should be noted that the Qur'an does not refer specifically to any text from the Bible to back up its claim. This is in sharp contrast with the New Testament, which gives many scriptural references from the Old Testament to support its claim that Jesus is the promised Messiah. Jesus' miraculous birth (Matt. 1:22–23; cf. Is. 7:14) as well as his place of birth (Matt. 2:1–6; cf. Mic. 5:2) had been foretold. His messianic mission had been announced (Luke 4:16–21; cf. Is. 61:1–2), as had his sacrificial death (Acts 8:29–35; cf. Is. 52:13 – 52:12) and resurrection (Acts 2:22–36; cf. Pss. 16:8–11; 110:1).

When called to believe in Muhammad as God's Prophet, Jews and Christians object that nowhere in their Scriptures is there any prophecy about him. Muslims respond that if the Scriptures do not validate the Qur'anic claim about Muhammad, then they must have been corrupted, wrongly interpreted, or falsified!

The theory of the falsification of the Bible appears to have been designed to vindicate the Qur'anic claim that Muhammad's coming was foretold in the Scriptures. Muslims have tried to trace this accusation of corruption back to the Qur'an and the Hadith, so we shall need to consider what these writings say. In this chapter our focus will be on the teaching of the Qur'an and in the next chapter we shall look at the relevant narratives in the Hadith.

The Qur'anic teaching about the Scriptures

In Mecca Muhammad faced much opposition. He seems to have ex-perienced serious doubts about his mission. In order to reassure him, God pointed him to those who had already been given the Scriptures:

> If you are in doubt about what We have revealed to you, enquire of those who read the Book before you. The truth has indeed come to you from your Lord.
> So do not for a moment include yourself with the sceptical. (10:94)

Those Arabs who were sceptical were also referred to the Jews and

Christians, who were expected to confirm that the new revelation was indeed from God:

> And before you, the apostles We sent were but men, to whom We granted inspiration:
>   If you do not realize this, ask those who possess the Message (*al-dhikr*). (16:43; cf. 21:7)

The Qur'an urges the 'People of the Book', that is, Jews and Christians, to receive the final revelation God had entrusted to Muhammad (2:41; 4:47). This call is based on the assumption that the Qur'an is God's revelation in Arabic (26:192–199; 46:12) confirming the preceding revelations, that is, the Torah and the Gospel (2:89, 91, 97, 101; 3:3, 81; 5:48; 6:92; 35:31). The question is, however: if the Bible had been corrupted, would the Qur'an have confirmed it?

Most of the 'People of the Book' did not respond positively to the Qur'anic call (2:41, 87, 89, 91, 101); they did not convert to Islam. Yet the Qur'an still urges Muslims to have faith in the Bible (3:84, 119; 4:136). Moreover, the Qur'an urges Jews and Christians to judge by what God has revealed in the Torah and the Gospel (5:45, 47). They should observe their Scriptures' teachings (5:66, 68), it says, for the Torah and the Gospel represent God's guidance and light (5:46). By doing so Jews and Christians would have no reason to fear on the Day of Judgment (2:62; 5:69).

It is against this background that we should examine those Qur'anic texts that are critical of the 'People of the Book'. Around twenty verses in the Qur'an challenge the attitude of the Jews towards their Scriptures. Very occasionally, Christians too are criticized for mishandling Scripture. The texts date from the time when Muhammad was in Medina and reflect the conflicts between Jews and Muslims there. Many criticisms are formulated in general terms (2:12, 59, 159, 174; 3:71, 187), but some are more specific. They claim that the Jews

- covered up the Muslim character of Abraham's faith in God (2:140; cf. 2:135; 3:65–67);
- knew that the direction for prayer, the *qibla*, had changed, yet refused to accept the replacement of Jerusalem by Mecca (2:144–146);
- showed some manuscripts of the Torah while hiding others (6:91);
- presented as divine revelation scriptures they had written for evil purposes (2:79);

- recited some religious writings in the same way as Holy Scripture so as to deceive the listeners (3:78);
- concealed parts of their Scripture (5:15).

The Qur'an uses several verbs to describe the dishonest attitude of 'the People of the Book' towards the Scriptures. These include *akhfa* (to conceal), *baddala* (to substitute), *katama* (to cover up), and *nasa* (to forget). The strongest verb is without doubt *harrafa* (to give something a wrong direction). In three out of four verses this verb is used in an expression that means literally 'to take the words out of their context' or 'to divert the discourse from its meaning', hence to misread, to mis-interpret, to distort, to pervert or to falsify.

In Islamic theology, the verb *harrafa* and its corresponding noun *tahrif* have become the technical words for the manipulation of the Scriptures and the result of this manipulation. We shall look at the four Qur'anic occurrences of *harrafa* and seek to understand what it really means. My exegesis of these verses will be based on the commentary of the Qur'an by Razi, which Muslims consider to be one of the most authoritative commentaries.

Sura 2:75

> Will you [O Muslims] entertain the hope that they [the Jews] will believe you?
>
> Don't you know that a party of them heard the Word of God, and *distorted* it knowingly after they understood it? (2:75; my emphasis)

The Qur'an states that the people of Israel were God's chosen people, yet they often disobeyed his commands and were punished (2:40–103). Sura 2:75 comes in the context of a long list of ways in which they had disobeyed God, and is the first of five verses describing how they had misused their Scriptures (2:75–79). The accusation is that somehow they had corrupted the word of God. The verb *harrafa* is translated here as 'distorted'.

In commenting on this verse Razi begins by quoting a famous Muslim theologian, al-Qadi 'Abd al-Jabbar (415/1024), who envisaged two ways of understanding the falsification of the Torah. The first is the falsi-fication of its *text* (*fi l-lafz*). This would have been impossible if the word of God (the Torah) had been passed down reliably, as was the case with the Qur'an.

An important concept in Islam is *tawatur*, 'successive transmission'. It refers to the existence of independent and unbroken chains of people who could be trusted to transmit a message accurately. The trustworthiness of a text is measured by whether we can find reliable people throughout history who would have passed it on to the next generation in its original form without distorting it.[2]

Prior to the successive transmission of the Torah it was possible for its text to be falsified, explains Razi. However, the scope of this falsification was necessarily limited, he says, for God would not have let his word be altered in such a way that it no longer remained truthful.

The second way in which the Torah could be falsified is by falsification of its meaning (*fi l-ma'na*). Razi suggests that this kind of falsification may have occurred prior to the coming of God's Apostle (Muhammad) because it was not immediately evident that God's word (the Torah) was pointing to him. But ever since the time of the Prophet, the corruption of the meaning of God's word has become impossible, just as it is now impossible for someone to misinterpret the Qur'anic teaching concerning food prohibitions (e.g. eating pork, dead animals and blood). At this stage Razi does not say which of the two interpretations – falsification of text, or falsification of meaning – he favours.

When did the falsification occur and what was corrupted? Again Razi envisages two possibilities. He suggests that it took place either in Moses' time, in which case it had nothing to do with Muhammad, or in Muhammad's time. In the latter case it is likely that what was perverted was either its teaching about Muhammad, such as his attributes in the Torah, or the laws (e.g. the legal punishment for adultery). The Qur'an, says Razi, does not indicate precisely what had been corrupted.[3]

Sura 4:46

Some Jews *displace* words from their (rightful) places, saying: 'We have heard but we refuse to heed. You had better listen to us – what is beyond your comprehension! Attend to us!' – thus twisting words with their tongues and making false imputations about religion.

It would have been better for them, and more appropriate, if they had said: 'We hear and obey. Hear what we say. Look at us.' But God has cursed them for their unbelief. There is scant faith in them. (4:46; my emphasis)

This text blames some of the Jews for corrupting God's Word. It is quite clear that this charge concerns only a certain group of Jews, who are accused of corrupting not the text itself but what it says. The exact meaning of some of the Jews' words is uncertain. They do, however, indicate that the Jews' response to the teaching of the Prophet was disrespectful and dishonest.[4] The verb *ḥarrafa* appears in the first sentence and is translated here as 'displace'.

So how did the falsification happen? Razi lists three possibilities:

(1) *Substituting a word for another word.* As an example of this, Razi points to what the Jews did with the punishment for adultery. They replaced the word 'stoning' with the more general word 'legal punishment' (*ḥadd*). This is what is referred to in sura 2:79: 'Woe to those who write the Book with their own hands, and then say: This is from God.' Some may ask: is it feasible to do this with a Scripture whose every letter and word have been passed down by means of successive transmission, as it is well known all over the world (lit. 'in the orient and in the occident')? Razi takes this objection seriously. It might be answered, he says, by recognizing that the population of the time was small in number and that the number of scholars was tiny.

(2) *Giving false arguments* (*shubah baṭila*) and wrong interpretations (*ta'wilat fasida*); and distorting the meaning by means of verbal subterfuge (*ḥiyal lafẓiyya*). This is what Muslim heretics do with the Qur'anic verses that contradict their doctrines. In Razi's view, this interpretation is more likely to be the right one (*aṣaḥḥ*).

(3) *Twisting the Prophet's sayings.* Having put some questions to Muhammad, the Jews used to report his answers incorrectly.[5]

Sura 5:13

> However, because of their [the Jews'] breach of the covenant, We laid them under a curse and hardened their hearts. They *displace* words from their (rightful) places and have forgotten part of the message that had been committed to them. (5:13; my emphasis)[6]

Here the Jews are blamed for breaking the covenant God had made with them through Moses. One way of breaking this covenant was by showing disrespect for God's word and dismissing its instructions.

Once again Razi considers that the falsification of Scripture is to be understood in terms either of the *distortion of its meaning* (*ta'wil baṭil*) or of the *changing of its words* (*taghyir al-lafẓ*). The first of these inter-pretations, says Razi, is to be preferred, for a Scripture that has been passed down by means of successive transmission is not liable to textual corruption.[7] Thus Razi states unequivocally his conviction about the authenticity of the Scriptures. His understanding of their falsification is based on his belief that just as in the case of Qur'an, the Scriptures have been handed down through *tawatur*, that is, multiple and uninterrupted chains of transmission.

Sura 5:41

> Apostle! Do not let those grieve you who race each other into unbelief: those who say with their lips, 'We have believed', whereas in their hearts do not believe, and those among the Jews who listen to what is false [or 'in order to lie'].
>
> They listen to [or 'on behalf of'] people who have not come to you.
>
> They *displace* words from their (rightful) places; they say, 'If such and such is the message brought to you, accept it. But if it is not, then be on your guard.' (5:41; my emphasis)[8]

The Prophet is instructed through these words not to lose heart because of the attitude of some Arabs and Jews. The former reverted to their previous religion because they had not genuinely converted to Islam. The latter not only had rejected Muhammad as Prophet, but were trying to demean his name and denigrate his message.

Razi observes that the meaning of the accusation levelled at the Jews depends on the way we interpret the Arabic letter *li* (which is why an alternative translation is shown in square brackets). One possible reading is that they accepted the false teaching of their leaders about Islam and, in doing so, falsified the Torah and defamed the person of Muhammad. Another possibility is that they had come to question Muhammad on behalf of other people with the intention of twisting his teaching by adding to it, taking away from it or changing it.

Razi explains the last part of this verse by referring to an encounter the Prophet had with some Jews in Medina.[9] A man and a woman from the Jewish community of Khaybar had committed adultery. Because of their distinguished social rank, the Jewish leaders did not want to stone them, as required by the Torah, so they sent messengers to Muhammad to ask him about the penalty for adultery. The messengers were commissioned to accept Muhammad's answer if he said the adulterers should be flogged, but to refuse it if he said they should be stoned. Muhammad's answer was that they should be stoned, because this is what the Torah required. The two accused were stoned to death at the command of the Prophet in front of his mosque. From this story Razi draws the conclusion that the Jews had corrupted their Scripture, for in the case of adultery they had replaced the death penalty with the lesser penalty of flogging.[10]

What, then, do these four texts conclude about the falsification of the Scriptures? To answer this, we shall consider four questions.

1. Who is blamed for mishandling the word of God?

Clearly the Jews, and not the Christians, are addressed in each of the four Qur'anic verses we have considered. This is confirmed by two facts:

(1) All the Qur'anic verses about the corruption of the Scriptures are found in Medinan suras (with the exception of 6:91 and 7:162, 165, which Qur'anic exegetes consider Medinan). This fact suggests that the historical context for the criticism is the conflict between the Muslim and Jewish communities in Medina.

(2) Those who are criticized are either *ahl al-kitab*, 'the People of the Book' (2:140, 159, 174; 3:71, 187; 5:15) or *al-yahud*, the Jews (2:42, 59, 75, 79, 146; 3:78; 4:46; 5:13, 41; 6:91; 7:162, 165). Only one verse speaks of *al-naṣara*, the Christians, as having 'forgotten part of the message that has been committed to them' (5:14; cf. 2:140).

2. When did the corruption occur?

The texts suggest that the falsification took place in Muhammad's time. This is confirmed by other verses (2:42, 79, 140, 146, 159, 174; 3:71, 78; 5:41; 6:91): for example:

> It is the wish of a section of the People of the Book to lead you
>   astray.
> But they shall lead astray (not you), but themselves, and they do
>   not perceive!
> You People of the Book!
> Why do you reject the Signs of God, of which you are witnesses?
> You People of the Book!
> Why do you clothe truth with falsehood, and conceal the Truth
>   while you have knowledge? (3:69–71)

There are a few verses that appear to indicate that contemporaries of

Moses had already mistreated God's revelation (2:59; 7:162, 165). Razi's interpretation is based on the events surrounding Muhammad's mission, although he does not rule out the possibility that falsification had taken place in Moses' time.

3. What has been corrupted?

Only one of the four texts mentions specifically 'the word of God' as having been corrupted (2:75). For Razi this refers either to what the Torah says about Muhammad or to the death penalty for adultery. Bearing in mind that the Qur'an uses the same word, *kitab*, 'the Book', for the Jewish, the Christian, and the Islamic Scriptures, which are all regared as God's word, the expression may also refer to the Qur'an itself. It is therefore possible that this verse actually alludes to the Qur'an being misquoted by the unbelieving Jews in their attempt to discredit it.

The three other verses speak of the falsification of 'the words' without any details. According to Razi, what was perverted could have been God's word to the Jews (the Torah) as much as Muhammad's words (his teaching).

4. How have the Scriptures been falsified?

The Qur'anic texts remain unclear about how the Jews corrupted their Scriptures. Razi, as we have seen, offers two interpretations:

(1) If it is to be understood in connection with the *meaning of the text*, any more falsification is impossible. Ever since the revelation of the Qur'an it has become impossible to misinterpret the teaching of the Torah concerning, for instance, the coming of Muhammad.

(2) If falsification is to be understood in connection with the *text itself* it can be only to a limited degree (e.g. the verse about stoning). Why? Because the Torah is first and foremost the word of God. Just as God is trustworthy, so must his word be.

Razi states openly that he supports the first interpretation. The reason is that 'a Scripture that has been passed down by means of successive transmission is not liable to textual corruption'. The fact is that the Scripture has enjoyed *tawatur*, and Razi does not dispute this fact, which was well established in his day.

Notes

[1] See Muslim, *faḍaʾil* 126:IV, p. 1255, no. 5813 [4343]; Bukhari, *tafsir* 61:1:VI, p. 389, no. 419 [4517].

[2] E.g. Person A (who could be trusted) first witnessed an event, then passed it on to person B (who also could be trusted). Person B then found Person C (another reliable person) who would carry on the accurate message to the next generation after B had died. Person C told it to Person D … and so on, until person X in the day when the message about the relevant event was put into writing. If we can find multiple chains of named people A, B, C … X, then *tawatur* is established.

[3] Razi, II.3, pp. 123–124.

[4] It is possible that 'We have heard but we refuse to heed' refers to the commitment the Jews made after God had revealed the Ten Commandments to Moses: 'We will listen and obey' (Deut. 5:27). Ironically the sound of these words in Hebrew, *we-shamaʿnu we-ʿasinu*, is very similar to the Arabic 'We have heard but we refuse to heed', *samiʿna wa ʿasayna*. These words may have been misunderstood by an Arabic audience.

[5] Razi, V:10, p. 95.

[6] In some translations this verse is numbered 5:14 rather than 5:13.

[7] Razi, VI:11, p. 148.

[8] In some translations this verse is numbered 5:44 rather than 5:41.

[9] Muslim, *ḥudud* 28:III, p. 919, no. 4214 [3212].

[10] Razi, VI:11, pp. 183–184.

3
The Hadith and falsification

Muslims believe in God and in his Prophet (61:10–12). They obey God as well as his final Messenger (4:13–14). The Qur'an describes Muhammad as *uswa ḥasana*, 'an excellent example' for all Muslims (33:21), but says very little about his life. His *sunna*, 'custom' or 'practice', is instead made known to us through many *hadith*, narratives or sayings.

The Hadith or 'Prophetic Tradition' is the record of the teaching and practice attributed mainly to the Prophet and sometimes to his companions. Sunni Muslims consider the Hadith as a major source for Islamic doctrine and practice, its authority being second only to the Qur'an. Shi'i Muslims have their own compilations of the Prophetic Tradition.

There are nine 'canonical' collections of the Hadith, all written in Arabic. These 'Nine Books', *al-kutub al-tis'a*, are divided into three groups:

- Bukhari (256/870) and Muslim (261/875). These compilations are considered more authoritative than the others. They have the same title: *Ṣaḥiḥ*, meaning 'authentic' or 'sound'.
- Abu Dawud (275/888), Ibn Majah (273/886), Nasa'i (303/905) and Tirmidhi (279/892). These, known as *Sunan* (pl. of *sunna*), are seen as fairly reliable.
- The compilations of Darimi (255/868), titled *Sunan*, Ibn Ḥanbal (241/855), titled *Musnad*, and Malik (179/795), titled *Muwaṭṭa'*, contain many narratives the authenticity of which is uncertain.

The collections of Abu Dawud, Bukhari, Ibn Majah, Malik and

Muslim have been translated into English. Bukhari's *Ṣaḥīḥ* is also available in an Arabic–English edition (nine volumes), as is Ibn Majah's *Sunan* (five volumes). Bukhari's compilation has some ten thousand narratives, more than in Malik's collection, but far fewer than in that of Ibn Ḥanbal. Most narratives occur in more than one collection and the same compilation often reports different versions of the same narrative. This vast body of literature, however, does not represent an exhaustive record. Many narratives, including 'authentic' ones, are not found in the nine compilations. They have been transmitted via other channels, especially via commentaries of the Qur'an (*tafsir*) such as the one by Ṭabari (310/923).

Muslim scholars use several criteria to assess the historical reliability of a narrative, the most important being the criteria of *tawatur*: the existence of independent and unbroken chains of trustworthy transmitters. This chain of transmission, *sanad*, starts with the Prophet Muhammad down to the 'traditionalists' (e.g. Bukhari), who put the narrative into writing.

Broadly speaking there are three degrees of reliability: 'sound', *ṣaḥīḥ*; 'fair', *ḥasan*; and 'weak', *ḍa'if*. A narrative falsely attributed to the Prophet is called *mawḍu'*, 'made up'. While the degree of reliability of some narratives is agreed upon, Muslims discuss the authenticity of many others without always reaching the same conclusions.

The Hadith echoes the teaching of the Qur'an, explains Qur'anic passages, and complements and details Qur'anic doctrine. Islamic beliefs and laws based on the Hadith include the following:

- circumcision (Bukhari, *libas* 64:VII, p. 516, no. 779 [5441]);
- the five canonical prayers (Bukhari, *ṣalat* 1:I, p. 211, no. 345 [336]);
- Muhammad's intercession on the Day of Judgment (Bukhari, *tawḥid* 19:IX, p. 373, no. 507 [6861]);
- Muhammad's nightly journey to heaven (Bukhari, *manaqib al-anṣar* 42:V, p. 143, no. 227 [3598]);
- Muhammad's miracles (Bukhari, *manaqib* 25:IV, pp. 496–505, nos. 771–782 [3306–3317]);
- God's ninety-nine most beautiful names (Bukhari, *tawḥid* 12:IX, p. 363, no. 489 [6843]);
- the death penalty for apostasy (Bukhari, *jihad* 149:IV, p. 160, no. 260 [2794]);
- the death penalty for sexual immorality (Muslim, *ḥudud* 12:III, p. 911, no. 4191 [3199]);

• Jesus' return to earth at the end of time (Bukhari, *anbiya'* 49:IV, p. 436, no. 657 [3192]).

Most narratives are sayings whose author is the Prophet himself; they are *hadith nabawi* or prophetic sayings. Some are known as *hadith qudsi*, divine sayings uttered by the Prophet under divine inspiration.[1]

The Hadith and falsification

Having looked at the importance of the Hadith, we now return to the subject of the previous chapter: what the Hadith has to say on the accusation that Jews and Christians falsified their Scriptures.

The Hadith accounts show that the Prophet and his companions knew some Christians and had many contacts with Jews in Arabia. Consequently we would expect the question of whether or not the Scriptures were falsified to be one of the major disputed issues. To our surprise and even disappointment, however, only a few narratives concern this question.[2] This scarcity is in itself significant. The authority of the Scriptures did not by and large pose much of a problem for the first Muslim community.

Ṭabari (310/923)

One hadith, or narrative, is recorded in the much respected commentary on the Qur'an by Ṭabari. In his exegesis of sura 5:68 he quotes Ibn 'Abbas, one of the Prophet's companions. A group of Jews had come to question the Prophet to find out whether he really believed the Torah:

> O Muhammad, 'Do you not claim that you walk in the steps of Abraham's community and religion, you believe in the Torah which we have and confess that it is God's truth?'
> The Messenger of God said, 'Of course I do but you have read into the Scripture things that are not there and you have rejected God's covenant with you, and you have concealed what you had been commanded to make known to the people. Therefore, I disown your innovations.'
> They replied, 'We abide by what is in our hands [the Torah]; we follow the truth and the guidance and we do not believe in you nor do we follow you.'
> Then God revealed this verse (5:68), 'Say, O People of the Book:

You have nothing to rely upon unless you stand by the Torah, the Gospel and what your Lord has revealed to you.'

Here the Prophet's positive answer is followed by a remark that describes the Jews' disloyalty towards their Scriptures by using three verbs: *aḥdatha* (to innovate), *jaḥada* (to reject) and *katama* (to conceal). None of these verbs, of which only the third is Qur'anic, indicates that the Jews had changed the text of the Torah. Does this suggest that the Prophet was so aware of the Jews' respect for their sacred texts that he did not question their authenticity?

Darimi (255/868)

The second hadith is reported by 'Abbad b. 'Abbad, a Muslim from the second generation. 'Umar, the second caliph, is quoted by 'Abbad as having called Muslims to honour the Qur'an and to abide by its teaching. He goes on to attack 'the People of the Book', and especially their leaders, who held on to their privileges to the detriment of the teaching of the Scriptures:

> If the doctors and the monks had not feared their rank and dignity would disappear through obedience to the teaching of the Scripture, they would not have falsified nor concealed them. When they infringed upon Scripture by their actions they tried to deceive their people regarding what they had done, for fear of seeing their prestige abolished and their corruption unveiled. So they have falsified the Scripture through their interpretation, and what they could not falsify they have concealed. In this way, they have hidden their actions in order to keep their prestige. In the same way they said nothing about the [evil] actions of their people through complaisance. 'God took a covenant from the People of the Book to make it known and clear to humankind and not to hide it' (Qur'an 3:187). But they have manipulated it and adapted it to their advantage.[3]

This narrative is full of Qur'anic words that betray the degree of its Qur'anic inspiration. The accusation against the doctors (*aḥbar*) and monks (*ruhban*) reminds us of the accusation against the Christians who took their leaders as their lords (9:31). These religious leaders ravished the people's possessions (9:34) instead of complying with God's covenant

(3:187; 5:13–14) by true obedience to the Torah and the Gospel (5:66–68). They covered up their behaviour through the falsification and concealment of Scripture.

The motives for the alteration of the Scriptures are made clear in this account. In order to perpetuate their domination over their subjects, and so as not to allow their lives to be seen as contrary to the Scriptures, the authorities of both communities had resorted to reprehensible practices.

The identification of two modes of alteration represents another interesting point in this narrative. We are told that the dignitaries falsified the Scriptures by deliberately *misinterpreting* their texts and by *concealing* what was too obvious to lend itself to misinterpretation. As this narrative is impregnated by the letter and spirit of the Qur'an, the light it sheds on the meaning of the Qur'anic texts is particularly valuable.

Bukhari (256/870)

Ibn 'Abbas noticed that some Muslims had talks with Jews on religious issues. He was concerned about the outcome of these relations and sought to deter Muslims from engaging in such discussions:

> Muslims! How do you ask the people of the Scriptures, though your Book [i.e. the Qur'an] which was revealed to His Prophet is the most recent information from God and you recite the Book that has not been distorted? God has revealed to you that the people of the Scriptures 'have changed with their own hands what was revealed to them, and they have said: This is from God, in order to get some worldly benefit thereby.' (2:79)

> Ibn 'Abbas added: Isn't the knowledge revealed to you sufficient to prevent you from asking them? By God, I have never seen any one of them asking you about what has been revealed to you.[4]

It is not too difficult to understand Ibn 'Abbas's concerns about the possible influence of the Jews on the growing Muslim community. By quoting a critical Qur'anic text about 'the People of the Book' (2:79) he seeks to discredit the Jews and to dissuade Muslims from talking with them. His argument is that the Qur'an, being the latest Scripture that God has revealed, is by that very fact more comprehensive than any previous revelation. However, one may ask: why should Muslims be discouraged from discussing with 'the People of the Book'? After all, does not the Qur'an point Muslims to them if they have a query about God's revelation (10:94; 16:43)?

According to one tradition, the Jews used to read the Torah in Hebrew and then explain it to the Muslims in Arabic. On seeing this the Prophet commented, 'Do not believe the People of the Book, nor disbelieve them, but say, "We believe in God and whatever has been revealed to us, and whatever has been revealed to you" ' (cf. 2:136; 29:46).[5] The Prophet was at least prepared to listen to Jews and Christians talking about their Scriptures.

In Bukhari there is another hadith about falsification, intended to explain the following Qur'anic verse:

> Those to whom We have given the Book know it as well as they
>   know their own sons.
> A group among them deliberately conceals the truth knowingly.
>   (2:146)

So what was 'the truth', how was it concealed, and by whom? The hadith gives us this answer:

> The Jews came to God's Apostle and told him that a man and a woman from among them had committed adultery.
>
> God's Apostle said to them: 'What do you find in the Torah about stoning?'
>
> They replied: 'We disclose their shameful act and lash them.'
>
> Then 'Abdullah b. Salam said: 'You are telling a lie; the Torah contains the penalty of stoning.'
>
> The Jews brought the Torah and opened it. One of them placed his hand on the verse about stoning and read the verses preceding and following it.
>
> 'Abdullah b. Salam told him: 'Lift your hand.' When he lifted his hand, the verse about stoning was written there.
>
> They said: 'Muhammad has told the truth, the Torah contains the verse about stoning.' Then God's Apostle gave the order that both of them be stoned to death, and they were.
>
> 'Abdullah said: 'I saw the man leaning over the woman to shelter her from the stones.'[6]

In this incident, the hadith indicates clearly that the text of the Torah had not been changed. The Jews are blamed for lying about what the

Scripture said in order to protect other Jews from being put to death. Thus the charge made against them in sura 2:146 is historically founded; but since the text itself is not in question, the scope of the Qur'anic accusation is limited.

Ibn Ḥanbal (241/855)

The final narrative stems from an observation that Mu'adh b. Jabal made upon his visit to a land inhabited by many Christians. He was sent by Muhammad to preach Islam in either Syria or the Yemen. The narrator is uncertain about the location, but this is not relevant to the meaning of the hadith, which has two variants, the first of which is as follows:

> Mu'adh saw Christians bowing (*tasjudu*) before their archbishops and bishops. He said to himself that God's Apostle is worthier of being exalted in such a way. When he came back [to Arabia], he said, 'O Apostle of God, I have seen that Christians bow before their archbishops and bishops. I have said to myself that you are worthier of being exalted.'
>
> He said, 'If I had to command anyone to bow I would order the woman to bow before her husband. The woman does not fulfil her duties towards God until she has entirely fulfilled her duties towards her husband so that if he asked her to give herself to him even when she is in labour she would consent.'[7]

Of the nine canonical compilations of the Hadith, Ibn Ḥanbal's collection is certainly the largest, which is partly why the authenticity of many sayings attributed to the Prophet has been questioned. However, the above narrative is also found in the collections of Abu Dawud and Ibn Majah, which are more reliable.[8] What Muhammad is reported to have said concerning a woman's duties towards her husband is no doubt shocking.

Regarding the second variant of the account, also contained in Ibn Ḥanbal's collection, there is no compelling reason to doubt its authenticity. When Mu'adh saw Christians bowing before their archbishops and bishops he asked them:

– Why do you do that?
– Because this is how the Prophets were greeted.
– Our Prophet is worthier of being greeted this way.

Having returned home Mu'adh asked the Prophet about this. He replied:

– They have lied about their prophets just as they have falsified their Scripture. God has given us a better way for greeting which is the way people in paradise greet one another [*al-salamu 'alaykum*, 'Peace be upon you'; cf. Qur'an 7:46; 10:10; 36:58].[9]

This narrative is the only one that criticizes Christians by name, *al-naṣara*, for tampering with their Scriptures. Without excluding Jesus, it is likely that the prophets referred to are the Jewish prophets. In Old Testament times it was not unusual to greet people by bowing low before them (cf. Gen. 23:7, 12; Exod. 18:7). Such a gesture indicated honour towards highly respected people such as kings (1 Sam. 25:23, 41; 2 Sam. 9:6.8; 1 Kgs. 1:16, 23, 31, 53), prophets (2 Kgs. 2:15; 2 Kgs. 4:37) and even parents (1 Kgs. 2:19). The Qur'an too reports that Joseph's brothers fell down before him in recognition of his leading position in Egypt (12:100; cf. Gen. 44:14).

It is true that Jesus taught his disciples not to let anyone call them 'lords', for they had only one Lord and they were all brothers (Matt. 23:8). Moreover, he showed them what kind of Lord he was by washing their feet (John 13:1–17). No Christian would want to dispute that not all Christian leaders walk in Jesus' footsteps in serving their people. If what this hadith means is that Christian leaders had corrupted the Scriptures by abusing their authority over their people, it echoes one of the criticisms of the Qur'an against them (9:31, 34). Christians must be open to hear such criticisms about inconsistencies in their lifestyle and practice.

In summary, then, the Hadith contains very few narratives on the subject of the falsification of the Scriptures. Those we have considered accuse Jews and Christians of falsely interpreting and teaching the Scriptures, but do not suggest that the *text itself* was corrupted.

Notes

1 Bukhari, *tafsir* 32:1:VI, p. 289, no. 303 [4406]; cf. Qur'an 32:17; Bukhari, *riqaq* 38:VIII, p. 336, no. 509 [6021]; Muslim, *dhikr* 22:IV, p. 1413, no. 6499 [4852].

2 The narratives considered in this chapter represent the only ones concerning the falsification of Scripture in the nine canonical compilations of the Hadith.

3 Darimi, *muqaddima* 56 [647].

[4] Bukhari, *shahadat* 29:III, p. 526, no. 850 [2488]; cf. ibid., *i'tiṣam* 25:IX, p. 339, no. 461 [6815]; *tawḥid* 42:IX, p. 460, no. 613 [6968] and p. 461, no. 614 [6969].

[5] Ibid., *i'tiṣam* 25:IX, p. 338, no. 460 [6814].

[6] Ibid., *manaqib* 26:IV, p. 532, no. 829 [3363]; cf. ibid., *ḥudud* 37:VIII, p. 550, no. 825 [6336]; Muslim, *ḥudud* 26:III, p. 918, no. 4211 [3211].

[7] Ibn Ḥanbal, *musnad al-kufiyyin* no. 151 [18591].

[8] Abu Dawud, *nikaḥ*: II, p. 574, no. 2135; Ibn Majah, *nikaḥ* 4:III, p. 116, no. 1853 [1843].

[9] Ibn Ḥanbal, *musnad al-kufiyyin* 151 18591.

4

What has been falsified?

As we have seen, there are two major ways of understanding what the
Qur'an and the Hadith teach about the corruption of the Scriptures.
Muslim theologians are divided into two groups as to which of these
views they hold. The first group claims that Jews and Christians have
misinterpreted the Scriptures, but that the text of these Scriptures, or at
least most of it, is authentic. The second group claims that the *text of the
Bible has been changed*; not that it has been changed entirely, but that it
has been changed in such a way that taken as a whole it is no longer
reliable.

The first view: the meaning has been falsified

Some of the greatest Muslim thinkers belong to the first group: Razi
(606/1209), Baqillani (403/1013), Avicenna (428/1037), Ghazali (505/
1111) and, more recently, Muḥammad 'Abduh (1323/1905).

Razi

Razi considers it unlikely that the text has been falsified. He gives two
reasons. The first is *theological* and is founded on one of God's essential
attributes: God is truthful and so must be his word. If God had let his very
word become unreliable, his truthfulness would be undermined. Razi's
second reason is *historical* and is based on the successive transmission,
tawatur, of the Bible: with its many manuscripts being disseminated all
over the world, the Bible has been handed down uninterruptedly, which

rules out the falsification of its text. Therefore the only consistent option for Razi is that the Jews had concealed the teachings of the Torah, for example those concerning the coming of Muhammad, or the legal punishment for adultery.

Ghazali

Ghazali is a well-known Muslim theologian and mystic who died in the twelfth century AD. His *Excellent Refutation of the Divinity of Jesus from the Plain Sense of the Gospel*[1] sets out to prove that Christians had misinterpreted those Gospel passages that appear to show Jesus as the Son of God. The fact that he bases his arguments on the text of Scripture indicates (unless we dismiss it as purely tactical) that he accepts their authority.

According to Ghazali, two principles are required for a correct interpretation of the Gospels. First, those texts acceptable on rational grounds must be taken *literally*, and those unacceptable rationally must be interpreted *metaphorically*. Secondly, every effort should be made to reconcile anything that appears to be contradictory.[2] When applied to Jesus the first principle means that since his divinity would contradict God's oneness, he can be 'the Son of God' only in a metaphorical sense. As for the second principle, one must choose: either Jesus is God or he is human. The fact that many texts underline Jesus' humanity leaves us with no doubt, says Ghazali, as to the real meaning of the apparently contradictory passages.[3]

Baqillani

Baqillani gives much more credit to the Christian Scriptures than to the Jewish Scriptures. In his major theological work he devotes a whole chapter to the Christian doctrines of the trinity of God and the divinity of Jesus Christ.[4] His aim is to provide an alternative interpretation of the Gospel texts and in so doing to prove that Christians have given unwarranted and wrong interpretations to their Scriptures. To achieve his objective Baqillani adopts a strictly rationalistic approach similar to that of Ghazali. As for the Jewish Scriptures, Baqillani associates the alteration of the Torah with the disappearance of the monarchy in Israel. He believes that the alteration is also due to errors in interpreting the Torah, in copying it, and in translating it from one language to another.

Muhammad 'Abduh

Muḥammad 'Abduh was a great Egyptian scholar of the nineteenth century. He was a reformer, calling for the renewal of Islamic thought while seeking to remain faithful to the teaching of Islam. In his renowned commentary on the Qur'an,[5] 'Abduh takes a view similar to that of Razi. He explains in relation to sura 2:159 that the dissemination of the Scriptures made it impossible for the text to be falsified. He blames only the Jews for the alteration of the Scriptures and remarks that, just as they had altered the Torah so as to reject Christ, so they had misinterpreted passages in the Torah and in the prophet Isaiah, which had in fact foretold the coming of Muhammad.[6]

'Abduh's exegesis of sura 2:185 provides him with the opportunity of comparing the Scriptures of Islam with those of Judaism and Christianity. The light of the truth shines far more brightly in the Qur'an, he says, than in the Torah or the Gospels. The Gospels indicate that the disciples themselves found it difficult to understand the teaching of Jesus, yet, 'Abduh adds, 'we believe that this is the authentic Gospel'.[7]

The Egyptian reformer makes another interesting parallel when he explains sura 3:78. Some Jews in Medina used to recite human writings as if they were Scripture, so as to deceive their people about Muhammad:

> There is among them a section who distort the Book with their tongues:
> As they read you would think it is a part of the Book, but it is no part of the Book;
> And they say, 'That is from God', but it is not from God. (3:78)

Applying this verse, 'Abduh explains that certain Muslims today falsify, *yuḥarrifuna*, the Qur'an with their own interpretations, trying to justify their conservatism (their unwillingness to reform) on the one hand, or their heretical views on the other. Some even claim that they do not have to found their religion on the Qur'an, but rather on what scientists say.[8]

The second view: the text has been falsified

According to the second group of Muslim theologians, the very text of Scripture, and not just its meaning, has been changed. This group includes Ibn Ḥazm (456/1064), Juwayni (478/1085) and, to some degree, Ibn Taymiyya (728/1328), who takes a middle position. Today most

Muslim apologists follow this school of thought. They seem to be unaware of the fact that their radical views concerning the alteration of Scriptures reflect only one trend within classical Islamic theology.

Ibn Taymiyya

Ibn Taymiyya, who died in the fourteenth century AD, questions the successive transmission of the Torah and the Gospel in his *Correct Answer to Those who Changed the Religion of Christ*:[9] 'Muslims claim that the Torah and the Gospel which the People of the Book today possess are not the products of successive transmission from Moses and Jesus. The chain of transmission of the Torah was broken first at the time of the destruction of Jerusalem and the expulsion of the Israelites from the city.'[10] The author claims that the present Torah was the work of one man, Ezra, who was not a prophet and whose aim was to reinforce his authority over the Jews. This appears to refer to two separate events, mistakenly identified as the same: the discovery of 'the book of the law' (probably an old manuscript of Deuteronomy) under King Josiah in 622 BC (2 Kgs. 22:8–13), and the reading of 'the book of the law of Moses' by Ezra in 515 BC (Neh. 8:1–8).

When considering the four Gospels, Ibn Taymiyya makes the point that they were written many years after Jesus ascended to heaven, that Mark and Luke were not among Jesus' apostles, and that Luke never saw Jesus. Therefore, he says, 'error is possible in the transmission by two, three, or four, especially when they erred concerning Christ himself, so that it even seemed to them that he was crucified'.[11]

Although Jesus had twelve apostles, commissioned to be his witnesses, Ibn Taymiyya considers that this was not enough to guarantee that Jesus' teaching was conveyed accurately: 'the apostles were *only twelve* men', he says.[12] He suggests that the alteration of the Gospels occurred shortly after they were written, 'when their copies were still a small number – one, two or four'.[13]

The author also argues that the divinity of Christ, the reliability of the Scriptures and the 'messengership' of the evangelists are mutually dependent. He sees this interrelatedness as a major flaw that undermines the Christian faith: 'Thus it must be said to them concerning this position, "You are not able to prove Christ's being God except by these books. You are not able to show the correctness of these books except by proving that the apostles are inerrant messengers of God. You are not able to prove that they are messengers of God except by proving that

Christ is God." Their position has thus become a vicious circle.'[14] It must be said, however, that the link between the credibility of the messenger and the reliability of the message applies to Islam as much as in Christianity. The credentials for Muhammad's prophethood lie with the Qur'an being an outstanding Arabic Scripture. The Qur'an, on the other hand, would not be God's word if Muhammad was not God's Prophet. Ultimately, none other than God can give evidence for the trustworthiness of his word. This requires, on our part, more than a mind to understand God's word; it requires a heart to trust God himself.

Holding to such views as he does, one would expect Ibn Taymiyya to give little credit to the Scriptures, but this is not so. He considers that the scope of their alteration is limited and so does not undermine their reliability: 'Some [Muslims] state that the texts of the two books [the Torah and the Gospel] which have undergone change are but a few, and this is the more likely view ... What is true is that in the Torah and the Gospel which the People of the Book possess today there is contained the judgment of God, although some of their texts have undergone corruption and change (5:41–43).'[15] If the Christian Scriptures have not undergone radical change, yet the religion of Christ has been altered by the church, this means that Christianity is no longer founded on the teaching of Christ but instead on the doctrine of the church, says Ibn Taymiyya. He blames the first church councils for having made up dogmas such as the Trinity and the divinity of Christ, and blames Christians for claiming inerrancy for the men of the Councils after the apostles.[16] The practices of the church show how far Christianity is from the religion of Christ, he says, and lists those with no basis in the Gospels: praying towards the east, eating pork, the use of pictures in churches, keeping a fifty-day fast, monasticism, the celebration of Christmas, Epiphany and the Holy Cross, and replacing circumcision with baptism.[17]

It is true that many of these practices, more typical of the Eastern Church, have no textual warrant in the Gospels. The question is, however, whether they contradict the teaching of Jesus. In Islam too, many beliefs and rituals have no basis in the Qur'an or Hadith (e.g. the festival of the Prophet's birth, the commemoration of 'Ashura, etc.).

Finding inconsistencies and contradictions: Juwayni and Ibn Hazm

The title of Juwayni's treatise indicates its polemical content: *Quenching the Thirst of Those who Seek the Truth about the Alteration of the Torah and the Gospel.*[18] Two and a half centuries before Ibn Taymiyya, Juwayni questioned the successive transmission of the Torah.[19]

Muslim authors often try to prove their case by referring to the text of the Bible. Juwayni points to the differences between the Torah used by the Jews and the Torah used by the Christians, that is, the Septuagint.[20] One example is the length of the age of the Patriarchs from Adam to Terah (Abraham's father), which varies between the Hebrew text and the Greek translation.[21]

Ibn Ḥazm, the author of a book dealing with the history of religions,[22] lists the contradictions he finds between the Torah and history (e.g. the duration of the Israelites' captivity in Egypt; Gen. 15:13; Exod. 12:40). He lists further contradictions between the Torah and geography (e.g. the location of the four rivers in Eden; Gen. 2:10–14), contradictions between the Torah and rationality (e.g. the creation of Adam in God's image; Gen. 1:26–27), and contradictions between the Torah and morality (e.g. Noah's drunkenness; Gen. 9:20–23). Above all, he lists contradictions between the Torah and the Qur'an.[23]

When we read the Gospels, we find they sometimes differ in their accounts of the same events. Some Muslims see these differences as contradictions. Their approach, both rationalistic and literalistic, leads them to find many textual discrepancies. Juwayni gives five examples of such discrepancies: Jesus' genealogies,[24] Peter's betrayal of Jesus,[25] Jesus' entry to Jerusalem,[26] the attitude of the two robbers towards Jesus on the cross,[27] and the events that took place immediately after Jesus died.[28]

For Ibn Ḥazm, too, the Gospels make no sense, as he sees them to be full of inconsistencies. How could 'the Son of God' be tempted by the devil? How could Jesus claim that he did not come to abolish the law (Matt. 5:17), yet at the same time make divorce unlawful and put an end to the law of retaliation (Matt. 5:31–32, 38–42)? How could Jesus possibly ask people not to speak about his miracles, since miracles are meant to accredit God's prophets and to lead people to follow them? Jesus never claimed to be more than a man (cf. John 20:17), says Ibn Ḥazm, yet his disciples made him God. It is impossible, indeed absurd, he says, to believe that God is the son of man, or that he is both the Son of God and the son of man, or that a human being gave birth to God.[29]

How, then, does Ibn Ḥazm understand the Qur'an and the Hadith when they speak positively about the Scriptures? The hadith that reports Muhammad's belief in the authenticity of the Torah is declared unauthentic. By contrast, those hadiths that accuse Jews and Christians of tampering with their Scriptures are judged reliable. The Qur'anic text describing the Torah and the Gospel as 'light and guidance' is seen as referring to the Scriptures prior to their falsification; and the invitation to Jews and Christians to stand by their Scriptures is seen as a call for them to believe in Muhammad, whose mission has been foretold in the Scriptures.

Ibn Ḥazm concludes that the Qur'anic teaching leaves us with no doubt as to the corruption of the Torah and the Gospel. He does not, however, consider this as meaning that they have been altered in every part. He makes the point that God in his sovereignty has decided to protect parts of these Scriptures to serve as a charge against Jews and Christians. We are warned that none of us should challenge God about his actions for, as the Qur'an says (13:41; 21:23), God does not have to give account of what he does.[30]

Summary

'The Bible has been corrupted.' This is how Muslims explain that, in spite of being predicted in the Scriptures, Muhammad is not acknowledged as God's Prophet by Jews or Christians. Muḥammad 'Abduh saw in the Jews' rejection of Jesus a precedent for their failure to recognize Muhammad's prophethood. Indeed, Jesus himself criticized the Jewish leaders for misinterpreting the Torah (Mark 7:8–13). He did not, however, challenge the reliability of its text. Christians therefore accept the authority of the Torah and consider it to be part of their own Scriptures. By contrast, the Islamic Scripture includes neither the Torah nor the Gospel, although the Qur'an confirms them both. Had these been part of the Islamic Scriptures, Muslims would have been in a position to compare the biblical teaching with that of the Qur'an and to reach their own conclusions.

The belief that the Bible has been altered has become widespread within the Muslim community, yet many have scarcely had any opportunity to look into it. Some Muslim scholars (Razi, 'Abduh) have rightly observed, on theological and historical grounds, that only the meaning of the Scriptures could have been corrupted. They see the Scriptures as authentic, but argue that some of the texts have been misinterpreted. In particular they refer to the texts concerning the coming of Muhammad and the person of Jesus. We shall need to look carefully at these references,[31] but in the next chapter I shall first respond to the most radical view, which holds that the biblical text has been falsified.

Notes

[1] Ghazali, *al-Radd al-jamil li-ilahiyyat 'Isa bi-ṣariḥi l-Injil* (1939). The attribution of this work to Ghazali is a matter of debate. R. Chidiac, who edited this text and translated it into French, accepts its authorship, as do L. Massignon, M. Smith and J. W. Sweetman. But M. Bouyges, W. M. Watt, and more recently H. Lazarus-Yafeh, are of a different opinion. See H. Lazarus-Yafeh, *Studies in al-Ghazzali* (Jerusalem: Magnes, 1975).

[2] Ghazali, *al-Radd*, p. 8.

[3] We shall return to Ghazali's interpretation of the Gospels in chapter 17.

[4] Baqillani, *Kitab al-Tamhid*, pp. 75–103.

[5] M. 'Abduh, *Tafsir al-Manar*.

[6] Ibid., vol. 2, pp. 48–50.

[7] Ibid., pp. 159–160.

[8] Ibid., vol. 3, p. 343.

[9] Ibn Taymiyya, *al-Jawab al-ṣaḥiḥ liman baddala dina l-Masiḥ*, pp. 137–369.

[10] Ibid., p. 215.

[11] Ibid., p. 216.

[12] Ibid., p. 236; my emphasis.

[13] Ibid., p. 239.

[14] Ibid., p. 216.

[15] Ibid., pp. 225–226.

[16] Ibid., pp. 217, 219, 221.

[17] Ibid., pp. 229, 233, 237, 253.

[18] Juwayni, *Shifa' al-ghalil fi bayan ma waqa'a fi-l-Tawrat wa-l-Injil min al-tabdil*.

[19] Ibid., pp. 44–46.

[20] The Septuagint (sometimes abbreviated as LXX) is the Greek translation of the Old Testament that was widely used by the early church (see chapter 1, n. 4). Subsequent translations of the Old Testament were often based on the Septuagint rather than on the Hebrew text. Bible translations today are based on the Hebrew text for the Old Testament and the Greek text for the New Testament.

[21] Juwayni, *Shifa'*, pp. 50–56; cf. Gen. 11:10–26.

[22] Ibn Ḥazm, *Kitab al-Fiṣal fi l-milal wa l-ahwa' wa l-niḥal*.

[23] Ibid., vol. 1, part 1, pp. 98–224.

[24] Juwayni, *Shifa'*, pp. 58–66; cf. Matt. 1:1–17; Luke 3:23–38.

[25] Ibid., pp. 68–72; cf. Mark 14:66–72; Luke 22:54–60.

[26] Ibid., pp. 72–74; cf. Matt. 21:1–7; Mark 11:1–5.

[27] Ibid., pp. 74–76; cf. Matt. 27:39–44; Luke 23:39–43.

[28] Ibid., pp. 76–80; cf. Matt. 27:51–53.

[29] Ibn Ḥazm, *Kitab al-Fiṣal*, vol. 1, part 2, pp. 1–69.

[30] Ibid., part 1, pp. 211–215.

[31] See chapter 17, 'Islamic interpretation of Jesus' claims', and chapter 20, 'Do the Scriptures foretell the coming of Muhammad?'

5

Why the biblical text has not been falsified

The charge that the Torah and the Gospel have undergone textual corruption remains unsubstantiated and contains serious flaws. In this chapter we shall consider four arguments in defence of the text of Scripture: (1) *theological*: the word of God must reflect who God is; (2) *scientific*: the manuscripts give evidence for the reliability of the Scriptures; (3) *rational*: the falsification of the Scriptures does not make sense; and (4) *biblical*: the Scriptures need to be read as they were intended.

The word of God must reflect who God is

Razi explains that textual corruption of the Scriptures would be inconsistent with the character of God, because God's word must reflect who God is. Since God is truthful and trustworthy, his word cannot be corrupted in such a way that it becomes unreliable. This key principle is repeated several times in the Qur'an: 'There is nothing that can alter the words of God' (6:34; cf. 10:64; 18:27). God who revealed his word guarantees that he will protect it from corruption: 'We have sent down the Message and We Ourselves watch over it' (15:9).[1] This principle is also found in the Bible: 'Your word, O LORD, is eternal; it stands firm in the heavens' (Ps. 119:89; cf. 1 Pet. 1:24–25). Jesus too confirmed that God's word is unchangeable and committed himself to the preservation of the Gospel: 'It is easier for heaven and earth to disappear than for the least stroke of a pen to drop out of the Law' (Luke 16:17). 'Heaven and earth will pass away, but my words will never pass away' (Matt. 24:35).

To believe that the Scriptures have undergone textual corruption would imply that God had failed in his promise to communicate his word to humankind. It would be incompatible with his sovereign power, which is central to his character. We must also ask why God would have taken the initiative to reveal his word if all along he knew that it would not be transmitted accurately. Would it make sense? Could it be reconciled with his wisdom?

The falsification of the Scriptures contradicts not only God's truthfulness, power and wisdom, but also his faithfulness. God is faithful to his word (Deut. 7:9). He solemnly declares that he himself guarantees its effectiveness:

> As the rain and the snow
>   come down from heaven,
> and do not return to it
>   without watering the earth
> and making it bud and flourish,
>   so that it yields seed for the sower and bread for the eater,
> so is my word that goes out from my mouth:
>   It will not return to me empty,
> but will accomplish what I desire
>   and achieve the purpose for which I sent it. (Is. 55:10–11)

Would God's word be effective if it were not preserved from alteration?

God is faithful not only to his word but also to his people. He revealed his word so that they would know the truth. Jesus promised his disciples that they would be guided in all truth (John 16:13). Surely God would be guilty of misleading his people if he had allowed his word to be twisted. If he had permitted it to be corrupted, what could we make of his faithfulness in keeping his promises?

The evidence of the manuscripts

The material evidence for the corruption or authenticity of the Scriptures lies with the manuscripts. The study of these manuscripts confirms the integrity of the Bible. Far from being a handicap, as mentioned earlier, the very existence of many manuscripts has enabled scholars to establish that the text of the Bible has been amazingly well transmitted. Writing in the fourteenth century, Ibn Taymiyya thought that for the authenticity of the Scriptures to be proven, every manuscript needed to be checked. This was not feasible at the time since they were scattered all over the world.[2] Today, however, the situation is very different. Scholars have unprecedented means and opportunities for communicating and comparing their findings. The manuscript experts, regardless of their religious convictions, agree that the Bible has been handed down with exceptional accuracy. The textual variations in no way call into question the integrity of the biblical text.[3]

Some Greek manuscripts of the whole Bible (Old and New Testaments) pre-date the birth of Islam. The Codex Sinaiticus (preserved in the British Museum in London) and the Codex Vaticanus (kept in the Vatican library) are from the fourth century. The Codex Alexandrinus (also in the British Museum) is from the fifth century. When compared with later manuscripts, these manuscripts show that the text of the Bible has not been changed as a result of Jews and Christians failing to accept Muhammad as God's Prophet.

Although there are many translations of the Bible, they are based on the same Hebrew and Greek manuscripts. The diversity in these translations helps us to understand God's word better. Each translation has its merits, and new translations are necessary because human languages represent living realities that evolve with people, time and space.

Today, thanks to the scholars who specialize in the study of the biblical manuscripts, we have the material evidence for the successive transmission of the Bible. Razi, who believed in the *tawatur* of the Torah, nevertheless suggested that the Jews had changed the legal punishment for adultery, replacing the death penalty for adultery with whipping the adulterers instead. We have seen that the Hadith does not support this view. Although the Jews did not implement the Torah's punishment for adultery, they did not change its text either.[4] It is worth noting that all existing manuscripts of the Torah require the death penalty for adultery (cf. Lev. 20:10; Deut. 22:22). Conversely, the Qur'anic verse about stoning, *ayat al-rajm*, is not found in the Qur'anic text but in the Hadith. Initially part of a Qur'anic revelation, this verse was mistakenly not preserved in the Qur'anic Codex.[5]

Falsification does not make sense

Muḥammad 'Abduh pointed out, as we have seen, that the widespread propagation of the Scriptures made it highly unlikely that anyone could have tampered with them. Any attempt was not only doomed to failure for practical reasons, but bound to be discovered and disowned. The animosity between Jews and Christians meant that if either community had tried to change the Scriptures they would have been denounced by the other.

Modifying the texts would have been an impossible task. Not only were the Scriptures widely scattered but they had been translated into different languages. By the time of Christ the Old Testament was available in Greek, and by the end of the third century most of the New Testament had been translated into Latin, Syriac and Coptic. The New Testament was also quoted in Christian writings as early as the second century.

One has to ask: why in the first place would 'the People of the Book' corrupt their own Scriptures? And would it make sense for any religious community to falsify what they hold most dearly?

The Scriptures must be read as they were intended

Many objections Muslims raise to the authenticity of the Scriptures stem from their *rationalistic* or *literalistic* reading of their texts. But neither of these approaches is warranted for a sound understanding of God's word in the Bible, or even of God's word in the Qur'an. Indeed, a rationalistic approach to God's word is not in line with Islamic teaching.

Because God is far above his creatures, his revelation is not to be judged by human criteria. Many things in the Qur'an appear to be quite irrational. Miracles are just one among many examples, such as the youths who slept in the cave for 309 years (18:25) and King Solomon talking with ants and the hoopoe (27:18–22). Mainstream Islamic theology defines faith (*iman*) as trusting God (*taṣdiq bi-llah*), not as understanding who he is. Similarly, does not *islam* mean submitting to God, which includes submitting our mind as well as our will?

This non-rationalistic approach to God's word is even more appropriate for understanding the Bible. For unlike the Qur'an the Bible is not just God's revelation of his *will* for humankind; it is God's revelation of *himself*. If the Scriptures are about who God is, their message is necessarily beyond the reach of the human mind alone to comprehend. Those seeking to understand the Scriptures will not rely exclusively on their own intelligence, for the ultimate interpreter of the Scriptures must be the very same God who is revealed in them. The Bible is the written account of God's self-disclosure in the history of Israel and supremely in the person of Jesus Christ.

It is equally unfitting for God's word to be read with a literalistic approach. When the Qur'an, for instance, speaks of God sitting on the throne (7:54: 10:3; 13:2; 20:5), or of God's hand (3:73; 48:10; 57:29), most Muslims do not take these expressions at face value. A literalistic approach to the Scriptures contradicts their very nature. The Bible, far more than the Qur'an, is a collection of different types of writing, and it is common to find several literary genres in the same book. Therefore, we must interpret a biblical text in its context and according to its literary genre.

We should avoid, for instance, giving a literal or scientific interpretation to a symbolic, poetic or apocalyptic text. Revelation, the last book in the Bible, is full of symbolic figures and images that need to be interpreted metaphorically and would not stand up to a literal interpretation. Or take a historical text: it will not necessarily be a rule for us to follow. Thus when we are told of the sinful actions of certain prophets, it is obviously not to discredit these men of God, and still less to point to them as examples to follow. The Bible recounts their sins because they were actually committed. This refusal to cover up the truth, however shocking or dishonourable for the men involved, confirms the authenticity of the Bible.

The primary focus of the Bible is to communicate God's truth. In the example just given there is an important truth: the fact that great men of God fell into sin shows how deeply ingrained it is in human nature. We are told this not to plunge us into despair but to lead us, as David was led, to repent and to trust in God's mercy alone for our salvation (see Ps. 51; 2 Sam. 12).

In Islam God's word basically means a Book: the Torah, the Zabur, the Gospel and the Qur'an. Prophets are God's messengers who speak in God's name, some of whom had been entrusted with Scriptures to pass on to their people. Thus the Qur'an is the word of God, and Muhammad is God's messenger who conveyed this word first to the Arabs and then to the rest of humankind. In Christianity, as we noted in chapter 1, things are not the same. The Christian understanding of God's revelation is significantly different from that in Islam. While the Bible is God's word in *written form*, Jesus Christ, who is called God's Word in the Qur'an (3:39, 45; 4:171), is the word of God in *human form* (John 1:1–14). 'In the beginning was the Word, and the Word was with God, and the Word was God … The Word became flesh and made his dwelling among us' (John 1:1, 14). The written word of God bears witness to Jesus Christ himself, for 'the testimony of Jesus is the spirit of prophecy' (Rev. 19:10). Thus Jesus is the embodiment of God's word.

Jesus is himself God's revelation to humankind. The gospel is the message (not the book) Jesus proclaimed, which he commissioned his twelve apostles to proclaim after him. Thus the gospel of Jesus Christ is recounted in the four Gospels, but equally in the rest of the New Testament writings. The Gospel narratives give us four perspectives on Jesus, his person and his mission. They are not intended to be comprehensive histories or detailed biographies, nor do they always report events in chronological order. They have a message to communicate, and the way things are reported serves to highlight aspects of Jesus' teaching and mission. It is Jesus who is the focus of these God-inspired records about God's involvement in human history.

As God's incarnate word, Jesus has a role in Christianity similar to that of the Qur'an in Islam. As God's messenger, Muhammad's status is comparable to that of Jesus' apostles, especially those who committed the gospel to writing. Muhammad was the recipient of God's word, as were the apostles. What made these people prophets is not primarily, as Ibn Taymiyya supposed, that Jesus is seen in the Gospels as God incarnate, but the fact that God chose them to be his messengers. Some of the New Testament writers (e.g. Mark, Luke and James), as Ibn Taymiyya rightly observed,[6] were not among Jesus' twelve apostles; and not all of them were, like Paul (cf. 1 Thess. 2:13), fully aware of being led by God to put his word into writing. Yet God oversaw the whole process of communicating his word through them.

Certainly God's revelation in Christianity is different from what Muslims expect it to be, but who are we to challenge God on the way he decides to reveal his word? Who are we to think that it is not fitting for the Scriptures to have been written in a way different from the Qur'an? Muslims and Christians need to acknowledge that God is free to reveal his word as he pleases. As a result, Muslims ought not to read the Scriptures with an Islamic perspective; nor should Christians read the Qur'an with a Christian one.

The fact that God decided to communicate his word to humankind implies that he committed himself to making his people identify this word as such. God's faithfulness to both his word and his people meant that it was he who led the Israelites, and Christians after them, to recognize his written word. He led them to discern, from among the abundant religious writings of the time, those writings that were truly his word. It was God who led his people to identify the books of Holy Scripture. It was not for Jews and Christians to judge on their own authority what was and what was not the word of God. Rather, by the power of the Holy Spirit they recognized what he had inspired.

In short, if we accept this Christian understanding of revelation, we cannot approach the Scriptures with the literalism of Ibn Ḥazm or Juwayni, or with the rationalism of Baqillani or Ghazali. What we need instead is a thorough and open-minded study of the Scriptures, enlightened by the Spirit of God who inspired them. Such a prejudice-free approach will cause most of the apparent discrepancies to disappear. Many numerical discrepancies in the Old Testament, for instance, can easily be accounted for as scribal errors. Some of the other apparent inconsistencies, however, will remain, mainly because of our ignorance. These difficulties in interpretation summon us to further research, greater humility and more trust in the divine author of the Scriptures. They should not be allowed to dim our vision of the clarity of the Scriptures' message. Otherwise, we find ourselves in a position where we are not able to see the wood for the trees.

Conclusion

So if the text of Scripture has not been changed, has it instead been misinterpreted by Jews and Christians? In other words, are the Torah and the Gospel really in line with Islam? Do they predict Muhammad's mission after all? As we noted earlier, the Qur'an makes no reference to any specific scriptural text to back up its claim that the Scriptures foretell the coming of Muhammad; the only reference is found in the Hadith. We shall return to this question in Part 4, where we consider the prophethood of Muhammad in more detail.

To sum up, then, the theory that the Scriptures have been falsified seems to have originated largely because the Islamic concept of revelation was applied to the Scriptures. It shows a misunderstanding of what the Bible is, and, more importantly, of who Jesus is: that is, God's word made human. Some Muslim intellectuals today are better informed regarding what revelation means to the Christian and are more ready to accept the authenticity of the Scriptures than their predecessors were.[7] It was earlier generations of Muslim thinkers who made an article of faith out of a few critical Qur'anic references to the attitude of 'the People of the Book' towards their Scriptures.

Notes

[1] The Arabic word for 'message' is *dhikr*. It is used for the Qur'an as well as for the Torah (see 21:48, 50, 105). Ibn Taymiyya quotes sura 15:9 and

applies it to the interpretation of God's word rather than to the text itself
(Ibn Taymiyya, *al-Jawab*, p. 238).

[2] Ibid., pp. 226, 230, 240.

[3] It can be said that no comparable work of antiquity has stood up so well
to the test of time. For example, Julius Caesar's *The Gallic War*, written
in the first century BC, has come down to us thanks to ten manuscripts,
the oldest of which dates from the ninth century. The Greek historian,
Thucydides, lived in the fifth century BC; the earliest manuscripts of his
History of the Peloponnesian Wars date from the ninth century. The same
is true of the *History* of the great Greek historian Herodotus. Today no
history scholar challenges the authenticity of these works. The textual
evidence for the authenticity of the Bible is far weightier.

[4] Cf. Bukhari, *manaqib* 26:IV, p. 532, no. 829 [3363].

[5] The word *hadd* (pl. *hudud*) is the Arabic word for legal punishment in
Islamic law. The present Qur'anic text requires one hundred lashes for
each of the adulterers (24:2). However, according to the Hadith this
sanction was abrogated and replaced with the verse about stoning which
requires the death penalty (cf. Bukhari, *hudud* 30–31:VIII, p. 536, no.
816 [6327]; p. 537, no. 817 [6328]; Muslim, *hudud* 15:III, p. 912, no.
4194 [3201]). The Hadith also refers to two suras not found in the
present Qur'an. One, it is said, 'resembled in length and severity to
Bara'at' (sura 9, known as *al-Tawba*), and the other 'resembled one of the
surahs of *Musabbihat*' (suras 57, 59, 61, 62 and 64). Of the latter, only
two verses have been preserved: 61:2 and 17:13 (cf. Muslim, *zakat*
119:II, p. 500, no. 2286 [1740]).

[6] Ibn Taymiyya, *al-Jawab*, p. 216.

[7] An example of a readiness on the part of both Christians and Muslims
to engage in a dialogue about the significance of Scriptures in Christianity and Islam is given in *The Challenge of Scriptures: The Bible and the
Qur'an*, by the Muslim Christian Research Group.

Part 2
Key doctrines

6

The greatness of God

Christianity and Islam are both monotheistic religions that state emphatically that there is only one God. The central doctrine in Islam speaks of the oneness of God, *tawḥid*. God is the Creator, the one who has made humankind 'in the finest form of creaturehood' (95:4; 64:3). He is eternal, personal, sovereign, powerful, wise, holy and just:

> God is He, besides whom there is no other god;
> Who knows (all things) both secret and open;
> He, Most Gracious, Most Merciful.
> God is He, besides whom there is no other god;
> The King, the Holy One, The Perfect One,
> The Trustworthy, The Ruler, The Mighty One,
> The Powerful, the Supreme:
> Glory to God! (High is He) above the partners they attribute
>   to Him.
> He is God the Creator, the Maker, the Bestower of Forms
>   (or Colours),
> To him belong the Most Beautiful Names:
> Whatever is in the heavens and on earth, declares His Praises
>   and Glory:
> And He is the Mighty One, the Wise. (59:22–24)

Islamic theology distinguishes ninety-nine names for God, known as 'the most beautiful names of God', *asma' Allah al-ḥusna* (cf. 7:180; 17:110; 20:7; 59:24). According to the Hadith: 'God has ninety-nine names, one-hundred less one; and he who has memorised them all by heart will enter Paradise. To count something means to know it by heart.'[1] Some of these names are:

al-waḥid	The One	*al-ḥayy*	The Living
al-qadim	The Eternal	*al-khaliq*	The Creator
al-qahir	The Sovereign	*al-qaḍi*	The Judge
al-qadir	The Powerful	*al-raḥim*	The Merciful
al-aḥad	The Unique	*al-hadi*	The Guide
al-ṣadiq	The Trustworthy	*al-rabb*	The Lord
al-ghafir	The Forgiving	*al-wahhab*	The Generous
al-salam	The Perfect	*al-muḥyi*	The Life-giving
al-ṭahir	The Pure	*al-awwal*	The First
al-ʿadil	The Just	*al-akhir*	The Last
al-ʿalim	The Knowing	*al-malik*	The King

The names of God certainly give us some idea of who he is. The supreme Name, however, which represents God himself, remains unknown (cf. 87:1). The existence and identity of this Name are much debated by Muslim theologians, but they all agree that God's self-revelation is limited to his will expressed in his word.[2]

And what about the name *Allah*? All Arabs, whether Jewish, Christian or Muslim, refer to God as *Allah*, since it is the only word for 'God' in Arabic. It is, for example, found in all Arabic translations of the Bible. According to most Arab linguists, the word is a contraction of the definitive article *al* and the Arabic name for God, *ilah*. Hence the name *Allah* refers to God as the only God, '*the* God'. The word *ilah* derives from a root carrying the ideas of adoration, protection, eternity, power and creation. Some linguists consider that *Allah* is a proper noun, that is, the name of God, which has no derivation. It is similar to the name of God in other semitic languages: Aramaic (*Elah*), Syriac (*Alaha*) and Hebrew (*El, Eloah, Elohim*).[3]

We shall now consider a few of God's names and attributes, seeing that he is transcendent and unique, merciful and loving, and the one who is Lord and Judge.

God is transcendent and unique

Just as in Christianity, Islam claims that God is *transcendent*, meaning that he is radically other than, and totally separate from, his creation.

The world is not an emanation of God. There is an essential discontinuity between the Creator and the universe he has made. This otherness of the Creator is clearly affirmed in the Qur'an:

> He is the Creator of the heavens and the earth:
> He has made for you pairs from among yourselves, and pairs
>   among cattle:
> By this means does He multiply you.
> *There is nothing whatever like unto Him,*
> and He is the One that hears and sees all things. (42:11; my emphasis)

From a biblical perspective, divine transcendence does not exclude all resemblance between God and humankind. The fact that God is fully divine and humankind fully human does not necessarily mean that the Godhead and humankind are to be defined in mutually exclusive terms. The separation between God's nature and human nature does not preclude some similarity in our respective attributes. Indeed the Bible says that God made us in his image:

> Then God said, 'Let us make man in our image, in our likeness,
> and let them rule over the fish of the sea and the birds of the air,
> over the livestock, over all the earth, and over all the creatures that
> move along the ground.'

> So God created man
>   in his own image,
> in the image of God
>   he created him;
> male and female
>   he created them. (Gen. 1:26–27)

Our creation in the image of God underlines our superior rank over all other creatures. It emphasizes the exclusive privilege we have, for we are called to enjoy an intimate relationship with our Creator. At the same time, God grants us power and responsibility to make full use of the earth and to look after it. Our dignity is based on our relationship with the one who created us to be, in a manner of speaking, his partners. This is illustrated, for example, in our ability to bear children and to relate to them in a way that reflects to some degree God's relationship with humanity.

The creation of human beings in the image of God is not a concept found in the Qur'an. The Qur'an does, however, describe humanity as God's *caliph* on earth (2:30). The Arabic word *khalifa* is used to refer to the men who succeeded Muhammad at the head of the Muslim nation. When it is applied to people in general, it indicates that the Creator has entrusted us with the responsibility of representation and of stewardship (cf. 38:26). Does not the fact of fulfilling such a function imply a very special closeness, and indeed a unique relationship, between God and his 'viceroy'? This point is highlighted by the text in Genesis.

In the Hadith the Prophet declares that 'God created Adam in His [or his] image'. But what does this saying, which undoubtedly echoes the biblical text, mean in Islamic tradition? Muslims have interpreted it in various ways. For the sake of clarity it is possible to distinguish three groups of theologians, corresponding, broadly speaking, to three versions of the saying.

(1) *The literalists.* Those who are known in early Islam as *al-mujassima*, 'the corporalists', give the hadith a literal interpretation: 'God created Adam in His own image with His length of sixty cubits.'[4] They draw the conclusion that God is a body, *jism*, and that man was made in the likeness of this body.

The Ḥanbalites are more moderate in their interpretation. They believe that, since the Qur'an talks about God's face (2:115), his hands (3:26) and his eyes (11:37), God has an image, *ṣura*. This language, they say, refers to a reality different from what we know, and so cannot be explained or defined, *bi-la kayfa*.

(2) *The rationalists.* These consider that the pronoun 'his' refers not to God but to Adam: that is, God created Adam in the image of Adam. This could mean that God did not change Adam when he punished him for his disobedience and expelled him from paradise. Or otherwise, it could mean that God created Adam as a grown-up person in the sense that, unlike all other humans, he did not go through the different stages of childhood.

According to another interpretation, 'his' stands for humankind in general. On seeing a Muslim beating a fellow Muslim, the Prophet observed, 'When any one of you fights his brother, he should avoid his face for God created Adam in his image.'[5] In other words, Muslims should show respect for the human face because it is a replica of the face of Adam, who is God's prophet and the father of humankind.

(3) *The spiritualists.* These interpret Adam's likeness to God in spiritual terms. Another variant of the above hadith says, 'Do not make

ugly the face, for the son of Adam has been created in the image of God [*'ala surati l-rahman*, lit. in the image of the Merciful].'[6] This saying is understood in the sense that human beings, unlike all other creatures, possess some of the divine attributes such as intelligence, language, life, science, power, will, sight and hearing. Thus the creation of humankind in God's image points to 'the high dignity of man and of his being the roof and the crown of His creation and of his being the vice-regent of the Lord upon the earth'.[7] The role of humankind as God's representatives, *khalifa*, implies a certain similarity between God and representatives.[8]

Apart from the Sufis (who represent the mystical trend within Islam), Muslims do not focus much attention on human creation in the likeness of God. Instead, they concentrate on underlining the otherness of God. For them, when comparing God's attributes and those of human beings, 'only the names are the same … there is no comparison between the Creator and the created thing'.[9]

The concept of the transcendence of God in Islam does not mean that he is absent from his creation or that he is distant from humankind. On the contrary, the Qur'an asserts that 'God is nearer to us than our jugular vein' (50:16).[10] He is waiting for us to turn to him:

> If My servants question you [Muhammad] concerning Me, in
>   truth I am near.
> I answer the call of the suppliant who cries to Me.
> So let them listen to My call: let them believe in Me so that they
>   may walk in the right way. (2:186)

Christianity emphasizes the transcendence of God too, though in a different way from Islam. In the Bible the otherness of God implies that there is no other god and that no-one is like God. But there is much more to the otherness of God. He is unique in that *the Creator is also the Saviour*. In no-one else can anyone find salvation:

> And there is no God apart from me,
> a righteous God and a Saviour;
>   there is none but me.
> Turn to me, and be saved,
>   all the ends of the earth;
>   for I am God, and there is no other. (Is. 45:21–22)

No-one would have imagined that God, who is our Judge, could also be our Redeemer. In Christianity, God reaches out to humankind to the fullest extent: he has become a human being! No closer to humanity can he ever be.

God is merciful and loving

Among God's most beautiful names, 'the Ever-Merciful', *al-raḥman*, and 'the Most-Merciful', *al-raḥim*, stand out. The first of these names replaces *Allah* in several places in the Qur'an. God shows his mercy through his innumerable blessings:

> If you count up the mercies of God, never would you be able to
>   number them.
> God is truly Most-Forgiving, Most-Merciful. (16:18)

The blessings God gives include spiritual gifts such as the forgiveness of sins, and material gifts such as daily bread. His mercy is such that the Hadith compares it to that of a loving mother:

> Some Sabi [i.e. war prisoners, children and women only] were brought before the Prophet and behold, a woman amongst them was expressing milk from her breasts to feed and whenever she found a child amongst the captives, she took it to her breast and nursed it.
>   The Prophet said to us,
>   – 'Do you think that this lady can throw her son in the fire?'
>   We replied,
>   – 'No, if she has the power not to throw it.'
>   The Prophet then said,
>   – 'God is more merciful to His slaves than this lady to her son.'[11]

The Bible speaks of God's mercy in a similar way:

> Can a mother forget the baby at her breast
>   and have no compassion on the child she has borne?
> Though she may forget,
>   I will not forget you! (Is. 49:15; cf. Is. 66:13)

The love of God in Christianity

The gospel of Jesus Christ is not just about God's mercy: it is about God's *love*; and divine love is far more embracing than divine mercy. A merciful person is not necessarily loving, whereas a loving person is always merciful. Without love, the mercy of God would only serve to reveal more clearly his majesty as Creator and Judge. But divine love means that he commits himself to us and reveals to us not only his word but his very self. Love is so essential to his character that the New Testament goes as far as to say that 'God is love' (1 John 4:8, 16). Jesus drew out the full implications of perfect love when he said: 'Greater love has no-one than this, that he lay down his life for his friends' (John 15:13).

Being a message about God's incredible love for us, the gospel is also about *our response* to his love. Jesus showed his disciples how to walk God's way. He called them to love God, to love their neighbours, and even to love their enemies.

'Teacher, which is the greatest commandment in the Law?'

Jesus replied: '"Love the Lord your God with all your heart and with all your soul and with all your mind." This is the first and greatest commandment. And the second is like it: "Love your neighbour as yourself." All the Law and the Prophets hang on these two commandments.' (Matt. 22:36–40)

You have heard that it was said, 'Love your neighbour and hate your enemy.' But I tell you: Love your enemies and pray for those who persecute you, that you may be sons of your Father in heaven. He causes his sun to rise on the evil and the good, and sends rain on the righteous and the unrighteous. (Matt. 5:43–46)

If God created all of us in his own image then we should not be surprised if he loves us all and considers us special to him. Does a father love only those of his children who obey him?

The love of God in Islam

What about the love of God in Islam? It is certainly not central to the Qur'anic message: what is at the forefront is God's oneness and mercy. The usual Arabic word for a loving person is *al-muhibb*, which is not one of God's most beautiful names. Instead, we have the name *al-wadud*, which occurs just twice in the Qur'an. It is linked with 'the Most-Merciful' (11:90) and with 'the Most-Forgiving' (85:14). For Ghazali (who was both a mystic and theologian), the word has almost the same meaning as 'the Most-Merciful'. The only difference is that in the case of *al-wadud* the one to whom mercy is shown is not seen as a weak or needy person:

> Its meaning is close to 'the Merciful', but mercy is linked with one who receives mercy, and the one who receives mercy is needy and poor. So the actions of the Merciful presuppose there being one who is weak to receive mercy, while the actions of the Loving-Kind do not require that … In fact, love and mercy are only intended for the benefit and advantage of those who receive mercy or are loved; they do not find their cause in the sensitiveness or natural inclination of the Lovingkind One.[12]

The Qur'an speaks of God's love for people (3:31; 5:54). It is a conditional love that depends on their obedience. Thus God loves those who fear him (3:76; 9:4), trust in him (3:159), are steadfast (3:146) and equitable (5:42), and fight for his cause (61:4). But God does not love the unbelievers (3:32), the evildoers (3:57), the proud (16:23) or the prodigals (7:31). Above all, God loves those who love him and follow the Prophet:

> Say: 'If you love God then follow me: God will love you and forgive you your sins. God is ever forgiving and merciful.'
> Say: 'Obey God and His Apostle. If you turn away – God has no love for unbelievers.' (3:31–32)

In the context of the Qur'an, God's love means that he is pleased with his obedient servants rather than knowing them in a personal and loving relationship. Sura 5:54, however, suggests that God's love for people comes before their love for him: 'Believers! If any of you turn back from his religion, soon will God produce a people whom He will love as they will love Him, – lowly with the believers, but mighty against the unbelievers.' Razi explains this in terms of divine empowerment: God loves people so as to enable them to love him.[13] Muslim theologians understand God's love in a metaphorical way: God loves believers in that he wants to reward them for their obedience, to forgive their sins and to honour them in the hereafter.[14]

This love God has for his obedient servants is depicted in a famous hadith known as *ḥadith al-nawafil* (the hadith about supererogatory deeds). In this *ḥadith qudsi* (divine hadith) God presents his love as the reward given to those who go the extra mile in their submission to his law:

> I will declare war against him who shows hostility to a pious worshipper of Mine. And the most beloved things with which My slave comes nearer to Me is what I have enjoined upon him. And My slave keeps on coming closer to Me through performing *nawafil* (praying or doing extra deeds besides what is obligatory) till I love him, so I become his sense of sight with which he sees, and his hand with which he grips, and his leg with which he walks; and if he asks Me, I will give him; and if he asks my protection I will protect him; and I do not hesitate to do anything as I hesitate to take the soul of the believer, for he hates death, and I hate to disappoint him.[15]

Remarkable as it is, this hadith teaches that God's love is his response to people's obedience. This stands in sharp contrast to the love God has shown in Jesus Christ: '*This is love: not that we loved God, but that he loved us* and sent his Son as an atoning sacrifice for our sins' (1 John 4:10; my emphasis). Jesus demonstrated the love of God in serving the needy, healing the sick, feeding the hungry and, above all, in giving his life for us.

God as our loving Father

The fatherhood of God is fundamental to his nature in the same way as his love. His fatherhood in relation to humankind reflects his eternal fatherhood in relation to Jesus Christ. The supreme revelation about God in the Scriptures is that he is the eternal Father. In a sense, this is God's highest name. 'How great is the love the Father has lavished on us, that we should be called children of God! And that is what we are!' (1 John 3:1). The Father–child relationship to which God calls us corresponds to the way we have been created, that is, in God's image. It is the fulfilment of our relationship with God.

From an Islamic perspective it is degrading for God to be considered a Father. The word is seen to carry with it the idea of a mother and a child: 'The very Creator of heavens and earth: How could He have a son when He has no consort? He created all things, and He has full knowledge of all things' (6:101; cf. 72:3). The Qur'an makes it clear that 'God is One, God the ever self-sufficing, unbegetting, unbegotten. None is like to Him' (112:1–4).

Obviously there is a misunderstanding here that demands at least two clarifications. First, the fatherhood of God means that humankind, being created in the likeness of God, enjoys a unique relationship with him unlike that of any other creature; but this in no way implies that God has a spouse or that humankind shares God's nature. Secondly, by calling God 'Father', Christians bear witness to the fact that God the Saviour, as revealed in Jesus Christ, has given them the immense privilege of being adopted as his sons and daughters. They have become sons and daughters of God not by natural birth but by adoption.

Viewed in this way, human relationships can be seen as a reflection of the relationship between us and God, in that every human being encounters in his or her fellow human being a creature made in the image of God. This reflection is most fully expressed in the special bond between a man and woman within marriage. In God's purpose marital love is meant to be the best human illustration of God's love for us and the love we should have for him. That is why God's love for his people is often compared metaphorically to a husband's love for his wife (cf. Is. 50:1; Jer. 2:2; Ezek. 16; Hos. 1–3).

God is Lord and Judge

In the Qur'an God is often described as 'the Lord of the Worlds' (1:2). He is 'the Lord of all things' (6:164), 'the Lord of the heavens and the earth' (13:16), and 'the Lord of the East and the West' (26:28).

Although God has been willing to delegate responsibility to his human creatures, he has not given up his authority. We are his servants, called to use our power within the limits defined by our divine master. The word *islam*, as we have seen, means submission, obedience, capitulation. It indicates how we should live in total dependence on our Creator. The Qur'an defines human beings as servants especially honoured by their Lord (21:26).

In the Bible too, lordship is one of the major attributes of God:

The LORD reigns for ever;
   he has established his throne for judgment.
He will judge the world in righteousness;
   he will govern the peoples with justice. (Ps. 9:7–8)

You are worthy, our Lord and God,
  to receive glory and honour and power,
for you created all things,
  and by your will they were created
  and have their being. (Rev. 4:11)

God's authority, however, is inseparable from his fatherly love. Consequently, true submission to God is the submission of a son or daughter, the result of our relationship with our heavenly Father. Christians seek to submit their lives to God in response to his love. In this sense Christians may be defined as 'Muslims'. Our submission to God and our communion with him are nevertheless seriously damaged by the reality of sin.

The lordship of God will be fully revealed on the last day. The Qur'an describes God as 'the King of the Day of Judgment' (1:4). The Qur'an, like the Torah, emphasizes that God is the just Judge of all people. On the last day, he will bring us to life and will summon us to appear before his throne. He will then judge us according to his perfect justice, rewarding those who have done what is good and condemning those who have done what is evil. The former will enjoy eternal paradise and the latter will suffer eternal punishment (39:70–75).

The decision between them (at judgment) will be in perfect
  justice,
and the cry (on all sides) will be, 'Praise to God, the Lord of the
  Worlds!' (39:75)

The central message of the Gospel, as compared with the Torah and even, by analogy, with the Qur'an, is not the reality of the Day of Judgment (cf. Matt. 25:31–46), but the fact that our Judge has become our Saviour. As we shall see in the next two chapters, this is what makes the Gospel such 'good news'.

Notes

[1] Bukhari, *tawḥid* 12:IX, p. 363, no. 489 [6843]; Muslim, *dhikr* 2:IV, p. 1409, no. 6475 [4835]. Not all the divine names are found in the Qur'an. In the Hadith we have two different lists that overlap to some extent (Tirmidhi, *da'awat* 82 [3429]; Ibn Majah, *du'a'* 10 [3551]). A non-canonical list is given in the English translation of Muslim's *Ṣaḥiḥ* (IV, p. 1409, no. 2912).

[2] Sura 87:1 invites the Prophet to praise God's supreme Name, which is understood by commentators as referring to God himself. For a summary of this debate see D. Gimaret, *Les Noms divins en Islam*, pp. 85–94.

[3] On the etymological derivations of *Allah* and the interpretations given by Muslim theologians to *ilah*, see Gimaret, *Les Noms divins en Islam*, pp. 121–131.

[4] Bukhari, *isti'dhan* 1:VIII, p. 160, no. 246 [5759]; Muslim, *janna* 28:IV, p. 1421, no. 6809 [5075].

[5] Muslim, *birr* 115:IV, p. 1378, no. 6325 [4731].

[6] The references to this version of the hadith are in Gimaret, *Dieu à l'image de l'homme*, p. 124.

[7] A. Ḥ. Siddiqi, in Muslim, IV, p. 1378, no. 2872.

[8] A thorough study of this hadith is found in Gimaret, *Dieu à l'image de l'homme*, pp. 123–136. It should be underlined that the three types of interpretations correspond schematically to three variants of this hadith, i.e. all these variants could be interpreted in one way or another, and have been by different theologians.

[9] M. M. Khan, in Bukhari, VIII, p. 160, n.1.

[10] The *jugular vein* – any of several large veins of the neck, conveying blood from the head.

[11] Bukhari, *adab* 18:VIII, p. 19, no. 28 [5540]; Muslim, *tawba* 22:IV, p. 1438, no. 6635 [4947].

[12] Ghazali, *The Ninety-Nine Beautiful Names of God*, pp. 118–119; cf. Gimaret, *Les Noms divins en Islam*, pp. 423–426.

[13] Razi, VI:12, p. 21.

[14] Cf. Razi on sura 85:14; XVI:31, p. 112.

[15] Bukhari, *riqaq* 38:VIII, p. 336, no. 509 [6021].

7

The problem of sin

The Bible and the Qur'an are both uncompromising in their de-nunciation of sin. The Qur'an, which strongly affirms God's unity, denounces above all other sins the sin of associating other divinities with God. This 'sin of association', *shirk*, is the only one God does not forgive:

God does not forgive the association of a partner to Himself:
a lesser sin than that He forgives to whom He wills. (4:48, 116)

The notion of unforgivable sin is also found in the words of Jesus (Matt. 12:31–32). This sin, described as the sin against the Holy Spirit, seems to refer to a refusal to believe in Jesus Christ's divine mission by someone who has received irrefutable proof of it.

What about other sins? In the Qur'an, sin is seen as disobeying God's will. This disobedience is due to both an ignorance of divine law and the inherent weakness of human nature: 'God wills to make things lighter for you. For man was created a weak creature' (4:28). We therefore need the revelation of God, which is a light on our way, as well as God's help to be able to walk in the right way (1:5–7).

From the perspective of the Qur'an, sin has consequences only for the one who commits it, for 'no liability of one soul can be transferred to another' (6:164; 17:15; 35:18; 39:7; 53:38). This is why Adam's sin is seen to have had no repercussions on his descendants. Adam repented and God accepted his repentance (2:36–37). According to Faruqi, Adam's disobedience was simply a misunderstanding of what was good and what was not: 'Adam, therefore, did commit a misdeed, namely thinking evil to be good, of ethical misjudgement. He was the author of the first human mistake in ethical perception, committed with good intention, under enthusiasm for the good. It was not a "fall" but a discovery that it is possible to confuse the good with the evil, that its pursuit is neither unilateral nor straightforward.'[1] All human beings, according to Islam, are born in a state of moral purity. Our disobedient acts do not fundamentally alter our status: although disobedient, we remain God's servants and are able to compensate for our bad deeds by doing good works.

In the Bible too, sin is defined as the breaking of the law of God (1 John 3:4). But Jesus taught his disciples a deeper understanding of the law. He said that someone is already guilty of committing a sin the moment they think of doing it. So he equated hatred with murder and lust with adultery, for both stem from an evil attitude of the heart:

> 'You have heard that it was said to the people long ago, "Do not murder, and anyone who murders will be subject to judgment." But I tell you that anyone who is angry with his brother will be subject to judgment.' (Matt. 5:21–22)

> 'You have heard that it was said, "Do not commit adultery." But I tell you that anyone who looks at a woman lustfully has already committed adultery with her in his heart.' (Matt. 5:27–28)

The seriousness of sin

Jesus' teaching highlights the sinfulness of humankind and underlines the seriousness of sin. Islamic teaching stands in sharp contrast to this. The Qur'an teaches that good deeds outweigh evil deeds. The divine punishment for an evil deed is just, whereas the reward for a good deed is exceedingly generous: 'Whoever has done what is good will have the like ten times over and he who has done what is evil will be repaid only the equivalent. None will be treated unjustly' (6:160; cf. 4:40; 10:27). The Hadith too highlights God's generosity. God appears to be far more pleased with people's good deeds than he is angry with their evil ones: 'If My slave intends to do a bad deed then (O Angels) do not write it unless he does it; if he does it, then write it as it is, but if he refrains from doing it for My sake, then write it as a good deed (in his account). (On the other hand) if he intends to do a good deed, but does not do it, then write a good deed (in his account), and if he does it, then write it for him (in his account) as ten good deeds (and multiply it) up to seven-hundred times.'[2] Here God's generosity seems to be at the expense of his holiness and justice. In being so lenient with sin, he appears to overlook sin and to condone evil. In the Bible God is not so indulgent: he does not tolerate sin, nor does he put up with evil. Our good works are worthless: they do not appease God's anger against sin, nor do they make up for our bad deeds:

> All of us have become like one who is unclean,
>   and all our righteous acts are like filthy rags;
> we all shrivel up like a leaf,
>   and like the wind our sins sweep us away. (Is. 64:6)

Sin is the breaking of God's law, but it is much more than that. What we do outwardly reflects what is deep in our hearts. Beyond the act of law-breaking, sin refers to our general disposition in relation to God. It speaks of a broken relationship with God and a life characterized by the desire for independence from God – an attitude that effectively says, 'I want to run *my* life, *my* way.' It is this sin that weakens us, leads us astray and is the source of our many acts of disobedience.

Original sin

Because of the solidarity that exists within the human family, Adam, the father of all humankind, was responsible not only individually but collectively. His disobedience had consequences for all his descendants and affected all the members of his family. This bias towards evil, inherited from the first father, is what Christians call *original sin* (see Rom. 8:2; 1 John 1:8). It alienates us from our Creator.

The concept of original sin is alien to Islam, but the Qur'an does give us a portrait of human beings that represents an eloquent description of our sinfulness. Man is described as weak (4:28), with a restless anxiety (70:19). He is hasty (17:11), forgetful (39:8), ignorant (33:72), perverse, thankless (14:34), contentious (18:54) and rebellious (96:6). Above all, it is said that 'the soul has an inward bias towards evil' (12:53). The Qur'an says that people are so evil that they all deserve God's condemnation. And if it were not for God's patience, he would have destroyed us all: 'If God were to punish men for their wrong-doing, He would not leave, on the earth, a single living creature: But he gives them respite for a stated term' (16:61). The Qur'an describes Adam and Eve's disobedience in terms that are in some respects parallel to the biblical account (Gen. 3; Qur'an 2:35–38; 7:19–24; 20:116–123). As a result of their disobedience, God expelled them from paradise:

> We said: 'Adam, have your dwelling-place, you and your wife, in the garden.
>
> 'Together feed there freely, wherever you wish. But this tree, neither of you must approach, lest you commit gross violation.'
>
> Satan, however, brought about their fall, causing them to be ousted from their state of life.
>
> For We said: 'Go out from here in mutual enmity. Out in the earth is a habitation and needful provision for a season.'
>
> Adam was made aware of words that came to him from his Lord, who turned relenting towards him. For truly He is the One who accepts repentance and Merciful.
>
> We said: 'Go down from here, all of you. Guidance will come to you from Me. There will be no fear for any who follow My guidance, nor any reason to grieve.' (2:35–38)

It is worth noting that, unlike verse 35, the Arabic text in verse 38 does not use the dual form of 'you' when addressing Adam and Eve, but the plural form, implying that God was speaking to more than two people.[3] So who else is included? Who else is to be punished and receive the promised guidance? Is it Satan? Most likely not, since God's guidance, *huda*, is not for Satan, who remains God's enemy for ever. God's guidance is, however, for all of humanity. If God is speaking not only to Adam and Eve, but to all their descendants, this verse may suggest that humankind as a whole was affected by the disobedience of our forefathers. If this is the case it would mean that the Qur'an points to the teaching of the Bible on sin and its consequences.[4]

Why are all humans so prone to do what is evil? Is it not because there is something irremediably wrong in humankind, something that affects all of us from the very beginning of our existence? Here is a remarkable hadith that speaks of our bias towards evil from the first day of our lives: 'There is none born among the offspring of Adam but Satan touches it. A child, therefore, cries loudly at the time of birth because of the touch of Satan, except Mary and her child.'[5]

Why sin matters

The Bible elevates men and women to a far higher status than the Qur'an by declaring that we are created in the image of God. Conversely, sin is considered as even more serious than in the Qur'an. Because of the 'fall', we cannot save ourselves by our good works. We are all alienated from God, separated from him, and cut off from the one who is the source of life.

> But your iniquities have separated
>   you from your God;
> your sins have hidden his face from you,
>   so that he will not hear. (Is. 59:2)

> There is no-one righteous, not even one;
>   there is no-one who understands,
>   no-one who seeks God.
> All have turned away,
>   they have together become worthless;
> there is no-one who does good,
>   not even one. (Rom. 3:10–12)

God had warned Adam about the outcome of his disobedience: 'you must not eat from the tree of the knowledge of good and evil, for when you eat of it you will surely die' (Gen. 2:17). Adam's disobedience brought God's warning into effect, for 'the wages of sin is death' (Rom. 6:23). The sin he committed was not just a 'mistake in ethical perception'; it was far more serious than that. Such was his disobedience that he was denied any access to the tree of life and expelled from paradise, according to both the Bible (Gen. 3:22–24) and the Qur'an (2:38; 20:123). Spiritual alienation condemns everyone to spiritual death. That is why, more than once, Jesus referred to people as 'dead' (Matt. 8:21–22; John 5:24–25; cf. Eph. 2:1).

Islam teaches that our sins cannot offend our Creator, who stands too far above us to be directly concerned by our disobedience. When we commit sin we wrong ourselves; God remains unaffected: 'Whoever transgresses God's bounds does evil to himself' (65:1; cf. 2:57; 7:160; 18:35; 35:32; 37:113). Our guilt lies only in our disobedience to our Lord's commandments. From the biblical point of view, however, sin is not just a transgression of God's law but an offence against God himself

(Ps. 51:4; Luke 15:18, 21). Sin affects God personally and does not leave him indifferent. But rather than causing his judgment to fall on humanity, God unfolds the infinite treasures of his love and power to save us from our otherwise hopeless situation.

Notes

[1] I. Faruqi, *Islam and Other Faiths*, p. 120.

[2] Bukhari, *tawḥid* 35:IX, p. 437, no. 592 [6947]; *iman* 31:I, p. 36, no. 40 [40]; Muslim, *dhikr* 22:IV, p. 1413, no. 6499 [4852].

[3] Unlike English, where we have one form for 'you' (for both singular and plural), Arabic has different singular, dual and plural forms. The dual form is used when referring to two people, and the plural form is used when referring to more than two.

[4] Razi interprets this text along these lines: he explains that the plural form is meant to include not just Adam and Eve but their descendants too. In a sense we have all been expelled from paradise as a result of the disobedience of our first parents (cf. Razi on 2:36: II:3, p. 17; and on 15:123: XI:22, p. 112).

[5] Bukhari, *anbiya'* 44:IV, p. 426, no. 641 [3177].

8

The meaning of salvation

Christianity and Islam both testify that God is good, that he wants the good of humankind and that he acts effectively to achieve this end. In other words, God wants to save us. He wants to save us from our sins. But salvation does not have the same meaning in Islam as in Christianity. The reason is simple. In Islam, humans are not seen as being in such a hopeless situation before God: we are seriously ill, but not spiritually dead. A Muslim scholar goes as far as to say that strictly speaking the concept of salvation does not exist in Islam:

> Islam holds man to be not in need of any salvation. Instead of assuming him to be religiously and ethically fallen, Islamic *da'wah* [mission] acclaims him as the *khalifah* of Allah, perfect in form, and endowed with all that is necessary to fulfill the divine will indeed, even loaded with the grace of revelation! 'Salvation' is hence not in the vocabulary of Islam. *Falaḥ*, or the positive achievement in space and time of the divine will, is the Islamic counterpart of Christian 'deliverance' and 'redemption'.[1]

When we speak of salvation in Islam, what is meant is the way Muslims fulfil their religious obligations so that on the Day of Resurrection they escape God's judgment, receive forgiveness and enter paradise. Salvation has four components: faith, obedience, repentance and the Prophet's intercession on the last day.

Faith and obedience

According to the Qur'an, salvation consists first of all in believing:

> Believers! Believe in God and in His Apostle,
> and in the Book which He has sent down upon His Apostle
> and in the Book He sent down aforetime.
> Whoever repudiates faith in God, and His angels, His Books and
>   His Apostles,
> and in the Last Day, has indeed gone far into error. (4:136;
>   cf. 57:28; 61:10–12)

Islamic doctrine is summarized in these five articles of faith: belief in God, his angels, his Books, his Apostles, and the Day of Judgment. However, faith is inseparable from practice (cf. 4:13–14). Foremost among the works of faith are the 'pillars' of Islam: the recital of the confession of faith ('I bear witness that there is no god but God, and that Muhammad is the Apostle of God'), ritual prayer, statutory almsgiving, annual fasting and the pilgrimage to Mecca.

A Muslim's salvation therefore depends on assent to the truths revealed in the Qur'an, as well as observance of religious duties and the moral ideal:

> Righteousness does not consist in the mere act of facing on the *qiblah* [direction] of the east or of the west. They have the true righteousness who believe in God and the last Day, in the angels and in the Scripture and the prophets, who spend their substance – prize it lovingly as they may – on their own kinsfolk, and orphans, the impoverished, the wayfarer and those who beg, and on the ransoming of slaves. Theirs is true righteousness who perform the prayer-rite and pay the *Zakat* [almsgiving], who fulfil their word when they have given a promise, who endure patiently under distress and hardship, and in time of danger. These are the ones whose faith is genuine: these are the truly God-fearing people. (2:177; cf. 64:9)

Repentance

A Muslims' obedience to God's law contributes significantly to their salvation for 'good deeds blot out the evil ones' (11:114). But what if they disobey God's commands? They must sincerely repent and ask for divine forgiveness: 'Believers! Turn to God in sincere repentance. Your Lord may absolve you of your evil doings and bring you into gardens where streams flow, on the Day when God will not confound the Prophet nor the believers with him' (66:8; cf. 4:99; 9:102). By returning to God in this way, Muslims have good reason to believe that God will relent towards them and blot out their errors. God is indeed the one 'who forgives transgression and accepts repentance' (40:3). The fact that the above Qur'anic text states that God *may* (Arabic *'asa*) forgive does not necessarily cast doubt on his willingness to forgive. The expression is meant, explains Razi in his exegesis of sura 9:102, to encourage people to seek God's forgiveness intently. It underlines that forgiveness is, on the one hand, an act of divine sovereignty and generosity, and on the other, something we must ask for with true humility.[2]

Muhammad's intercession

In the Qur'an God's forgiveness is related to three of the four components of salvation: faith, obedience and repentance (19:60; 20:83; 25:70; 28:67). The fourth, the intercession of the Prophet, is not mentioned in the Qur'an; it is founded instead on several narratives in the Hadith. This intercession is seen as a privilege God has granted Muhammad and an expression of God's mercy towards Muslims. It is based on Muhammad's being the last Prophet (33:40) and on the fact that God has already forgiven his sins (48:1–3; 94:1–3).

On the last day, Muhammad's will ask God to grant forgiveness to the Muslims who need it most: 'My intercession will be for those of my nation who committed major sins.'[3] In response to the Prophet's intercession, God will forgive many Muslims, and they will come out of hell and enter paradise: 'Some people will be taken out of the Fire through the intercession of Muhammad, they will enter Paradise and will be called *al-jahannamiyyin* (the people of Hell).'[4]

Forgiveness and punishment

God is called 'the best of those who forgive' (7:155), but he cannot be bound by the obedience or disobedience of his creatures. He has every right to grant forgiveness as he pleases: 'He forgives whom He pleases, and punishes whom He pleases' (2:284; 3:129; 5:18, 40; 48:14). So, with the exception of the 'sin of association', *shirk*, nothing can limit divine mercy. Salvation is always a divine prerogative and favour, even when granted to believers; although they may have followed the teachings of Islam perfectly, they will have done nothing more than carry out their duties to their Creator.

The salvation promised by the Qur'an is eschatological: it will be revealed only on the last day, when people's actions will be judged on their true merits. The Qur'an uses the image of scales to illustrate the justice of divine judgment. In general, those whose good works outweigh their bad works will go to paradise, whereas those whose bad works outweigh their good works will go to hell:

> Those whose balance (of good deeds) is heavy, they will attain
>   salvation.
> But those whose balance is light, will be those who have lost their
>   souls;
> In Hell will they abide. (23:102–103; cf. 7:8–9; 101:6–8)

Salvation is thus associated more or less closely, depending on the theologians, with good works. But what if Muslims' evil deeds outnumber their good works? Here is where God's sovereign mercy comes in. He may decide to forgive them their evil deeds, either directly or in response to the Prophet's intercession. If he does forgive, they will go to paradise; otherwise they will first have to atone for their sins in hell and then enter paradise after that. Unbelievers, however, will suffer eternal punishment.

If the sovereign Judge decides to grant his forgiveness he will just need to say one word for his will to be done:

> It is He who gives Life and Death.
> If He decrees anything He only says: 'Be' and it is. (40:68)

Salvation in Islam, then, depends both on God's sovereignty and our natural capacity to do his will, both on his mercy and our ability to compensate for our evil deeds.

God's sovereignty in salvation is not accepted unanimously by Muslim theologians. For the Mu'tazili theologians, forgiveness is inextricably linked to a believer's obedience and repentance after disobedience. If these conditions are met, God *must* forgive; if they are not, he *must* punish them. God's forgiveness is limited to minor sins; any major sin must be punished (if it has not been repented of). People who have committed one major sin (including Muslims) will suffer eternal punishment if they do not repent. To believe that God could act otherwise would be to deny his justice. Therefore, the salvation of believers is their due as a reward for their good works. Furthermore, according to the Mu'tazilis, only repentant Muslims will benefit from the Prophet's intercession. Muhammad will not ask God to grant forgiveness to sinful Muslims but rather to increase his blessing on well-deserving Muslims. Thus 'the unearned blessing of any man or people, the Qur'an utterly rejects as not consonant with God's nature and His justice; the Muslims being no more unfit for such favouritism than any other people'.[5]

The role of good works

According to the Bible, a person's salvation is tied to faith in God and in Jesus Christ. This faith, if genuine, necessarily results in a change of life of which good works are the outward sign (cf. Eph. 2:10). These works are not merely an obligation and do not earn merit as in Islam. They are, as it were, an echo of God's love in the Christian's life: 'We love because he first loved us' (1 John 4:19). Jesus summarized the whole of the law of Moses and the teachings of the prophets in two commandments: 'Love the Lord your God with all your heart and with all your soul and with all your mind ... Love your neighbour as yourself' (Matt. 22:37, 39). In the words of Jesus as in the writings of his disciples, these two commandments become one, for the second follows on from the first: 'If anyone says, "I love God," yet hates his brother, he is a liar. For anyone who does not love his brother, whom he has seen, cannot love God, whom he has not seen. And he has given us this command: Whoever loves God must also love his brother' (1 John 4:20–21).

How does the Bible, and especially the New Testament, measure the distance separating men and women from God? By measuring how far we are from the love God expects of us. For religious persons, their sin is often to manipulate God's law to suit their own purposes. They obey the letter of the law but forget its essence, which is love. They use their obedience as a weapon, sometimes to justify themselves before God, and sometimes to condemn their neighbour. The major purpose of the law, however, is to reveal to us the gravity of our sin and to bring us into complete reliance on God for our salvation: 'No-one will be declared righteous in his sight by observing the law; rather, through the law we become conscious of sin' (Rom. 3:20). Therefore, none of us can rely on our good deeds; they will not bring us salvation.

The meaning of repentance

John the Baptist prepared the way for Jesus, preaching a message of repentance: 'Repent, for the kingdom of heaven is near' (Matt. 3:2). Following on from this, Jesus began his mission with a solemn appeal for repentance and faith: 'The time has come … the kingdom of God is near. Repent and believe the good news!' (Mark 1:15). Repentance is at the heart of Jesus' message: 'I tell you … unless you repent, you too will all perish' (Luke 13:3).

So what does repentance mean? In contrast to the Qur'an, which 'none shall touch but those who are purified' (56:79), Jesus did not hesitate to mix with people who were considered 'sinners' by the religious authorities of his day. Those known for their strict observance of the law were indignant at Jesus' behaviour. So Jesus told them, 'It is not the healthy who need a doctor, but the sick. I have not come to call the righteous, but sinners to repentance' (Luke 5:31–32). It is not that the religious leaders did not need to repent, but that they were not even aware of their need. That is why Jesus told them, 'I tell you the truth, the tax collectors and the prostitutes are entering the kingdom of God ahead of you' (Matt. 21:31).

In Jesus' words, repentance means the decisive act by which we turn around so as to live from this time on in total dependence on him. Genuine conversion means this inner change of direction, which marks the end of a life of sin and the beginning of a new life. We draw near to God, just as we are, without the merit of any good works, but relying solely on God's love made known in Jesus Christ.

The meaning of the cross

God has indeed shown the full measure of his love for us in the person of Jesus Christ. On the cross Jesus bore the punishment we deserve, dying in our place, taking upon himself the penalty for our sins:

> For Christ died for sins once for all, the righteous for the unrighteous, to bring you to God. (1 Pet. 3:18)

> You see, at just the right time, when we were still powerless, Christ died for the ungodly. Very rarely will anyone die for a righteous man, though for a good man someone might possibly dare to die. But God demonstrates his own love for us in this: While we were still sinners, Christ died for us. (Rom. 5:6–8)

And because of this, God can forgive us completely without denying his justice: 'God presented him as a sacrifice of atonement, through faith in his blood ... he did it to demonstrate his justice at the present time, so as to be just and the one who justifies those who have faith in Jesus' (Rom. 3:25–26). This text refers to the sacrificial system, which was an important part of the law given to Moses. The law prescribed different types of sacrifices to be offered, first in the tabernacle and later in the temple of Jerusalem. Animal sacrifices included 'a young bull without defect as a sin offering' and 'a ram ... without defect as a guilt offering' (Lev. 4:3; 5:18). These two sacifices were offered for sins committed unintentionally (Lev. 4 – 5). Sins in general were atoned for on the Day of Atonement, *yom kippur*, which played (and still plays) an important role in the religious life of Israel (Lev. 16). God ordained these sacrifices because the penalty for sin is death (Gen. 2:16–17; Ezek. 18:20; Rom. 6:23). Animal sacrifices, however, cannot redeem human life but only foreshadow the atoning sacrifice of Jesus Christ:

> The law is only a shadow of the good things that are coming – not the realities themselves. For this reason it can never, by the same sacrifices repeated endlessly year after year, make perfect those who draw near to worship. If it could, would they not have stopped being offered? For the worshippers would have been cleansed once for all, and would no longer have felt guilty for their sins. But those sacrifices are an annual reminder of sins, because it is impossible for the blood of bulls and goats to take away sins ... And ... we have been made holy through the sacrifice of the body of Jesus Christ once for all.
>
> Day after day every priest stands and performs his religious duties; again and again he offers the same sacrifices, which can never take away sins. But when this priest had offered for all time one sacrifice for sins, he sat down at the right hand of God. (Heb. 10:1–12)

Christians see the sacrifice of Jesus as the perfect sacrifice offered once for all for the forgiveness of sin. John the Baptist, who came to prepare the way for Jesus, according to the Gospel (John 1:19–28) and the Qur'an (3:39), described Jesus as 'the Lamb of God, who takes away the sin of the world' (John 1:29).

The idea of an atoning sacrifice for sin is alien to Islam. However, the Qur'an does refer to the sacrifice of a cow, from which the second sura gets its title 'The Cow'. God commanded Moses to offer 'a cow neither old nor a heifer … a golden cow, of bright colour to delight the eyes … a cow that has not been broken in to plough the land nor to water the tillage, one fully sound and unblemished' (2:67–71). From a Christian perspective, this sacrifice, of which the Torah speaks in more detail (Num. 19:1–10), points to 'the precious blood of Christ, a lamb without blemish or defect' (1 Pet. 1:19). Another sacrifice reported in the Qur'an is that offered by Abraham. God redeemed his son with 'a great sacrifice' (37:107). Muslims commemorate this event each year by the 'feast of the sacrifice', *'id al-adha*.

The resurrection of Jesus from the dead testifies to the fulfilment of his redeeming mission. Through raising him from the dead God demonstrated that he had accepted his sacrifice, and by exalting him to his right hand he declared him to be the Saviour of the world (John 4:42; 1 John 4:14). Jesus Christ is qualified to be our intercessor, not merely because he was a sinless prophet, but because of his atoning death. He now intercedes before God on behalf of all who believe in him: 'If God is for us, who can be against us? … Who will bring any charge against those whom God has chosen? It is God who justifies. Who is he that condemns? Christ Jesus, who died – more than that, who was raised to life – is at the right hand of God and is also interceding for us' (Rom. 8:31–34). The gospel is therefore *good news* in that it tells us that instead of condemning us according to his justice, God acquits us because of what Jesus has done. This salvation solves the dilemma implicit in Muslim theology: that is, either God pardons sinners without practising his justice, or he condemns them without showing his mercy.[6] The cross of Christ reveals God's mercy as well as his justice. It points to God's love for the sinner as well as his consistent hatred of sin.

It is in the cross that God's will to save men and women, rather than to punish them, finds fulfilment. Punishment is only, to use Luther's vivid expression, 'the work of God's left hand'. The Hadith attributes a similar saying to God: 'My mercy has surpassed my anger.'[7]

The gospel tells us of how God has demonstrated his *mercy*. But it is not only his mercy he has shown, for in Jesus Christ, God has also demonstrated his *sovereignty*. The very existence of evil in creation was, in a sense, a challenge to God's supreme power. Was he still in control of the world he had made? This question finds no adequate answer in Islam, for we would expect a powerful God not only to punish evildoers, but to eradicate evil completely. God's victory over evil and death was displayed through the death and the resurrection of Jesus Christ. Thus creation as well as salvation gives evidence that God still holds the destiny of the world in his hands.

Salvation now and then

Because God is the author of our salvation, and because he has already achieved our salvation through Jesus Christ, we do not have to wait until the Day of Judgment for his verdict on our lives. Even in this life we can be sure we have received his forgiveness and that we are right with him. For 'there is now no condemnation for those who are in Christ Jesus' (Rom. 8:1).

While on earth Jesus revealed God's love for people by forgiving their sins (Mark 2:1–12; Luke 7:36–50; John 8:1–11). In doing so he was making the point that God is determined to save humankind. The name *Jesus* means *God saves*: 'you are to give him the name Jesus, because he will save his people from their sins' (Matt. 1:21).

God fulfils his promise and saves us as soon as we turn to him and trust in what he has done for us in Jesus Christ. Because we know this promise to be true in our lives, those of us who trust him know the reality of his peace here and now. 'Therefore, since we have been justified through faith, we have peace with God through our Lord Jesus Christ, through whom we have gained access by faith into this grace in which we now stand. And we rejoice in the hope of the glory of God' (Rom. 5:1–2). Those who have been saved also produce good works that testify unmistakably to their life-changing experience.

On the Day of Judgment God will bring to completion his work of salvation in the lives of his people (see Rom. 5:9; 8:24). The fact that salvation is not yet fully ours in this life means that people may, and will, succumb to sin. Does this undermine our salvation? No – as long as we confess our sins and rely on God's appointed intercessor, we can remain assured of God's unfailing love:

> If we claim to be without sin, we deceive ourselves and the truth is not in us. If we confess our sins, he is faithful and just and will forgive us our sins and purify us from all unrighteousness … I write this to you so that you will not sin. But if anybody does sin, we have one who speaks to the Father in our defence – Jesus Christ, the Righteous One. He is the atoning sacrifice for our sins, and not only for ours but also for the sins of the whole world. (1 John 1:8 – 2:2; cf. Heb. 4:15; 7:26)

Completely undeserved

Salvation in Islamic teaching is based, to a lesser or greater degree, on divine reward. Paradise is promised to 'those who believe and work righteousness' (2:25; 3:15, 195; 4:57; 5:85, 119). Hell will be the fate of those 'who oppose God and His Apostle' (9:63, 68; 39:70–75). By contrast, Christianity is not just about God's eternal retribution. It is first of all about his redeeming love. If God's judgment were based on his justice alone, no-one would be saved, for God's verdict is that 'There is no-one righteous, not even one' (Rom. 3:10). No-one deserves to be saved, nor can anyone earn salvation.

The gospel points us to God's offer of salvation. It is a *universal* offer, available to all. It is an *unconditional* offer, not dependent on our merits or achievements. It is an *uncompromising* offer, satisfying God's justice and not compromising with sin. The promise of eternal life is for all who put their faith in Jesus Christ: 'For it is by grace you have been saved, through faith – and this not from yourselves, it is the gift of God – not by works, so that no-one can boast. For we are God's workmanship, created in Christ Jesus to do good works, which God prepared in advance for us to do' (Eph. 2:8–10).

How does God demonstrate his greatness?

The fundamental difference between salvation in Islam and in Christianity is explained by the fact that Islam does not acknowledge our moral downfall and consequently the necessity of our redemption. In Islam, people, though sinners, can present themselves before a merciful God with their own moral record and thus be hopeful of their salvation. Furthermore, the idea that God would want to identify himself with humankind through Jesus Christ, in order to take our sins upon himself and thus make possible our salvation, seems to Muslims totally unworthy of the Creator. It offends their sense of divine greatness and majesty. For Christians, however, our redemption reveals how God's sovereignty, mercy and justice have become a historical reality. These divine attributes are often glorified in the Qur'an, yet because love is not God's over-arching attribute there, as it is in Christianity, God does not reveal himself as the saving God. The gospel, however, tells the story of God's greatness being displayed uniquely in his suffering love.

God, and even more so his suffering love shown in Christ, which transcends all understanding (cf. Eph. 3:19), remain an unfathomable mystery. Christians seek not so much to understand this mystery as to worship him who is at its source. Submitting their reason to their Creator, they confess their inability to understand him in the depths of their being.

The Qur'an speaks of the overwhelming blessings God has in store for his obedient servants: 'No soul knows what things, yet hidden from them, await them to their entire delight in reward for their deeds' (32:17). God speaks of the unbelievable blessings he has in store for them in the following hadith: 'I have prepared for my faithful servants that which no eye has seen, no ear heard and which no man's heart has sensed. The proof of this may be found in the Book of God. Man is ignorant of the bliss which God has in store for him.'[8] It is striking to note that this hadith echoes, practically word for word, verses from the prophet Isaiah in the Old Testament (Is. 52:15; 64:3). The New Testament quotes them as a commentary on the wisdom of God, unfolded in the redemption of humankind through the death of Jesus Christ:

> No eye has seen,
>   no ear has heard,
> no mind has conceived
>   what God has prepared for those who love him. (1 Cor. 2:9)

In Islam God's unspeakable blessings refer to the recompense deserving people will receive in the hereafter as a reward for their obedience. By contrast, the same words in the Bible describe how God saves humankind in the most unexpected way, through the crucifixion of 'the Lord of glory' (1 Cor. 2:8). Salvation as a free gift is God's most precious blessing. Through it we receive all the privileges that come from entering into a new relationship with God. We become one of God's children, forgiven by him, loved by him, and knowing the assurance of eternal life.

Notes

[1] I. Faruqi, *Islam and Other Faiths*, pp. 316–317.

[2] Razi, VIII:16, p. 140.

[3] Abu Dawud, *sunna* 21:III, p. 1326, no. 4721 [4114]; Tirmidhi, *qiyama* 11 [2359]; Ibn Majah, *zuhd* 37:V, p. 528, no. 4310 [4300].

[4] Bukhari, *riqaq* 51:VIII, p. 371, no. 571 [6081]; cf. ibid., *tawḥid* 25:IX, p. 408, no. 542 [6896].

[5] Faruqi, *Islam and Other Faiths*, p. 126, n. 20.

6 Mu'tazili theologians consider God's justice as the overarching divine attribute, whereas for the Ash'aris God's sovereignty and mercy take precedence over everything else.

7 Bukhari, *tawḥid* 15:IX, p. 369, no. 501 [6855].

8 Ibid., *tafsir* 32:1:VI, p. 289, no. 303 [4406]; cf. *tawḥid* 35:IX, p. 435, no. 589 [6944].

9

The kingdom of God

Both Islam and Christianity teach that to some degree the kingdom of God has been established on earth. The coming of Jesus Christ for Christians and the revelation of the Qur'an for Muslims have ushered human history into a new phase. The birth of Islam (3:154; 5:50; 33:33; 48:26) and the revelation of the gospel (Acts 17:30) have brought the era of ignorance to an end. In its place a new era has begun, with the coming of the kingdom of God among all the peoples of the world, and especially among believers. It is not that God had previously refrained from exercising his royal sovereignty. He has always been king, but never before had he intervened in such a decisive fashion.

God's kingdom: among the Muslim nation

The Qur'an describes God as 'the King of heaven and earth' (2:107; 3:189). The kingdom of heaven and earth belongs to him and he rules over the Islamic nation through a law. To understand the concept of the kingdom of God in Islam we need to focus on this law. It is based on the teaching of the Qur'an and the Hadith. The Qur'an presents the Prophet Muhammad as a model for all believers (33:21) and the Hadith provides information about his life and teaching. As we begin to look into the law it is appropriate, therefore, to recall the main stages of Muhammad's life.

Muhammad's life

For twelve years (610–622) Muhammad preached to the people of Mecca, calling them to believe in one God. This message provoked much hostility from his polytheistic fellow citizens, with only a few dozen responding positively.

In 622 Muhammad decided to leave Mecca with some of his companions and emigrated to Yathrib, a city two hundred miles away, since known as Medina. There were three 'Arabized' Jewish tribes there, whose supremacy was strongly contested by the other Arab tribes. These groups, who had invited Muhammad and his companions to settle in their town, were more receptive to his message. The number of Muslims grew rapidly. At the same time, conflict arose and hardened with the Jews of Medina, who, together with the polytheistic Arabs of Mecca, were accused of conspiring against Muhammad. In this context the Prophet took on new responsibilities in the social and political organization of the growing Muslim community. The content of the Qur'anic revelation also evolved, taking into account elements of this new situation.

In 624 the struggle against the Jews of Medina reached a turning point in the Muslims' favour. From this time on, Muhammad's political authority was firmly established among his own followers and considerably feared by his enemies in Mecca. There were several battles between the two factions, until the Muslims finally won the victory. They triumphantly entered Mecca in 630, having obtained the surrender of its leaders.

Muhammad's military victory over his enemies reinforced the recognition of his prophetic mission, which was finally affirmed by the restoration of monotheistic worship in the temple of the *Ka'aba*. Many Arab tribes embraced the new religion and in the next few years the number of Muslims increased greatly, gaining an ever-stronger influence throughout the region. In 632 Muhammad died, having been hailed by the majority of Arabs not only as a Prophet, but also as a great social reformer, an exceptionally charismatic politician and a talented military leader.

The history of the first Muslim community, from its origins until the death of Muhammad, had a decisive effect on Islamic law. As well as being religious in character, it covers social, political, and even military matters. It will be useful to give a few examples from the Qur'an, the principal source of the law.

Social law

The social legislation centres on family life. Men and women must remain chaste before marriage (24:30–33). Marriage is a 'sign', pointing people to their Creator (30:21). It is a covenant between husbands and their wives (4:21) and must be preserved from all immorality (16:92; 17:32; 25:68; 42:37).

According to the Qur'an, adulterers – men and women – are to be punished with one hundred strokes of the whip (24:2). In the Hadith, however, we find what is known as *ayat al-rajm*, 'the verse about stoning', which has abrogated the Qur'anic sanction. This verse prescribes for married adulterers 'one hundred lashes and stoning to death', and for unmarried people 'one hundred lashes and exile for one year'. These punishments can be inflicted only 'when proof is established [by four witnesses], or if there is pregnancy, or a confession'.[1]

People who slander married Muslim women are to be punished by eighty strokes of the whip (24:4). Muslim men must not marry polytheistic women, but they may marry Jewish or Christian women (2:221; 5:5). They must also avoid marrying non-consenting women and near relations (4:19–25). The husband has authority over his wife, and, in the event of conflict between them, a specific procedure is recommended (4:34–35). Polygamy is authorized but limited to four wives, who must be treated without discrimination (4:3). Women who are prisoners of war have a different status from free wives (4:3; 23:6; 70:30). A husband must abstain from sexual intercourse with his wife during her menstruation (2:222). Although the grounds for divorce are not stated, detailed rules and regulations are laid down in the case of a breach of a marriage contract (2:227–232; 2:236–237, 241; 33:49; 65:1). Divorce is thus lawful, but according to the word of the Prophet, 'of all the lawful acts, the most detestable to God is divorce'.[2]

Children are a blessing from God, whether they are male or female. It is therefore forbidden to kill newborn baby girls, as was done among the Arabs before Islam (6:137, 140, 151; 17:31; 60:12). Babies should be breast-fed for a period of two years (2:233). In their turn children should respect their parents, showing affection and acting kindly towards them (2:83, 180, 215; 4:36; 6:151; 17:23; 29:8; 31:14; 46:15). Parents' attachment to their children, as to their material possessions, can become a severe test if it takes precedence over their faith in God (8:28; 64:14–15). They must therefore take care that their natural affection does not divert them from the way of God (63:9). With regard to succession, the rights of under-age orphans must be safeguarded, and the distribution of inheritance is governed by precise instructions (4:6–12, 176).

Religious law

On the religious level, Muslims are subject to five obligations known as 'the Pillars of Religion', *arkan al-din*:

1. *Shahada*: the recitation of the confession of faith: 'I bear witness that there is no god but God, and that Muhammad is the Apostle of God (*ashhadu an la ilaha illa-llah wa anna muḥammadan rasulu-llah*).
2. *Ṣalat*: prayer five times a day in the direction of Mecca, preceded by ritual ablutions (4:144; 5:6).
3. *Zakat*: statutory almsgiving, associated with prayer in numerous Qur'anic texts.
4. *Ṣawm*: annual fasting during the month of Ramadan (2:183–187).
5. *Ḥajj*: the pilgrimage to the temple of Mecca, at least once in a lifetime for those who are able (3:97).

Certain foods are prohibited (2:173; 5:3; 6:145; 16:115), as well as fermented drinks, games of chance (2:219; 5:90–91) and usury (2:275; 3:130).

The Qur'an warns apostates that they will suffer eternal punishment, but apostasy law based on the Hadith goes further. According to one hadith, the death penalty is required in three cases: 'The blood of a Muslim who confesses that none has the right to be worshipped but God and that I am His Apostle, cannot be shed except in three cases: In *qiṣaṣ*[retaliation] for murder, a married person who commits illegal sexual intercourse and the one who reverts from Islam and leaves the Muslims.'[3]

Love for God

Three Qur'anic verses speak about people's love for God:

> There are men who take (for worship) others besides God, as
>   equal (with God):
> They love them as they should love God.
> Those of faith are overflowing in their love for God. (2:165)

> Say: 'If you do love God, follow me: God will love you and forgive you your sins: For God is Oft-Forgiving, Most Merciful.' (3:31)

> Believers! If any of you turn back from his religion,

Soon will God produce a people whom He will love as they will
  love Him,
Lowly with the believers, but unbelievers mighty against the
unbelievers. (5:54)

Because a loving relationship suggests a relationship between people
equal to one another, most Muslims consider that it is not fitting for
humans to love God. Thus Razi explains, in his exegesis of sura 2:165,
that 'in saying that we love God what we mean is that we love obeying
him and serving him or that we love his reward and his beneficence'.[4] In
the Sufi tradition, however, the emphasis is on loving God personally;
that is, for who he is and not just because of his promise to reward his
faithful servants.

Just as the love of God is limited to believers, so Muslims are portrayed
as gentle or 'lowly with the believers', but stern or 'mighty against the
rejecters' (5:54). The characteriztic of Muslims' relationships with each
other is mercy rather than love: 'God bestows His mercy only on those
of His slaves who are merciful.'[5] The closest Islamic parallel to the
biblical command to 'Love your neighbour as yourself' (Matt. 22:39) is
the following hadith: 'None of you will have faith until he wishes for his
(Muslim) brother what he would like for himself.'[6] Clearly the biblical
command is more comprehensive and forceful.

Political law

On the political level, Islam claims to govern interpersonal relationships.
The law of retaliation given in the Torah (Lev. 24:17–21) remains in
force: 'life for life, eye for eye, nose for nose, ear for ear, tooth for tooth'
(5:45; cf. 2:178, 179, 194).

Submission to the political order of Islam does not necessarily imply
assent to its doctrinal content. The Qur'an distinguishes between
external submission and inner faithfulness to Islam, as witnessed in its
words to the Arab tribes who hastened to rally to Islam following the
Muslims' victory over the polytheists of Mecca:

The desert Arabs say: 'We have believed.'
Say: 'You have not believed: you should rather say: "We have
  become Muslims."
Faith has not entered your hearts.' (49:14; cf. 48:11)

Indeed, true faith consists in believing in God body and soul and renouncing everything to follow his way (cf. 9:24).

Resolute commitment to the cause of God and his messenger is called *jihad*. A saying attributed to the Prophet has it that 'the *mujahid* [fighter] is he who enters the fight against his own soul' so as to please God.[7] In the event of God's cause being in danger, Muslims are under an obligation to take up arms and fight the enemies of Islam, even if they are reluctant to do battle (2:216–218; 4:77). The Prophet gives battle first (9:73) and must urge Muslims to follow him (8:65). Indeed, it is preferable to engage in combat rather than to expose the Muslim community to sedition and run the risk of seeing God's cause defeated (2:191–193; 8:39). Armed combat or holy war is therefore the extreme form of *jihad*. Its aim is to defend Islam from its enemies. Muslims, nevertheless, must not act as aggressors or transgress the rules of combat (2:190); for whether they win or lose, they will ultimately be victorious: 'Do not ever think of those who are killed in the cause of God as being dead – rather as living in the presence of their Lord and in His providence' (3:169; cf. 2:154; 3:195; 4:74).

The comprehensive character of Islamic law constitutes proof for many Muslims of its perfection and superiority over the Torah and the Gospel. Provided the Islamic nation follows this law, which is seen as a real constitution, the Muslim nation will form a single nation (21:92; 23:52). It will be an exemplary nation (3:110), moderate (2:143), well balanced, neither repressive nor lax, neither utopian nor pragmatic. Islamic Law is consequently a law of good compromise, making it possible to reconcile God's demands with people's abilities, for God does not ask of man what he is not able to perform (2:233, 286; 6:152; 7:42; 23:62).

God's kingdom: among the Christian people

In the Bible, the universal sovereignty of God is stressed as it is in Islam. God is called 'the God of heaven and ... of earth' (Gen. 24:3; Matt. 11:25), the one whom 'The heavens, even the highest heaven, cannot contain' (1 Kgs. 8:27).

Jesus and the kingdom

Jesus' preaching and that of his disciples pointed to the imminent coming of the kingdom of God (Matt. 4:17; 10:7). The gospel is called 'the gospel of the kingdom' (Matt. 4:23; 9:35; 24:14). 'After John was put in prison, Jesus went into Galilee, proclaiming the good news of God. "The time has come," he said. "The kingdom of God is near. Repent and believe the good news!"' (Mark 1:14–15).

By his presence, his teaching and his actions, Jesus revealed the kingdom of God (Matt. 12:28). He gave this warning to those who hoped or expected that God's kingdom would be established with visible power and splendour: 'The kingdom of God does not come with your careful observation, nor will people say, "Here it is," or "There it is," because the kingdom of God is within you' (Luke 17:20–21). This kingdom, which Jesus readily compared in his parables with things or events from everyday life, is thus in no way spectacular, at least as long as the 'end' has not taken place (Matt. 10:22; 24:6, 13–14). Jesus spoke of an end to the period of history inaugurated by his coming, and said he would then come to establish the kingdom of God 'with power' (Mark 9:1). Moreover he called it 'his' kingdom (Matt. 16:28).

Jesus referred to the time separating his first coming from his advent in glory and the full establishment of the kingdom of God as 'the times of the Gentiles [or the nations]' (Luke 21:24). This time, the duration of which is known only to God (Mark 13:32), is the period he has allocated to allow all the nations of the earth to have access to his salvation (Rom. 11:25–26). Jesus' mission has indeed made the kingdom of God accessible to all nations. Until then it had been limited to Israel.

At no time in his earthly ministry did Jesus seek to impose his kingdom or his gospel, but his popularity increased nevertheless. On one occasion he had to slip away from the crowd when they were about to carry him off and make him king by force (John 6:15). When he was arrested he put up no resistance. To the great dismay of his disciples, he preferred to allow himself to be killed rather than resort to violence, even in self-defence (John 18:10–11). Standing before the Roman governor who questioned him, Jesus explained the meaning of his kingdom: 'My kingdom is not of this world. If it were, my servants would fight to prevent my arrest by the Jews. But now my kingdom is from another place' (John 18:36).

Throughout his trial, despite being subjected to all kinds of humiliation, Jesus adopted this same attitude. He had no vindictive word for his persecutors and no thought of revenge. Nailed to a cross bearing an inscription proclaiming that he was 'King of the Jews', Jesus was ridiculed by the soldiers: 'If you are the king of the Jews, save yourself' (Luke 23:36). One of the two criminals crucified with him railed: 'Aren't you the Christ? Save yourself and us!' (Luke 23:39). Though they mocked him and challenged his authority, all that Jesus' enemies heard from his lips was, 'Father, forgive them, for they do not know what they are doing' (Luke 23:34).

The kingdom, law and politics

Until the time of Jesus, the Israelites had lived under a theocratic government. All aspects of their lives were regulated by God's law. Here is a striking parallel with the way in which law governs the Muslim nation. The regulations governing marriage were comparable and so too the arrangements about divorce (Deut. 24:1–4). Generally speaking, immorality, notably adultery, was more severely repressed in the Torah, which provided for punishment by death in many cases (Lev. 20:10–18). No restriction was placed on polygamy and many of God's most distinguished men, such as David, were themselves polygamous (2 Sam. 5:13). The Torah also ordered Israelites to honour their parents (Exod. 20:12) and provided for the death penalty in the case of a severe violation of this commandment (Lev. 20:9).

In Jesus' time, the *Ten Commandments* concerning the uniqueness of God and the prohibition of all forms of idolatry had lost none of their force:

I am the LORD your God, who brought you out of Egypt, out of the land of slavery.

[1]. You shall have no other gods before me.

[2.] You shall not make for yourself an idol in the form of anything in heaven above or on the earth beneath or in the waters below. You shall not bow down to them or worship them …

[3.] You shall not misuse the name of the LORD your God, for the LORD will not hold anyone guiltless who misuses his name.

[4.] Remember the Sabbath day by keeping it holy …

[5.] Honour your father and your mother, so that you may live long in the land the LORD your God is giving you.

[6.] You shall not murder.

[7.] You shall not commit adultery.

[8.] You shall not steal.

[9.] You shall not give false testimony against your neighbour.

[10.] You shall not covet your neighbour's house. You shall not covet your neighbour's wife, or his manservant or maid-

servant, his ox or donkey, or anything that belongs to your
neighbour. (Exod. 20:1–17)

Almsgiving, prayer and fasting were upheld in the Jewish tradition as
fundamental religious practices. The temple in Jerusalem attracted
crowds of pilgrims from Israel and from all the other regions where the
Jews were dispersed. There were other noteworthy parallels between
Muslim and Mosaic law on questions of ritual purity (Lev. 15),
forbidden foods (Lev. 11) and usury (Exod. 22:24; Lev. 25:35–37; Deut.
23:20–21).

On the political level, the nation of Israel had its hour of glory during
the reign of David, who was simultaneously king, military leader and
prophet. His name is associated not only with the many psalms he
composed but with the conquest of the city of Jerusalem which he made
the capital of his kingdom (1 Chr. 11:4–9). Sadly he is also famous for
marrying Bathsheba after he had committed adultery with her and had
her husband murdered (2 Sam. 11). However, later he deeply repented
from his sin (2 Sam. 12:1–15). Because of the succession of wars that
marked his reign, God refused to let David carry out his plan to build
him a house; that is, a temple (1 Chr. 28:3). God did not want the
holiness of his house to be compromised by the violence that had sullied
the life of a man formerly chosen as 'a man after his own heart' (1 Sam.
13:14).

David's example illustrates the fact that the religious and political
realms cannot easily be mixed without the former being affected by the
negative aspects of the latter. There is a radical antagonism between
God's holiness and our sinfulness. This is experienced every day by the
believer and seems to be aggravated by the exercise of power. For, if
power corrupts, 'absolute power corrupts absolutely'. Israel's history
strikingly illustrated this antagonism and prepared the way for Jesus to
utter his famous sentence distinguishing two kinds of power: 'Give to
Caesar what is Caesar's, and to God what is God's' (Matt. 22:21).

Another more fundamental reason for Jesus' statement that his
kingdom would not be placed in the political sphere lies in the spiritual
nature of the kingdom. By definition, the laws of a nation apply to *all* its
citizens, who must obey them willingly or unwillingly. Access to the kingdom of God, however, cannot be obtained by force or external allegiance.
The bitter fruit of such enforcement would be hostility to anything
religious or would otherwise lead to hypocritical religion. True adherence
to faith can only be the result of a free decision to accept God's message.

Forgiveness, love and humility

The gospel, which brings the promise of God's forgiveness to all those who believe in Jesus Christ, includes the golden rule of unlimited forgiveness: 'Then Peter came to Jesus and asked, "Lord, how many times shall I forgive my brother when he sins against me? Up to seven times?" Jesus answered, "I tell you, not seven times, but seventy-seven times" ' (Matt. 18:21–22). Forgiveness, received from God and extended to others, is therefore the rule of life for Christian people. It goes without saying that it can be kept only by those who are prepared to forgive. Not that they are any more capable than others of doing so, for it is really beyond human ability, but, as St Augustine said, God gives that which he commands.

Living in God's kingdom also means loving our enemies, and this precludes all forms of holy war.

> You have heard that it was said, 'Love your neighbour and hate your enemy.' But I tell you: Love your enemies and pray for those who persecute you, that you may be sons of your Father in heaven. He causes his sun to rise on the evil and the good, and sends rain on the righteous and the unrighteous. If you love those who love you, what reward will you get? Are not even the tax collectors doing that? And if you greet only your brothers, what are you doing more than others? Do not even pagans do that? Be perfect, therefore, as your heavenly Father is perfect. (Matt. 5:43–48)

Jesus taught that life in God's kingdom implies the indissolubility of marriage, except in the case of conjugal infidelity (Matt. 5:31–32), and implies monogamy (Matt. 19:1–11). This life has its true expression in humility, unseen by others:

> Be careful not to do your 'acts of righteousness' before men, to be seen by them. If you do, you will have no reward from your Father in heaven.
>
> So when you give to the needy, do not announce it with trumpets, as the hypocrites do in the synagogues and on the streets, to be honoured by men. I tell you the truth, they have received their reward in full. But when you give to the needy, do not let your left hand know what your right hand is doing, so that your giving may be in secret. (Matt. 6:1–4)

But when you pray, go into your room, close the door and pray to your Father who is unseen. (Matt. 6:6)

But when you fast, put oil on your head and wash your face, so that it will not be obvious to men that you are fasting, but only to your Father, who is unseen ... (Matt. 6:17–18)

Here Jesus is saying that living for God is not just a question of the obligations we should carry out, but of the inner attitudes and thoughts of our hearts and minds. Our religious devotions, whether giving, praying or fasting, are to be practised not to bring attention to ourselves, but rather to bring glory to God.

This inner dimension of faith also finds expression in worship. Unlike Jews and Muslims, Christians are not required to pray in a specific geographical direction. 'God is spirit,' said Jesus, 'and his worshippers must worship in spirit and in truth' (John 4:24). The same applies to the notion of purity, which is first of all, in the teaching of Jesus, purity of heart. Vigilance is important, therefore, regarding not so much 'what enters the stomach' as 'what comes out of the heart': 'Nothing that enters a man from the outside can make him "unclean" ... What comes out of a man is what makes him "unclean". For from within, out of men's hearts, come evil thoughts, sexual immorality, theft, murder ...' (Mark 7:19–21). It is in the light of this teaching that Jesus' attitude should be understood, especially regarding the use of money (Matt. 6:24) and the drinking of wine (John 2:1–12).

Having exposed evil from its roots, it is understandable that Jesus did not seek to establish laws, but sought instead to eliminate evil wherever it was found (cf. Luke 12:13–15). Laws can and should evolve according to the specific situations in which they apply. It is essential only that they be just and protect the rights of the most deprived. The 'advantage' of the gospel, which contains no laws, is precisely that it allows each generation and each group or nation the freedom and responsibility to apply justice, taking into account contemporary and historical circumstances.

Although the kingdom of God is apart from any political, social and economic structure in the world, Christian people are called to be active witnesses of the kingdom in both word and deed. This will never be an easy task, since the aim is to reflect God's own character: 'Be perfect, therefore,' said Jesus to his disciples, 'as your heavenly Father is perfect' (Matt. 5:48). Far from being a middle-of-the-road religion, adapted to human weakness as Islam claims to be, Christianity points us to the one who can set us free from the prison of our sin. The kingdom of God Christians seek to spread is open to all who, having lost hope in their own lives, are born into a new life. As Jesus said, 'no-one can see the kingdom of God unless he is born again' (John 3:3).

Notes

[1] Muslim, *ḥudud* 12, 15:III, p. 911, no. 4191 [3199], and p. 912, no. 4194 [3201]; Bukhari, *ḥudud* 30, 31:VIII, p. 536, no. 816 [6327], and p. 537, no. 817 [6328].

[2] Abu Dawud, *ṭalaq* 3:II, p. 586, no. 2173 [2008].

[3] Bukhari, *diyat* 6:IX, p. 10, no. 17 [6370]. Other hadiths confirm that the Muslim who renounces his religion must be put to death (cf. Bukhari, *jihad* 149:IV, p. 160, no. 260 [2794]; *istitaba* 2:IX, p. 45, no. 57 [6411]).

[4] Razi, II:4, p. 185.

[5] Bukhari, *tawḥid* 2:IX, p. 351, nos. 473 [6828], and 474 [6829]; *adab* 18:VIII, p. 18, no. 26 [5538].

[6] Ibid., *iman* 6:I, p. 19, no. 12 [12].

[7] Tirmidhi, *faḍa'il al-jihad* 2 [1546].

Part 3
Jesus Christ

10

The crucifixion: illusion or reality?

Jesus Christ enjoys a very special status in Islam. In the Qur'an he is mentioned in fifteen suras and ninety-three verses.[1] Muslims honour him as one of God's greatest prophets and some Muslims are named after him. The Prophet Muhammad considered his relationship with Jesus to be unique: 'I am the nearest of all people to the son of Mary, and all the prophets are paternal brothers, and there has been no prophet between me and him.'[2] Among the Sufis, who represent the mystical trend within Islam, Jesus has an especially privileged position. Ibn 'Arabi describes him as 'the Seal of the Saints',[3] compared with the Prophet Muhammad, who, according to the Qur'an, is 'the Seal of the Prophets' (33:40). In contemporary Arabic literature there are a number of works devoted to him.[4]

The theme of Jesus' person, his death and resurrection, takes us to the heart of the debate between Christians and Muslims. If there is one fundamental matter on which Christianity and Islam seem totally opposed, one question over which the Bible and the Qur'an appear utterly irreconcilable, and one issue that will always cause debate between Christians and Muslims, it is certainly Jesus Christ. Controversies focus on two points in particular: his *divinity* and his *death on the cross*.

Before considering the question of Jesus' death, it will be useful, and indeed necessary, to begin by outlining what the Qur'an teaches about him.

Jesus in the Qur'an

The title of sura 3, *Al 'Imran* (The household of 'Imran), is derived from
the name the Qur'an gives to Mary's father. As soon as Mary was born,
her mother committed her to God's protection. God received the child
with favour and entrusted her to Zechariah, who was a priest in the
temple of Jerusalem. Mary grew up in the temple under his care. Often
Zechariah would find her with food, which she claimed God had
provided for her (3:35–37).

One day as Zechariah was praying in the sanctuary asking God to give
him a child, the angels called out to him (3:38–41; 19:2–15; 21:89–90).
They foretold the birth of his son, *Yaḥya*, John the Baptist, who, they
said, 'will confirm the truth of a Word from God, a prince of men and
chaste, a prophet numbered with the righteous' (3:39).

The virgin Mary too was told by the angels that she would give birth
to a son (3:42–51; 19:16–21):

> Behold! the angels said:
> 'O Mary! God gives you glad tidings of a Word from Him: his
> name will be the Messiah Jesus, son of Mary, held in honour in this
> world and in the age to come, and he will have his place among
> those who are brought near [to God's Throne].
> 'He will speak to the people in childhood and in his mature
> years, and he will be among the righteous.' (3:45–46)

The name *Jesus* (via the Greek *Iēsous*) comes from the Hebrew *Yeshua*,
which means 'God saves'. In the Qur'an the name for Jesus is not *Yasu'*,
the Arabic transliteration of *Yeshua*, but *'Isa*. According to Razi, *'Isa* is the
Arabic equivalent of Jesus' name in Hebrew.[5] It is used twenty-five times
in the Qur'an and on sixteen of these occasions in the phrase *'Isa bin
Maryam*, 'Jesus, son of Mary'.

From the cradle Jesus defended his mother against the accusation of
adultery and declared that he was a servant of God and a prophet
(19:27–33).[6] He came into this world in a miraculous way thanks to the
breathing of God's Spirit into his mother's womb:

> And (remember) her who guarded her chastity:
> We breathed into her of Our Spirit,
> and We made her and her son a Sign for all peoples. (21:91;
> cf. 66:12)

The sending of Jesus into the world is seen as an act of mercy and a sign from God to all people (19:21). Mary too is seen as a sign from God, since she and her son were both recipients of God's favour (21:91; 5:113). God instructed Jesus in the Scriptures and in wisdom, in the Torah and in the Gospel (3:48; 5:113). The Scripture especially entrusted to Jesus was the Gospel, which, as a faithful servant of God (19:30), he preached as a guide and a light for our paths:

> We sent Jesus the son of Mary, confirming the Torah that had come before him:
>
> We sent him the Gospel: in it was guidance and light, and confirmation of the Torah that had come before him: a guidance and admonition to those who fear God. (5:46; cf. 3:3)

Those who follow Jesus are described as those who have hearts full of compassion and mercy (57:27). As an Apostle of God sent to the people of Israel (3:49), Jesus was set before them as an example (43:57, 59). He was blessed by God wherever he went (19:31). He called the Israelites to worship God (3:50; 19:36; 43:64), confirming the Torah, but overruling some of its prohibitions (3:50). Strengthened by the Holy Spirit (2:87, 253; 5:113), he performed miracles with God's permission, healing the blind and the lepers and raising the dead (3:49; 5:113).

Although God accredited Jesus through many *bayyinat*, 'signs', not many people believed in him (43:63; 61:6). Jesus succeeded in gathering around him only a handful of men whom God protected against their enemies (61:14).[7]

> When Jesus realized the unbelief in them he said: 'Who will be my supporters on behalf of God?'
>
> The disciples replied: 'We are the supporters of God. In God we have put our trust. Witness [O Jesus] our surrender [lit. that we are Muslims].' (3:52)

Apart from these men who pledged their support to God (hence their description as *ansaru llah*, 'God's supporters'), the Israelites as a whole opposed Jesus and planned to put him to death. But the Qur'an tells us that God too had his plans:

> And [the Jews] plotted and planned, and God too planned, and the best of planners is God. (3:54)

The text continues to tell us that God stepped in, foiled the Jews' plot and vindicated Jesus. But how did he do it? How did God vindicate Jesus? We shall find an answer to this question by looking at the four Qur'anic texts that speak about Jesus' death.

Four texts about Jesus' death

Sura 19:33

In sura 19, entitled 'Mary', we have the account of the birth of John the Baptist (19:2–15), followed by the annunciation and the birth of Jesus (19:16–33). While Jesus was still in the cradle, he presented himself as someone who would always enjoy God's blessing: 'Blessed am I in the day of my birth, my day of death and my day of resurrection to life' (19:33). This blessing that Jesus called upon himself is almost identical to the blessing God pronounced on John the Baptist: 'Blessed be he on the day of his birth and the day of his death and the day when he is raised to life' (19:15). The verbs used in both these verses include

- *walada*, 'to beget';
- *mata*, 'to die', the most common verb denoting death in Arabic;
- *ba'atha*, 'to raise to life', one of the two verbs denoting resurrection in the Qur'an. The other is *qama*, 'to rise again'.

The use of the same verbs and the repetition of the same blessing for Jesus and for John the Baptist, his forerunner, suggest that Jesus would die and be raised to life at the end of time in the same way as John or anyone else.

John's death came about when he was beheaded by King Herod as a result of his denunciation of the king's sinful life (Matt. 14:3–12). Would Jesus too be put to death as a result of his faithful preaching of God's word? Let us consider another text.

Sura 5:119–120

Sura 5, entitled *al-Ma'ida*, 'The Table', draws its title from an episode in which Jesus, at the request of his followers, asks God to send down a table from heaven (5:115–118). This episode, which may remotely refer to the Last Supper, is followed by a text about the final judgment. On that day, it says, God will ask Jesus about what he taught during his mission:[8]

God said, 'Jesus, son of Mary, did you ever say to people, "Adopt me and my mother as two gods in disregard of God Himself?" '

To which he replied, 'Glory be to you. It is not in me to say what I have no warrant for. If I had ever said such a thing You would have known it. For You know my innermost being and I do not know Yours. I said to them only what you commanded me to say, namely, "Worship and serve God, my Lord and your Lord." As long as I was among them I bore witness to them and when You took me to Yourself it was You who were watcher over them. For You are a witness to all things.' (5:116–117)[9]

In this text Jesus confirms that during his life he obeyed God faithfully, speaking only what God had commanded him to say. Jesus then says to God, 'You took me to Yourself.'

This statement 'You took me to Yourself' uses the verb *tawaffa*, which literally means 'to receive', 'to take back', or 'to collect' (a debt). It has become the most common verb in Arabic to express the action of 'causing someone's death'. It is used of God, since he is 'the one who gives people life and death' (2:258; 3:156). This shift to a more euphemistic meaning has its parallels in many other languages because people have always tried to lessen the horror of death. Moreover, for believers, including Muslims and Christians, death is seen as the moment when the Creator calls his creatures to himself. This meaning is well attested in the Qur'an. God calls to himself the souls of people while they sleep, keeps those whose death he has decreed, and sends back the others until the day when he finally calls them to himself (cf. 4:97; 6:60–61; 39:42).

So, in his reply to God, Jesus refers to his death in completely natural terms. However, this is not how Muslims interpret *tawaffa* in this text. For Razi, it does not refer to Jesus' death, but to his being raised to heaven by God. With no other comment, he points us to sura 3:55.[10]

Sura 3:55

The third text tells us how God foiled the Jews' plot against Jesus:

And [the Jews] plotted and planned, and God too planned, and the best of planners is God.

Then God said: 'Jesus, I am causing you to die and I will exalt you to Myself, vindicating you from the unbelievers over whom your followers will have the victory at My hands and then, at the resurrection, is the homecoming of you all. I will be the arbiter of all your disputes.' (3:54–55)

Here again, in God's words to Jesus, we have the verb *tawaffa*, meaning 'to cause to die' or 'to take back'. It is followed by the verb *rafa'a*, meaning 'to lift up' or 'to exalt'. The order in which these verbs appear suggests that 'lifting up' means resurrection from death towards the One who causes people to die and rise again. If this is the meaning of the verse, then God's triumph over the Jews is his lifting Jesus to himself after raising him from the dead.

Razi reports that some Muslims (including Ibn 'Abbas) interpreted *tawaffa* in the sense of 'to cause to die'. Thus God, who knew that the Jews were planning to kill Jesus, made Jesus die, then raised him from the dead and lifted him up to himself. According to some, Jesus was dead for three hours; others say seven hours, while others say he was raised to heaven immediately after he died.[11] This interpretation, however, is not popular among Muslims today.

The traditional Islamic understanding is that Jesus did not die, but that God raised him to himself; Jesus will come back to earth and, having completed his mission, will die a natural death. But how does this fit with sura 3:55? Two interpretations have been suggested.

(1) For some, who understand *tawaffa* in the sense of 'to recall', this verse does not refer to the death of Jesus at all, but to his ascension to heaven. God 'recalled' Jesus to himself by lifting him up. If this is the meaning of the word, why is it followed by another verb meaning basically the same thing? The answer given is that the first verb is general, the second more specific: God calls people in different ways, some through death and others through lifting them to himself alive as in the case of Jesus. It is worth noting, however, that this interpretation of *tawaffa* – God calling to himself a person in bodily form – is found nowhere in the Qur'an. The verb used for the ascension of Enoch (Idris) to heaven is *rafa'a* (19:57).

(2) Others take the verb *tawaffa* as referring to Jesus' death, but make the point that the conjunction 'and' does not require that one event occur after the other. Hence they give this interpretation: Jesus was raised to heaven alive and will come back and die at the end of time. It must be noted, however, that neither the verse in question, nor indeed any other text in the Qur'an, allows for any events involving Jesus in the period between his ascension and the last day. All this verse says is that the

disciples of Jesus will be given victory over their enemies, over those who do not accept that he is a prophet of God.[12]

Sura 4:157–159

The traditional Islamic understanding of how Jesus was rescued by God is based primarily on sura 4:157–159, and also on several narratives in the Hadith. Sura 4, entitled 'Women', contains a long polemical argument directed against the Jews of Medina. There are six charges made against them, namely that they broke the covenant with God, they did not believe in God's signs, they put to death many prophets, they hardened their hearts and they dishonoured Jesus' mother by making false accusations against her. Worst of all, they boasted, saying that they had overcome Jesus:

> They claim, 'We killed the Messiah Jesus, son of Mary, the Apostle of God.'
> But they killed him not, nor did they crucify him. They were under the illusion that they had. Those who differ about this matter are full of doubts. They have no real knowledge but follow only conjecture. Assuredly, they did not kill him.
> On the contrary, God raised him to himself, and God is all-powerful, all-wise.
> And there are none of the People of the Book who will not believe in him before his death. On the Day of Resurrection he [Jesus] will be a witness against them. (4:157–159)

So, in response to the boasting of the Jews, the Qur'an contends that, contrary to what they thought, they had not succeeded in killing Jesus or crucifying him.

Notice that Jesus is described here as 'the Apostle of God'. Razi explains that it was either the Jews who called him this or it was God. If the Jews, they may have been using the title derisively. If God, he would have been seeking to vindicate Jesus in the very verse in which he is shown hatred by the Jews.

Razi continues to explain that Jesus was not killed by the Jews, but that instead they killed someone whom God had made to look like Jesus.[13] 'Those who differ about this matter', he says, are either the Jews who no longer felt sure that they had really killed Jesus, or the Christians.[14] Jesus had, in fact, been lifted up to heaven by God.

According to sura 4:159, 'there are none of the People of the Book who will not believe in him before his death'. All Jews and Christians, it says, will believe in Jesus one day. Two interpretations have been suggested as to how this will happen. It all depends on whom the pronoun 'his' refers to in the words 'before his death'.

(1) If 'his death' refers to the death of individual Jews and Christians: Before they die they will meet with the angels who will convince the Jew that Jesus is God's prophet, and the Christian that Jesus is not God's Son. Neither, however, will be saved because they will have come to believe in Jesus too late.

(2) If 'his death' refers to the death of Jesus: Before Jesus dies at the end of time, Christians and Jews will all believe in him the way Muslims do today.

At the final judgment, Jesus will testify against Jews and Christians, for all of them will have failed to believe in him in one way or another.[15]

Difficulties with the traditional Islamic interpretation

The traditional interpretation of sura 4:157–159 raises many questions. In his exegesis of sura 3:55, Razi cites no fewer than six 'problems', *ishkal*.[16]

(1) To believe that God turned someone's likeness into that of someone else amounts to sophistry, to living in a world where no-one can be sure of anything. If no-one can rely on the senses to know the truth, no-one can know the truth. This would ultimately lead to the collapse of divine laws, the invalidation of prophecy and the nullification of *tawatur*. The latter principle is based on the fact that the first transmitter of a tradition was an eyewitness. If the perceivable reality is itself specious, no testimony can be trustworthy and no evidence can be relied on. So, for instance, says Razi, how can we be sure that it was Muhammad and not somebody else who was teaching what is believed to be the Prophet's teaching?[17]

(2) The Qur'an says that God appointed Gabriel to be with Jesus and to support him (5:110). Knowing that the tip of one of his wings is capable of fighting against the whole world, Gabriel would surely have been able to stop the Jews from killing Jesus. Moreover, Jesus had the power to raise the dead and to heal the blind and the leper. Was he not able to overcome his opponents by killing them or by disabling them from causing him harm?

(3) God was capable of rescuing Jesus by raising him to heaven

without making someone look like him. Why cause an unfortunate person to be killed?

(4) If God had turned someone's appearance into Jesus' likeness before lifting Jesus up to heaven, he would have made people wrongly believe that Jesus was put to death. This means putting people in a position characterized by ignorance and confusion, which is not worthy of God's wisdom.

(5) Christians all over the world, in spite of their deep love for Christ and 'excessive' beliefs about him, testify that they have seen him slain and crucified. If we deny this we actually discredit what has been established by *tawatur*. Discrediting what has been established by successive transmission necessarily results in discrediting Muhammad as prophet, and Jesus, and even their very existence and the existence of all prophets. To do this would be absurd.

(6) According to testimonies handed down by successive transmission, the one who was crucified was alive for a considerable time before he died. If he had not been Jesus, surely he would have expressed his dismay. He would have claimed in all sorts of ways that he was not Jesus, but someone else. Everyone would have known that he had been crucified by mistake.

Let us consider how Razi answers these objections.

(1) His response to the first is threefold First, it is quite possible that God did not turn the likeness (*shubha*) of a man into that of Jesus, but created another man in the very image (*sura*) of Jesus, this man being crucified instead of him. This means that although Jesus was not crucified, people rightly identified the man who was crucified as Jesus! One could still object that the result would have been exactly the same, that is, God would have acted deceptively by misleading people and causing them to believe that *Jesus himself* was crucified.[18]

Secondly, many Muslim theologians interpret the Qur'anic text (4:157) in a way that does not imply that God turned the likeness of a man into that of Jesus. As the Jewish leaders could not find Jesus (because he had been lifted up to heaven), they seized a man and crucified him in order to avoid a riot among the people. In doing so they made people think that Jesus was being crucified. People believed them because they did not know Jesus personally due to the fact that he rarely mixed with people.

A strange explanation indeed! Jesus was the most popular person among his people, not least because of his many miracles. And what about those Christians who claimed that they had seen Jesus slain? Did they not know him well enough? The answer given is yes, but as they were just a few, they could have decided together to lie about Jesus. Razi provides no reason why Jesus' disciples would have agreed on such a lie.[19]

Thirdly, other Muslims claim that God did make someone look like Jesus, but that it was morally justified. Razi reports four accounts concerning the person who was put to death. In three cases the crucifixion of this man was well deserved, for he agreed to cooperate with the Jewish authorities in having Jesus arrested and killed. In one of these three cases the man was a disciple of Jesus (namely Judas Iscariot).[20] In the fourth case, Jesus tells his disciples that if one of them would agree to take his place, that person would surely enter paradise. One disciple takes up this offer, is turned into Jesus' likeness, and is crucified.[21] This part of the answer does not really address the problem raised by the first objection.

Razi's answers to the other objections are fairly short and to some extent dismissive.[22]

(2) If God had let Gabriel repel Jesus' enemies, or if he had empowered Jesus to do so, this miracle would have been too compelling; people would have been forced to believe, and forced belief is not genuine belief.

(3) If God had lifted Jesus up to heaven without making someone look like him, this miracle also would have been too compelling.

(4) Jesus' disciples were present and they knew that it was not Jesus who had been crucified. They tried to remove the confusion in people's minds by making them realize that someone else, not Jesus, had been crucified. In other words, the disciples did their best to dispel a misunderstanding caused by God!

(5) The people who were there were few; hence the possibility of their being under the illusion that Jesus was crucified. Therefore, the text of the Gospels, which is based on the testimony of just a few people, cannot be relied on. (This explanation actually contradicts the previous one: the four Gospels were written both by Jesus' disciples: Matthew and John, and by people who based their accounts on the testimony of Jesus' disciples: Mark and Luke.)

(6) If the person who was crucified was willing to take Jesus' place, he may well have hidden his identity. (But this answer still leaves us with a serious problem: how was this other person able to conceal his real identity from those who knew Jesus well? If he did succeed because he was fulfilling God's plan, God would have acted deceptively by using a human accomplice.)

In brief, concludes Razi, there are no clear-cut answers to the objections Christians have raised, only possible solutions. The bottom line for Razi is this: since the trustworthiness of Muhammad in all he conveyed has been established with unequivocal and supernatural evidence, these objections should not be allowed to contradict the irrefutable text of the Qur'an.

The traditional Islamic understanding of Jesus' death has been challenged more recently by the Aḥmadiyya movement, a Muslim group founded by Mirza Ghulam Aḥmad (1839–1908). According to this group (who have been declared to be non-Muslims by orthodox Muslims), Jesus was put on the cross, but did not die there. Although it looked as if he had died, he revived and went to India where he preached the gospel. He eventually died at the age of 120 and was buried in Kashmir.[23] This view has been made popular by the Muslim polemicist Ahmed Deedat in his booklet *Crucifixion or Cruci-fiction?* He argues that Jesus did not actually *die* on the cross and so was not 'crucified' in the full sense of the word.

An alternative interpretation

In making the case for the crucifixion of Jesus, it must be said that my aim is not to discredit the Qur'anic text but to try to understand what it means. As we have seen, Muslims themselves do not agree on how to go about interpreting the Qur'anic passages relating to the death of Jesus. I fully acknowledge that ultimately it is the responsibility of Muslims to understand their Scripture in the way they think best. I can only offer my understanding of this issue, the truth of which is far more important for Christians than for Muslims.

In contrast to Jesus' divinity, which is denied by many Qur'anic verses, his crucifixion is denied clearly in only one text (4:157–159). It is in the light of this text that the other Qur'anic verses are interpreted. If sura 3:55 were considered on its own, it would rather depict Jesus' elevation to heaven after his death. This was the view of some Muslims in the first generation. The question, therefore, is whether it is possible to understand sura 4:157–159 in a way that fits the apparent meaning of sura 3:55.

I believe there is a possible explanation that does justice to both texts. In sura 4:157, we have the statement, 'But they *killed* him not, nor did they *crucify* him'. The first verb used here is *qatala*. It denotes the action of causing someone to die violently ('to slay', 'to murder'). The second verb, *ṣalaba*, expresses the act of crucifying someone, thus condemning him to a dreadful, shameful death, and making him appear an odious criminal. This is in line with what the Torah says: 'If a man guilty of a capital offence is put to death and his body is hung on a tree, you must not leave his body on the tree overnight. Be sure to bury him that same day, because anyone who is hung on a tree is under God's curse' (Deut. 21:22–23; cf. Gal. 3:13).

The Jews wanted to subject Jesus to such a shameful death (cf. Matt. 27:20–23). But did they succeed? They certainly thought they did, but they were under an illusion, for God saved his servant, cleared his name of guilt and justified him by raising him from the dead and lifting him up to be with himself. This amazing act of divine intervention threw the Jews into confusion. Once they realized that the tomb was empty, they no longer knew if they had really killed Jesus. 'Assuredly, they did not kill him' because God had subsequently brought him back to life, vindicated his name and honoured him by raising him to himself.

If we accept this interpretation, the verb *rafaʿa*, 'to lift up' (4:158), would refer to God raising Jesus from the dead as well as raising him to heaven. The thrust of this text about Jesus would in some way be similar to what we find in another Qur'anic text concerning those who die as martyrs. Just as God honoured Jesus by lifting him up to heaven, he honours the martyrs by bringing their souls to himself: 'Do not ever think of those who are killed in the cause of God as being dead – rather as living in the presence of their Lord and in His providence, rejoicing in the blessing God has brought them' (3:169–170).

Again I would stress that this alternative interpretation is only a possible interpretation. It does, however, allow us to interpret the verb *tawaffa* in sura 3:55 in its common usage as 'to cause to die'.

Reasons for the Islamic teaching

Some Muslim commentators make a connection between sura 4:159, which says that everyone will believe in Jesus before his death (interpreted as Jesus' death), and sura 43:61, in which Jesus is called a 'sign [for the coming] of the Hour [of Judgment]'. The Qur'an says that Jesus will speak 'in his mature years' (3:46). The fact that he was lifted up when he was only about thirty years of age suggests that he had not yet completed his mission. From these texts commentators draw the conclusion that he will return to earth to take his mission a step further in the footsteps of Muhammad. He will enforce Islamic law and be highly successful, unlike the first time when he was nearly defeated by his enemies. He will then die and his death will be the signal for the last judgment.

This interpretation is based on several hadiths, not all of which have been recorded in the canonical compilations. One of these traditions describes Jesus' mission at the end of time:

> God's Apostle said: 'By Him in whose hands my soul is, surely the son of Mary will soon descend amongst you as a Just Ruler: He will break the cross, kill the pig and bring war to an end. Money will be in such abundance that nobody will accept it, and a single prostration to God (in prayer) will be better than the whole world and whatever is in it.'
>
> Abu Hurayra [who narrated this hadith] added: 'If you wish, you can recite: "And there are none of the People of the Book who will not believe in him before his death. On the Day of Resurrection he [Jesus] will be a witness against them"' (cf. 4:159).[24]

Thus Jesus will return to earth before the Day of Resurrection. He will fight against *al-Masih al-Dajjal*, the false Messiah (the Antichrist), and will overcome him. He will then establish a reign of peace on earth and will rule over humankind. At that time everyone will convert to Islam and Islamic law will be implemented among the nations. Jews and Christians will believe in Jesus the way Muslims do today. The Jews will recognize that he is a prophet and Christians will be convinced that he is not the Son of God. The destruction of all crosses at Jesus' command will make Christians realize that he was not crucified. Jesus will marry and have a family. Once his mission is completed, he will die a natural death and will be buried at Medina next to Muhammad. The death of Jesus will be the signal for the general resurrection.[25]

Islam therefore contests the historicity of Jesus' crucifixion. Given that the Qur'an accuses the Jews of having put to death many prophets before Jesus (cf. 2:61, 91; 3:21, 112, 181; 4:155; 5:73), the question is: why did God let them kill these prophets, yet allegedly prevent them from doing the same to Jesus? Perhaps it is because of Jesus' exceptionally high rank among the prophets? That he was not just a prophet, *nabi*, but an Apostle, *rasul*, entrusted with Holy Scriptures? The Qur'an does not provide us with a clear answer. I suggest that behind the Islamic denial of Jesus' crucifixion are two reasons, both relating to God's character, namely that (1) God is faithful to his messengers, and (2) God is invincible.

God is faithful to his messengers

The Qur'an states that God is faithful to his servants. He gives victory to those who seek to make his cause victorious (22:40; 40:51).

> O you who believe!
> If you will aid (the cause of) God,
> He will aid you, and plant your feet firmly. (47:7)

That is how it was with Abraham, Lot, Noah (21:51–77), Moses (28:18–28), and lastly, with Muhammad, who overcame his enemies. If God had allowed such a great prophet as Jesus to be handed over to his executioners and put to death, God's faithfulness, let alone his justice, would have been denied. Jesus' message, which is God's message, would have been discredited. Consequently God had to rescue Jesus and save him from the unjust, shameful and cruel death to which the Jews had condemned him.

God is invincible

In the Qur'an the Jews are not merely seen as unbelievers, but are often described as God's enemies. The diatribe in sura 4 is not directed against Christians, but against the Jews who refused to believe in Jesus. The Jews declared that they had put Jesus to death because he claimed to be the Messiah, the Apostle of God. The fact that they killed him proved in their opinion that he had not been sent by God. Sura 4:157–159, as traditionally understood, replies to this argument by rejecting what the Jews said. Contrary to what they believed, they had not succeeded in putting Jesus to death, and this proves that Jesus really was the man he claimed to be.

The Qur'anic answer implicitly shares the Jews' assumption that it is not possible for Jesus to be *both* God's Apostle *and* to have been crucified. The Jews say: Jesus was not sent by God, since we killed him. The Qur'an replies: Jesus was not killed by the Jews, because he was one of God's greatest messengers. Had he been crucified, God himself would have been defeated. By spoiling the murderous plans of the Jews and rescuing Jesus from their hands God vindicated his own name. He demonstrated, as sura 4:158 states, that he is indeed extremely powerful and wise.

We are faced here with two positions diametrically opposed to each other: the Jews' explanation that 'Jesus *was not* sent by God, which is why he *was* crucified'; and the Islamic explanation: 'Jesus *was* sent by God, which is why he *was not* crucified.'

In an attempt to see the issue more clearly, it is helpful to consult the Gospels, which were written by Jesus' own disciples and by people who relied on them. An attentive reading of the Gospels enables us to discover a third explanation, that differs from the other two. This may be stated as follows: 'Jesus was sent by God; nevertheless he was crucified.' Indeed, the Gospels teach that it was precisely through Jesus' death on the cross that he fulfilled his mission as Messiah.

Notes

[1] Jesus comes in fourth position, in terms of how much the Qur'an speaks about biblical prophets, after Moses, Abraham and Noah.

[2] Bukhari, *anbiya'* 48:IV, p. 434, no. 651 [3186].

[3] Ibn 'Arabi, *al-Futuhat al-makkiyya*, vol. 2, p. 49. As 'Seal of the Saints', Jesus is one of three; cf. M. Chodkiewicz, *The Seal of the Saints: Prophethood and Sainthood in the Doctrine of Ibn 'Arabi*, ch. 8: 'The Three Seals', pp. 116–127.

[4] Since the 1980s several studies on Jesus have been published in contemporary Islamic literature. Among the most significant are, in Arabic, *al-Masih fi l-fikri l-islami l-hadith wa fi l-masihiyya* [Christ in contemporary Islamic thought and in Christianity] by M. Khawwam; in English, *Muslim Perceptions of Christianity* by H. Goddard; and, in French, *Jésus et les musulmans d'aujourd'hui* by M. Borrmans. With a slightly different perspective K. Cragg's *Jesus and the Muslim: An Exploration* remains a reference book on this topic.

[5] Sura 3:45; Razi, IV:8, p. 43.

[6] The miracle of Jesus speaking in the cradle is found, not in the four Gospels, but in the apocryphal gospel known as the *Pseudo-Matthew*. Razi knows that Christians (and Jews) deny this miracle. They deny it, he says, on the ground that if it really had happened it would have been reported by successive transmission (*tawatur*). Muslims' response to this, he says, is twofold. First, if the miracle did not really take place, Mary's innocence would not be proved and the Jews would have condemned her to death for adultery. Secondly, those who witnessed this miracle were just a few, which explains why it was not reported on a large scale. See Razi's exegesis of sura 3:46 in IV:8, p. 46, and sura 19:33 in XI:21, p. 185.

[7] The name given to Jesus' disciples in the Qur'an is *al-Ḥawariyyun*. The derivation of the word is unknown and Razi envisages several explanations in his exegesis of sura 3:52 (IV:8, pp. 56–57). As for Christians in general, they are called *al-Naṣara*, either because they follow Jesus of Nazareth, *al-Naṣiri*, or, more likely, because like the first disciples they support (*naṣara*) Jesus against his opponents. It has also been suggested that the word refers to a Christian group in Arabia known as the *Nazareans*.

[8] In some translations these verses are numbered as 5:119–120, rather than 5:116–117.

[9] Razi knows that Christians deny that they worship Jesus and Mary as two gods. So why does the Qur'an accuse them of worshipping Jesus and Mary? Razi's answer is this: Christians believe that it was not God but Jesus and Mary who created the miracles they performed. This belief amounts to stating that Jesus and Mary are somehow two gods. What Razi attributes to Christians is very surprising indeed. Christians are well aware that Mary is credited with no miracles at all in the four Gospels. As for Jesus, he did acknowledge that his miracles derive from God: 'I have shown you many great miracles from the Father' (John 10:32; cf. John 5:36, 10:25; 14:10). The disciples of Jesus too recognized that it was God who enabled him to perform miracles (see Acts 2:22).

[10] Razi, VI:12, p. 113.

[11] Ibid., IV:8, p. 60.

[12] In recent years some Muslims have suggested, on the basis of sura 3:55 and sura 5:117, that after God had rescued Jesus from death, Jesus spent the rest of his life hiding until he died a natural death. They understand the raising up of Jesus in a spiritual and moral sense; that is, God honoured Jesus in raising his soul to himself and through giving him victory over his enemies, who failed to crucify him. This view gives little credit, if any, to the hadiths about Jesus' mission on earth at the end of time. Muslims who hold this view think that the lifting up of Jesus in his body to heaven is a Christian idea alien to Islam. They believe that Jesus was an ordinary prophet who will be raised from the dead like all people on the resurrection day (cf. Kawwam, *al-Masiḫ*, p. 351).

[13] According to L. Massignon, a leading French scholar, this interpretation began to appear in Sunni commentaries in the second half of the second Islamic century, after certain extremist views of Shi'i Muslims had been applied retrospectively to Jesus. The author also mentions several Muslim theologians and philosophers who believed that when Jesus' body died, his divine soul rose to God. Among these Muslims are

Ikhwan al-Safa, Abu Hatim al-Razi, Mu'ayyad al-Shirazi and Ghazali himself (*Opera Minora*, vol. 2, pp. 532–536). On the other hand, Shahrastani (in *Kitab al-Milal wa l-nihal*) reports on some extremist groups of Shi'i Muslims who claimed divinity for Imam 'Ali and his successors. Whenever one imam met with a violent death, these groups claimed that it happened to someone else who looked just like him. They did so in order to let the imam appear to have escaped the tragic fate to which his enemies wanted to subject him (pp. 509–510). The sixth imam, who died in 148/765, is said to have likened his son's fate to that of Jesus (p. 494). It is worth noting that for the imamite Shi'ites ('the Twelvers'), the twelfth imam, Muhammad al-Muntazar, is still alive. He went into hiding in the will of God (in 260/874) but will one day return and 'fill the earth with equity as it is now filled with iniquity'.

[14] Razi explains that the Christians were divided into three groups as to how to interpret Jesus' death in connection with his humanity and his divinity (the Melkites, Nestorians and Jacobites). The differences between these three groups relate to the Symbol of Chalcedon (451) and its definition of the union between the human and the divine natures of Jesus Christ. The Melkites agreed with the Creed, whereas the Nestorians and Jacobites (or monophysites) disagreed.

[15] Razi, VI:11, pp. 78–83.

[16] Ibid., IV:8, pp. 62–63.

[17] Clearly Razi takes this objection very seriously, as he mentions it again in his exegesis of sura 4:157 (VI:11, pp. 79–80). The objection is based on the assumption held by Muslim theologians that the five senses are the surest means by which to know the truth. Moreover, to perceive something through one's senses results in knowing the truth about it, necessarily and undoubtedly (cf. Baqillani, *Kitab al-Tamhid*, pp. 382–383; D. Gimaret, *La Doctrine d'al-Ash'ari*, pp. 155–181). The Arabic word for 'sophistry' is *sufsata'iyya*.

[18] Razi, IV:8, p. 63.

[19] Ibid., VI:11, p. 79.

[20] The idea that Judas Iscariot, rather than Jesus, was crucified has become quite popular among Muslims, partly due to the combined influence, on the one hand, of the so-called *Gospel of Barnabas*, and, on the other, of *Tafsir al-Manar*, a highly respected commentary on the Qur'an by M. 'Abduh and his disciple R. Rida. Some Muslims have suggested that Judas, when he had fully realized how cowardly he was in betraying his master, repented of his act, disguised his identity and decided to take Jesus' place on the cross in order to redeem himself (see

Khawwam, *al-Masīḥ*, pp. 308–312).

[21] Razi, VI:11, pp. 79–80.

[22] Ibid., IV:8, p. 63.

[23] For a Christian perspective on this issue by a former Aḥmadiyya Muslim, see S. Masood, *Jesus and the Indian Messiah*.

[24] Bukhari, *anbiya'* 49:IV: p. 436, no. 657 [3192]; cf. Bukhari, *fitan* 26:IX, p. 185, no. 245 [6598]; Muslim, *fitan*: IV, p. 1501, no. 6924 [5157], and p. 1520, no. 7023 [5233].

[25] Contemporary Muslims, who claim that Jesus died two thousand years ago, do not believe that he will return to earth at the end of time. The way they interpret the Qur'anic texts, which conflicts with the traditional understanding of Jesus' future ministry, is found in Khawwam, *al-Masīḥ*, pp. 352–357.

11

Peter and the crucifixion

Jesus' disciples, all of them Jews, were the first to face the dilemma that *either Jesus was God's prophet and Messiah*, in which case he would have triumphed over his enemies, *or he was not*, which explains why he was defeated and put to death by his opponents.

The reason for Jesus' death is revealed to us in the Gospels as the disciples gradually discover who their master is. To appreciate how they come to accept his death and view it as the bedrock of his mission, we shall follow the development of Peter's thinking. Among the disciples Peter is best known to us and seems to have been the spokesman for all his friends. He was also part of Jesus' 'inner circle', together with James and John. We shall see how he changed his ideas about Jesus. Initially, Peter's image of God, reflected in his perception of Jesus, was not very different from that of Islam.

Following Jesus

Peter was not Jesus' first disciple; he met Jesus through his brother Andrew, who had been a disciple of John the Baptist. John was baptizing on the banks of the River Jordan when he saw Jesus coming towards him: 'Look, the Lamb of God!' John exclaimed (John 1:36). His testimony immediately touched the hearts of Andrew and another disciple. They began to follow Jesus right away and spent the day with him (John 1:37–39).

In his delight at this meeting, Andrew went straight to his brother, then called Simon, and told him, 'We have found the Messiah.' He brought

Simon to Jesus, who said to him, '"You are Simon son of John. You will be called Cephas" (which, when translated, is Peter)' (John 1:41–42).

Simon does not seem to have made much of a response. Did he believe what his brother said? Was his silence due to doubt or to amazement, or was it something else?

Simon was a fisherman like his brother. He must have been deeply touched the day Jesus chose to get into his boat to teach the crowd from there on the shores of the Sea of Galilee. When the teaching was over, Jesus ordered him to take the boat out into deep water and to let down the nets for a catch.

Simon replied, 'Master, we've worked hard all night and haven't caught anything. But because you say so, I will let down the nets.'

The result was astonishing: the catch was so enormous that another boat had to be called over to help. Even then, both boats began to sink. Seized with great fear, Simon fell at Jesus' knees and exclaimed, 'Go away from me, Lord; I am a sinful man!'

Jesus reassured him and explained his future mission in simple and striking terms, 'Don't be afraid; from now on you will catch men' (Luke 5:1–11).

It was in this familiar setting of the Lake of Tiberias (another name for the Sea of Galilee) that Simon was to face a further overwhelming experience, which happened at night. That day, Jesus had provided food for an enormous crowd. When the people had eaten, their enthusiasm knew no bounds. Jesus ordered his disciples to get into the boat and to go ahead of him to the other side of the lake. He sent the crowd away and spent some time alone in prayer. At dawn he went to join the disciples, who were being buffeted by violent waves. When they saw him walking on the water, they were terrified. 'It's a ghost!' they cried.

'Take courage! It is I. Don't be afraid,' Jesus answered. Simon was immediately reassured, and asked Jesus if he might walk towards him on the water. He began to walk on the water, but could not believe what was happening. Afraid, he sank, crying out, 'Lord, save me!' Jesus seized him by the hand: '"You of little faith," he said, "why did you doubt?"'

In their amazement the disciples exclaimed, 'Truly you are the Son of God' (Matt. 14:22–33).

Learning who Jesus is

Jesus taught the crowds and performed many miracles, signs pointing to who he was and why he had come. The disciples were getting to know him more intimately. A decisive turning point came at Caesarea Philippi when he decided to reveal his identity more clearly to them:

'On the way, he asked them, "Who do people say I am?"'

'They replied, "Some say John the Baptist; others say Elijah; and still others, one of the prophets."'

'"But what about you?' he asked. 'Who do you say I am?"''

Jesus' question seems to have taken the disciples by surprise. They hesitated to give their own opinion about him, a hesitation that makes Peter's direct, spontaneous reply all the more striking: 'Peter answered, "You are the Christ."'

Perhaps the most remarkable feature of this account is Jesus' firmness when he warns his disciples not to divulge his messianic identity: 'Jesus warned them not to tell anyone about him' (Mark 8:27–30). Why did Jesus want to keep this confidential? Why did he not want everyone to know who he was? We have Jesus' own answer in the words that follow.

Learning the way of suffering

For the first time Jesus revealed openly to his disciples the nature of his mission. He told them that he would be put to death by the religious authorities and explained to them that his death was a necessary part of his mission. 'He then began to teach them that the Son of Man must suffer many things and be rejected by the elders, chief priests and teachers of the law, and that he must be killed and after three days rise again' (Mark 8:31).

Peter, who was the first to proclaim that Jesus is the Messiah, was also the first to find intolerable the idea that his master's mission should end in suffering and death: 'Peter took him aside and began to rebuke him. "Never, Lord!" he said, "This shall never happen to you!"' (Matt. 16:22).

Having congratulated Peter for recognizing him as the Messiah (Matt. 16:17), Jesus could now only blame him for uttering these words of rebuke, inspired as they were by the devil: 'Get behind me, Satan! You are a stumbling-block to me; you do not have in mind the things of God, but the things of men' (Matt. 16:23).

Peter's idea, surely a well-intentioned one, was that somehow God would find a way to save his Messiah from death. This, however, was quite unacceptable to Jesus. He described Peter's idea as literally *scandalous*, that is, according to the word's original meaning, an obstacle that would certainly cause him to stumble on the path of the mission for which he had come. But Jesus did not stop there; he called his disciples to walk in his footsteps, calling them to walk in the way of the cross: 'If anyone would come after me, he must deny himself and take up his cross and follow me. For whoever wants to save his life will lose it, but whoever loses his life for me will find it' (Matt. 16:24–25).

For Jesus, death was to be the path to life, and being brought low the way to be exalted. The disciples, however, found it difficult to accept such teaching and they were deeply troubled at hearing their master telling them again that he had to die and rise again (Matt. 17:22–23). They did not understand his words, but did not dare to question him about their meaning (Mark 9:32). This in no way lessened Jesus' determination to carry out his mission to the end.

At Capernaum, on the other shore of the Sea of Galilee, Jesus was joined by the crowd he had fed the previous day. He had no illusions about the crowd's motives: 'you are looking for me, not because you saw miraculous signs but because you ate the loaves and had your fill', he said. Jesus invited his hearers instead to seek the kind of food that would not perish: '"Do not work for food that spoils, but for food that endures to eternal life, which the Son of Man will give you …"

'"Sir," they said, "from now on give us this bread."

'Then Jesus declared, "I am the bread of life. He who comes to me will never go hungry, and he who believes in me will never be thirsty"' (John 6:26–27; 34–35).

When they heard these words, the Jewish authorities, who feared Jesus' popularity, grumbled against him. To them, he was only 'Joseph's son', a mere human being.

But Jesus repeated, 'I am the living bread that came down from heaven. If anyone eats of this bread, he will live for ever.'

These words, spoken in the synagogue at Capernaum, were deeply disturbing to many, including his own disciples, who said, 'This is a hard teaching. Who can accept it?' Outraged, many deserted him.

Jesus turned to the Twelve and asked them to choose: 'You do not want to leave too, do you?'

The question prompted an immediate reply from Peter: 'Lord, to whom shall we go? You have the words of eternal life' (John 6:22–71).

In his reply Peter admitted that it was not easy to be a disciple of Jesus, but at the same time he recognized that it would be impossible for him to be otherwise.

Learning the way of service

The final period of Jesus' ministry is marked by the fulfilment of his mission as Messiah. On the evening of his arrest, he gathers his twelve disciples around him. After sharing a meal together, Jesus ties a cloth round his waist, dressing as a servant would have done in his day. He pours water into a basin and proceeds to wash his disciples' feet. But Peter refuses outright to let his master wash his feet: 'No, you shall never wash my feet!'

The impulsive disciple cannot imagine that his Lord should humble himself to such an extent. We might think his indignation justified, but it is nevertheless condemned by Jesus: 'Unless I wash you, you have no part with me.'

This stern warning completely changes Peter's attitude, for he does not want to lose his master: 'Then, Lord, not just my feet but my hands and my head as well!' (John 13:1–20) Doubtless, by this symbolic gesture Jesus is illustrating the meaning of his imminent death. The giving of his own life is the supreme testimony of his love for his disciples. Through his death, the final act of his earthly life, he will pass over the threshold into his heavenly glory. By humbling himself so completely, he will fulfil his messianic mission perfectly. In short, it is by becoming the servant of all that he will become the Lord of all.

As soon as the meal is over, Jesus tells his disciples that they will all abandon him the moment he is arrested. But Peter protests, 'Even if all fall away, I will not.' In a triumphant mood, Peter thinks, no doubt sincerely, that such cowardice would be unworthy of him. Is he still hoping to be able to snatch his master away from a death that seems more and more inevitable, yet which he is still unable to accept?

Jesus does not leave his impetuous disciple under any illusion: 'I tell you the truth, today – yes, tonight – before the cock crows twice you yourself will disown me three times.'

Peter, who has not thought himself cowardly, is even less ready to believe that he can be a traitor. If Jesus really has to die, he says he will go with him to death: 'Even if I have to die with you, I will never disown you.'

Is this enthusiasm an expression of genuine loyalty or real courage? Or is it presumption or even despair? Is he so frightened by the idea of his master's death that he even prefers to die with him rather than to be left to his own devices? In any case, the text tells us that 'all the others said the same' (Mark 14:27–31).

Seeing his hour approaching, Jesus takes with him Peter and two other disciples. He takes them apart and shares his sense of foreboding with them: 'My soul is overwhelmed with sorrow to the point of death. Stay here and keep watch.' He goes a little further and, filled with anguish over what awaits him, he pleads with God, '*Abba*, Father, everything is possible for you. Take this cup from me. Yet not what I will, but what you will.' When he comes back to the three disciples, he finds them asleep. In a voice that must have been hoarse with suffering, he says to Peter: 'Simon, are you asleep? Could you not keep watch for one hour?' Having struggled to make his disciples accept the necessity of his death, Jesus now struggles within himself. Even though he knows it will be a terrible death, he accepts it as the highest expression of submission to the will of his Father (Mark 14:32–42).

The Gospel narratives recount in detail the circumstances surrounding Jesus' arrest and his appearance before the Jewish Supreme Court. Identified by a kiss from Judas, one of his disciples, Jesus is arrested by Roman soldiers. At that moment Peter seizes his sword, and with a violent, but ill-judged gesture, he strikes the High Priest's servant and cuts off his right ear. Jesus heals the man immediately and speaks to Peter: 'Put your sword back in its place, for all who draw the sword will die by the sword. Do you think I cannot call on my Father, and he will at once put at my disposal more than twelve legions of angels? But how then would the Scriptures be fulfilled that say it must happen in this way?' (Matt. 26:52–54). Jesus has no doubt at all about his relationship to his Father. He knows that if he asks God to rescue him, he certainly will do so. On the other hand, Jesus is perfectly aware that the events now taking place are part of his mission as foretold in God's word. He freely chooses to carry out this divine mission.

As Jesus predicted, all his close disciples (except John) abandon him and flee. The soldiers take him to the High Priest, where his trial is to be held (Matt. 26:47–56). When interrogated by the High Priest, the highest dignitary in Israel, Jesus unhesitatingly identifies himself as the Messiah announced by the ancient prophets. Having thus proved his own guilt in the eyes of his judge, he is condemned to death and submits to all kinds of torture, mockery and injuries (Matt. 26:57–68).

Learning from failure

Peter follows at a distance and is present in the background of Jesus' trial. Eventually he is recognized by one of the High Priest's servants. She challenges him: 'You also were with Jesus of Galilee.'

But Peter denies it. 'I don't know what you are talking about,' he says.

Another girl says, 'This fellow was with Jesus of Nazareth.'

Again Peter protests his innocence and denies any connection with Jesus.

Finally he is cornered by the whole group: 'Surely you are one of them,' they press him, 'for your accent gives you away.'

Peter's typical Galilean accent has betrayed him (Matt. 26:73). The people's denunciation makes him angry, and he begins to call down curses on himself and swears to them, 'I don't know the man!'

Immediately the cock crows, reminding Peter of the words Jesus spoke earlier. He breaks down and weeps. Now he begins to understand (Mark 14:66–72). Faced with a dramatic event, the human heart can break or become stronger. At that moment Simon's certainly breaks. Only later will he become strong and earn the name Jesus gave him – Peter, which in Greek means 'rock'.[1]

Death, resurrection, ascension

Jesus appears before Pilate, the Roman governor. Under pressure from a crowd stirred up by the religious authorities, Pilate reluctantly confirms the sentence pronounced by the Jewish High Court (John 18:28 – 19:16). Carrying the cross on which he will be put to death, they take Jesus out to a little hill near Jerusalem. At a place called Golgotha, they crucify him and he dies between two robbers, like a common criminal. His cross bears a sign that reads: 'JESUS OF NAZARETH, THE KING OF THE JEWS', written in Hebrew, Latin and Greek.

John, Jesus' disciple known as 'the one whom Jesus loved', is the only one of the twelve present at his master's crucifixion. Four women from among Jesus' friends are also there, among them his mother Mary (John 19:17–42).

The third day after Jesus' death, some of the women go to the tomb to embalm his body, but find the tomb empty and go away dismayed to report their discovery to the disciples (Luke 24:1–12). Peter and the beloved disciple hurry there and find it just as the women have said (John 20:1–10).

After this, Jesus appears to Peter (Luke 24:34) and to Mary Magdalene (John 20:11–18). He joins two of his disciples and walks with them along the road to Emmaus. The two, who are at first kept from recognizing him, tell how bewildered they are at what has happened to Jesus of Nazareth:

He was a prophet, powerful in word and deed before God and all the people. The chief priests and our rulers handed him over to be sentenced to death, and they crucified him; but we had hoped that he was the one who was going to redeem Israel. And what is more, it is the third day since all this took place. In addition, some of our women amazed us. They went to the tomb early this morning but didn't find his body. They came and told us that they had seen a vision of angels, who said he was alive. Then some of our companions went to the tomb and found it just as the women had said, but him they did not see.

Jesus replies without telling them who he is: 'How foolish you are, and how slow of heart to believe all that the prophets have spoken! Did not the Christ have to suffer these things and then enter his glory?' Later, as a result of Jesus breaking bread and giving thanks, the eyes of the two disciples are opened and they realize that the man they have been talking with is none other than Jesus (Luke 24:13–35)!

The same day, Jesus appears to his disciples when Thomas is not with them (John 20:19–23). When they later tell Thomas that they have seen the Lord, he boldly declares, 'Unless I see the nail marks in his hands and put my finger where the nails were, and put my hand into his side, I will not believe it.'

A week later the disciples were in the house again, and this time Thomas is with them.

Though the doors were looked, Jesus came and stood among them and said, 'Peace be with you!' Then he said to Thomas, 'Put your finger here; see my hands. Reach out your hand and put it into my side. Stop doubting and believe.'

Thomas said to him, 'My Lord and my God!'

Then Jesus told him, 'Because you have seen me, you have believed; blessed are those who have not seen and yet have believed.' (John 20:25–29)

Later, Jesus appears to seven of his disciples on the shore of the Sea of Galilee. After a night's fishing when they have caught nothing they are discouraged. Without saying who he is, Jesus suggests they throw their net on the right side of the boat. They do as he says and, to their surprise, there is an enormous catch! John, the beloved disciple, is the first to recognize Jesus. But it is Peter who jumps into the water to join the

Master. After a meal shared with his disciples, Jesus puts the same question three times to Peter: 'Simon son of John, do you truly love me more than these?'

Peter replies unhesitatingly, but without daring to compare himself to the others: 'Lord, you know all things; you know that I love you.'

By this triple confession, Jesus tactfully restores the disciple who has denied him three times, and he goes further in making him responsible for the other disciples. Peter will carry this responsibility until the day when, like Jesus, he will sign his faithfulness to God with his own blood. According to tradition, Peter died on a cross, his final testimony of love for his master (John 21:1–19).

Jesus spends a total of forty days on earth teaching his disciples before he ascends to heaven: 'After his suffering, he showed himself to these men and gave many convincing proofs that he was alive. He appeared to them over a period of forty days and spoke about the kingdom of God' (Acts 1:3).

Preaching the death and resurrection of Jesus

Ten days after Jesus ascends to heaven, his disciples receive the Holy Spirit as he promised them. Peter stands up and speaks powerfully in front of a vast crowd of Jews who have gathered in the dusty streets of Jerusalem for the feast of Pentecost. He challenges them, speaking to them about the death and resurrection of Jesus Christ: 'This man was handed over to you by God's set purpose and foreknowledge; and you, with the help of wicked men, put him to death by nailing him to the cross. But God raised him from the dead, freeing him from the agony of death, because it was impossible for death to keep its hold on him' (Acts 2:23–24; cf. Acts 3:13–15; 4:10–12).

Peter is a changed man! Now he is deeply convinced and proclaims aloud that God's will has been accomplished through Jesus' death. The Jews have not caused Jesus' mission to fail, he declares. Quite the reverse! Through their guilty rejection of the Messiah, God's plan has been carried out without their knowledge. God did not give Jesus into the hands of his enemies, but raised him from the dead, thus taking 'revenge' on those who had rejected the one God sent. The crucifixion of Jesus was not his final defeat, but his greatest victory. By his death and resurrection, Jesus has for ever conquered death!

Teaching the way of suffering

The New Testament contains two letters Peter wrote to teach and encourage the young Christian community. His first letter deals at length with Jesus' death and its significance for all his followers. He urges readers undergoing trials not to be discouraged but to walk in the steps of their Saviour, who was himself badly treated in this world. Such difficulties encountered by Jesus' disciples, Peter explains, can be a source of closer communion with their Lord:

> For it is commendable if a man bears up under the pain of unjust suffering because he is conscious of God. But how is it to your credit if you receive a beating for doing wrong and endure it? But if you suffer for doing good and you endure it, this is commendable before God. To this you were called, because Christ suffered for you, leaving you an example, that you should follow in his steps.
>
> 'He committed no sin,
>   and no deceit was found in his mouth.'
>
> When they hurled their insults at him, he did not retaliate; when he suffered, he made no threats. Instead, he entrusted himself to him who judges justly. He himself bore our sins in his body on the tree, so that we might die to sins and live for righteousness; by his wounds you have been healed. For you were like sheep going astray, but now you have returned to the Shepherd and Overseer of your souls. (1 Pet. 2:19–25)

It is hard to believe that these lines were written by the same man who previously had such difficulty in accepting the suffering and death of Jesus. What a long road Peter had to travel before realizing that Jesus' death was at the very heart of Jesus' mission as the saving Messiah. Peter's realization came about as the result of his daily companionship with his master. He became aware that Jesus was a unique prophet in many respects: his teaching, his claims, his authority, his humility and his miracles. No doubt the fact that Jesus appeared to Peter, risen from the dead, also played a decisive role in Peter's change of direction and his new perception of Jesus as the Messiah. Peter came to see that it was only because Jesus triumphed over death *by suffering himself* that he was able to become the conquering king.

Note

[1] Of the four Gospels, Mark's recounts Peter's denial with the most detail. According to tradition Peter himself contributed to the writing of this Gospel.

12

Evidence for Jesus' death and resurrection

As our journey with Peter shows, there is plenty of evidence for Jesus' death. We shall now relate this evidence to the objections raised by Islam, helpfully summarized by Kenneth Cragg: 'If, despite the inconclusiveness we have reviewed, there is a Qur'anic consensus to say "To Jesus at the Cross death did not happen," there is also an Islamic consensus to say, further, "It need not happen, and, moreover, it should not happen." It did not historically, it need not redemptively, and it should not morally, happen to Jesus.'[1]

Let us, then, examine the issue historically (looking at the evidence for Jesus' death), redemptively (looking at the purpose for Jesus' death), and morally (looking at the implications of Jesus' death).

The historical evidence for Jesus' death

The reliability of the Gospels

Nearly half of the verses in the Qur'an about Jesus relate to his birth. This is especially significant when we compare it with the few verses connected with the end of his life on earth. There are four texts about Jesus' death: two refer to his death as an ordinary death (5:120; 19:33), one has been interpreted in different ways (3:55) and one seems to deny categorically the killing and the crucifixion of Jesus (4:157–158). The last text, which is fairly concise, is not a historical account describing the events as they took place. It is part of an anti-Jewish polemic whose primary aim is not to deny the crucifixion of Jesus as such, but to vindicate Jesus as God's prophet before the Jews who defamed his name.

It must be emphasized that the Qur'anic text was written about six hundred years after the events. The four Gospels, however, were written within sixty years or so of Jesus' ascension to heaven. Two Gospels, Mark and John, are silent about everything connected with Jesus' birth. Matthew and Luke report the event in some detail but without giving it undue weight (two chapters out of twenty-eight in Matthew and two out of twenty-four in Luke). When we move on to the remaining part of the New Testament, there is practically no mention of Jesus' birth. In contrast, there are repeated references to his death and resurrection. The circumstances of Jesus' death are related in all four Gospels (two chapters in each).

The events culminating in the crucifixion of Jesus are reported in the Gospels with a lot of detail and a realism that only eyewitnesses could relate. Contrary to what Razi supposed, these eyewitnesses were more than a few. In addition to the Roman soldiers, there were many people who gathered to see what was going on (Luke 23:48). Jesus' own mother and his beloved disciple were within shouting distance of the cross (John 19:25–27). Two of Jesus' disciples, Joseph of Arimathea and Nicodemus, buried Jesus' body (John 19:38–42), and some women who knew Jesus well followed them and 'saw the tomb and how Jesus was laid in it' (Luke 23:55). How could Jesus' mother and his disciples have thought that somebody else was he? Would those who had been so close to him have been able to make such a mistake?

The honesty of the disciples

We have seen that the Gospel accounts underline the enormous difficulty Jesus' disciples had in accepting the idea of his violent death. They accepted it only when obliged to do so as the reality of the event impressed itself upon them. For indeed they could not believe that it was possible for their master to suffer in such a way. The death of their 'hero' signified in their minds the failure of his mission. How well we can understand the disciples! Which of us, in their place, would have reacted otherwise?

If the thesis that Jesus had not been crucified was in the least plausible, his disciples would surely have been the first to support it. But they did not have that option open to them. The evidence was such that they had to accept the reality of Jesus' death. They could not do otherwise. The difficulty they had in admitting his death only gives greater weight to the authenticity of their witness. Why would the writers of the Gospels have lied – as Razi suggests without giving any reason to explain such a lie – about an event they initially found extremely difficult to accept?

The flight of Jesus' disciples at the time of his arrest is reported in all four Gospels. Moreover, none of these books is silent about Simon's denial or attempts to excuse him. It is not pleasant for anyone to admit to cowardice, much less to confess to treachery (see Mark 14:43–51, 66–72). Unless Jesus had really been arrested, condemned and crucified, it would be hard to understand why his disciples would have confessed that they had behaved at times in such a miserable way. Might they too have been victims of an illusion? The Qur'an does not go so far as to affirm that, since it attributes an illusion only to the Jews who sought to put Jesus to death. Razi thinks that, being so close to Jesus, the disciples could not have been under any illusion about what had happened. Either he is not aware of, or he dismisses, the fact that it is the witness of these same disciples we find in the Gospels, and they all agree that Jesus was crucified.

Finally, what could have made Jesus' disciples say that their Lord had been raised from the dead if he had simply been taken up into heaven? From a historical point of view, resurrection from the dead followed by ascension to heaven was something totally unknown to them. They would have been more inclined to accept the idea of Jesus' rapture to heaven in a way similar to Enoch (Gen. 5:24; Heb. 11:5; Qur'an 19:57) and Elijah (2 Kgs. 2:9–11). Yet here there was no alternative for them; they had to accept that their master had been put to death and then raised to life.

The testimony of Jesus

Shortly before his arrest, Jesus is described to us in the Gospels in a state unusual for him. Unlike Socrates, who swallowed his hemlock serenely, Jesus was deeply troubled as he looked towards his imminent death. He was in great anguish, and from the bottom of his heart implored God to spare him this cup of pain if at all possible. Jesus had never before appeared so close to us, so human, to his disciples. He too would have preferred to avoid such a dreadful fate. He asked some of his disciples to keep watch and pray, but they struggled to keep awake and soon fell asleep.

Now why would the Gospels have reported an event so terrifying for Jesus and so humiliating for his disciples if it had not really taken place?

Furthermore, how can we reconcile this extreme vulnerability in the face of death on Jesus' part with his identity as the Son of God? It would have been more convenient and more acceptable to human reason to deny either Jesus' death or his divinity. The fact that his disciples affirmed both of these lends more credibility to their accounts. We are in a situation where in a sense the more a testimony seems improbable, the more it is likely to be true. The witness reports what he has seen without troubling himself to consider whether his testimony will be received or rejected, and without trying to modify what he reports so as to make it more credible.

Jesus knew he could ask God to rescue him, but then the Scriptures that foretold his sufferings would not be fulfilled (cf. Matt. 26:52–54; John 19:28). Jesus knew that without his death his mission would not be completed. His prayer was that, through it all, God's name would be exalted: 'Now my heart is troubled, and what shall I say: "Father, do not let this hour come upon me"? But that is why I came – so that I might go through this hour of suffering. Father, bring glory to your name!' (John 12:27–28, GNB). Jesus hung on the cross for several hours. Before he died he uttered a few short sentences, one of which clearly identified him as the son of Mary (John 19:26–27), proving that it really was he and not one of his disciples (e.g. Judas Iscariot) or anyone else.

On the day Jesus rose from the dead he appeared to several people including his disciples. (Judas was not among them; he had committed suicide after betraying Jesus. See Matt. 27:3–5.) If Jesus' disciples had been wrong in believing that their master had died, would he not quickly have put them right when he appeared to them? But since they were as sceptical about his resurrection as they had been about the need for his crucifixion, Jesus sought to convince them that it was really he who had been crucified:

> While they were still talking about this, Jesus himself stood among them and said to them, 'Peace be with you.'
>
> They were startled and frightened, thinking they saw a ghost. He said to them, 'Why are you troubled, and why do doubts rise in your minds? Look at my hands and my feet. It is I myself! Touch me and see; a ghost does not have flesh and bones, as you see I have.'
>
> When he had said this, he showed them his hands and feet. And while they still did not believe it because of joy and amazement, he asked them, 'Do you have anything here to eat?' They gave him a

piece of broiled fish, and he took it and ate it in their presence.

He said to them, 'This is what I told you while I was still with you: Everything must be fulfilled that is written about me in the Law of Moses, the Prophets and the Psalms.'

Then he opened their minds so they could understand the Scriptures. He told them, 'This is what is written: The Christ will suffer and rise from the dead on the third day, and repentance and forgiveness of sins will be preached in his name to all nations, beginning at Jerusalem. You are witnesses of these things.' (Luke 24:36–48; cf. John 20:19–29)

Strengthened by this discovery of Jesus' resurrection, which for them was so extraordinary and so unexpected, the disciples spent forty days in his company before he was taken up to heaven. Jesus appeared to several other people and on at least one occasion appeared to five hundred disciples at the same time (1 Cor. 15:3–8).

The writings of early historians

Historians must also have their say in this debate. Tacitus (an early second-century Roman historian) describes Christians as those who received their name from 'Christ who had been executed by sentence of the procurator Pontius Pilate in the reign of Tiberias' (*Annals* 15:44).[2] Flavius Josephus (a first-century Jewish historian), in his *Antiquities of the Jews*, also wrote about Jesus and his crucifixion: 'Pilate, at the suggestion of the principal men amongst us, had condemned him to the cross.'[3]

So, when considering from a historical point of view whether the crucifixion of Jesus was an illusion or reality, we are not short of evidence. The reliability of the Gospels, the honesty of the disciples, the testimony of Jesus, and the writings of early historians cannot easily be dismissed.

The redemptive purpose of Jesus' death

Jesus presented his death to his disciples as something unquestionably necessary: 'From that time on Jesus began to explain to his disciples that he *must* go to Jerusalem and suffer ... and that he *must* be killed and on the third day be raised to life' (Matt. 16:21; cf. Mark 8:31; Luke 9:22; 17:25; 24:7; my emphasis).

So why was his death necessary? First, it was because he had to fulfil the prophecies about his suffering (see Is. 53; Zech. 13:7; Pss. 16:8–11;

22:1, 16; 31:5; 34:20; 69:21; Luke 22:37). But why did the Scriptures prophesy his suffering in the first place? The answer is found in who we are as human beings, and in who God is.

Humans are sinful and redemption is required

We saw in chapter 7 that according to Islamic teaching people are sin*ners* because they commit sin, but they are not sin*ful*, that is, they are not spiritually dead. Sin is seen as an act of *disobedience to God* rather than evidence of a *broken relationship with God*. In Islam, as we have seen, human beings are not regarded as irreparably unrighteous or irretrievably lost; hence there is no need for redemption and the death of Christ is unnecessary. The Bible, however, presents humans as morally corrupt. Because sin has pervaded all areas of our lives and has led us to death, we are in a desperate situation. Redemption is necessary – it is our only hope.

Jesus presented his mission not primarily as that of a *prophet*, but as that of a *redeemer*:[4] 'the Son of Man did not come to be served, but to serve, and to give his life as a ransom for many' (Mark 10:45).

God is just, yet forgiving

Both Islam and Christianity hold that God is both just and forgiving. The question is how to reconcile these two divine attributes. In other words, how can God forgive people without compromising his justice? If he forgives sinners, will he not condone their sins? And if he punishes them, will he not be merciless?

Apart from 'the sin of association', *shirk*, sin is not as serious in Islam as it is in Christianity. Hence this question does not seem to be such a crucial one for Muslims. All Muslims would point out that people can make up for their evil deeds with their good ones (11:114). As we noted in chapter 8, Sunni Muslims also appeal to God's sovereignty. God has the right to do whatever he wants and his human creatures have no right whatever to challenge him: 'He cannot be questioned for His acts, but they will be questioned for theirs' (21:23). God is therefore free 'to forgive whom he will and to punish whom he will' (2:284; cf. 3:129; 5:20, 43; 48:14). As we have seen, for Mu'tazili Muslims, however, God's justice requires that he punish every major sin; if people do not repent they will suffer eternal condemnation, even if they have committed only one major sin. Therefore, they believe, God's forgiveness covers only minor sins (4:31).

The Bible teaches that people cannot redeem their evil deeds with good works: '[God] does not leave the guilty unpunished' (Exod. 34:7; cf. Exod. 23:7; Num. 14:18; Deut. 5:11). We all deserve God's judgment. However, God loves us and wants to forgive us. His justice and forgiveness have been reconciled through the death of Jesus, 'the Lamb of God, who takes away the sin of the world' (John 1:29). Jesus' death was an atoning sacrifice for *all* our sins, major and minor – if such a distinction can be made (1 John 2:2). On the cross Jesus took upon himself the sin of the world for which he was temporarily abandoned by God (Matt. 27:45–46). Because Jesus died on behalf of others, God, without undermining his justice, can grant his pardon, *and he will*, to all those who look to Jesus as their Saviour and Lord.

Jesus made sure that his disciples knew why he was going to die. On the eve of his death he had a meal with them and at the end of the meal, now known as the Last Supper, he explained to them the meaning of his impending death. He did this dramatically through the sharing of bread and a cup of wine:

> While they were eating, Jesus took bread, gave thanks and broke it, and gave it to his disciples, saying, 'Take and eat; this is my body.'
> Then he took the cup, gave thanks and offered it to them, saying: 'Drink from it, all of you. This is my blood of the covenant, which is poured out for many for the forgiveness of sins.' (Matt. 26:26–28)

The bread pointed to his broken body, and the wine to his blood, soon to be shed. In this, Jesus demonstrated that he is the mediator of a new covenant between God and his people: a covenant based on his sacrificial death. As the leader of a new humanity, Jesus is the new Adam, who rescues humankind from the death into which the first Adam led us (Rom. 5:12–19).

The moral implications of Jesus' death

Muslims consider that the moral implications of Jesus' death are unacceptable and that they are out of line with God's moral standards. But as we begin considering these implications, it must be emphasized that Jesus' death completely satisfied God's justice, the very basis for God's moral standards.

'Jesus was innocent!'

Muslims object that it would have been immoral for Jesus, who was sinless, to suffer on behalf of others. This argument would be pertinent if Jesus had been *forced* to do what he did. The New Testament clearly indicates, however, that Jesus freely chose to offer his life for our redemption (Phil. 2:7–8; Heb. 10:5–10), a decision motivated by his love for us and in perfect harmony with God's will. Are we going to contest this wonderful demonstration of God's love just because it does not fit our own understanding of who he is? After all, is God not sovereign to express his love in the way he thinks best?

'People should be responsible!'

The Qur'an stresses people's individual responsibility on the Day of Judgment. Everyone will be rewarded or punished according to their own deeds (6:164; 99:7–8). The Bible teaches the same: 'The soul who sins is the one who will die. The son will not share the guilt of the father, nor will the father share the guilt of the son. The righteousness of the righteous man will be credited to him, and the wickedness of the wicked will be charged against him' (Ezek. 18:20). This means that all would die if God treated us only according to his justice and not according to his love, for 'There is no-one righteous, not even one' (Rom. 3:10; Ps. 14:3).

The fact that salvation depends entirely on God's redeeming love, however, does not mean that our responsibility is not fully engaged. Each of us needs to respond individually to God's redeeming work in Christ. Our responsibility is engaged as we examine, on the one hand, our spiritual and moral predicament, and on the other, God's revelation in Christ.

'It's just too easy!'

It is argued that if God saves people without any condition other than believing in Christ, why should people refrain from sinning? If there is no punishment to be afraid of, how will people be deterred from doing wrong? The answer is that Christian living is based not on fear of God's condemnation, but on God's amazing love and our response to his love. If we truly love God we shall do our best to please him; we shall want to keep his commands. Furthermore, would it make sense to ask for God's forgiveness and to go on sinning deliberately? Clearly such an attitude would be not only inconsistent but hypocritical (cf. Rom. 6).

Genuine believers are committed to let God transform their lives. They are committed to do to others what God has done to them: 'Forgive us our sins *as we forgive* those who sin against us' (Matt. 6:12; my emphasis and translation). Christian living must indeed reflect the very character of God. Jesus said to his disciples, 'Be perfect, therefore, as your heavenly Father is perfect' (Matt. 5:48). Is it easy to live such a Christian life, maintaining God's highest standards?

The uniqueness of Jesus' resurrection

The resurrection of Jesus from the dead, an established historical fact, is unique. The people Jesus raised from the dead were raised only to face death again, but Jesus was raised to eternal life, never to face death again. What God did with Jesus he did with no other prophet, let alone any other human being. The theological significance of this unparalleled event is not to be ignored.

First, by raising Jesus from the dead, God declared that Jesus was successful in his mission. Jesus offered his life as a sacrifice for sin, and God accepted this sacrifice and was pleased with it. The redemption that brings us reconciliation with God was achieved: Jesus 'was delivered over to death for our sins and was raised to life for our justification' (Rom. 4:25).

Secondly, God vindicated Jesus, not by delivering him from the hand of his enemies, but by raising him from the dead (Acts 2:23–24; Phil. 2:5–11). In doing so God showed his faithfulness to his prophet. He also demonstrated in the most unexpected way that he is an invincible God. Through the death of Jesus, God won the supreme victory over evil, sin and death. As an ancient eastern Christian hymn puts it, 'Christ rose from the dead having through his death vanquished death so as to grant eternal life to those who lay in their tombs' (cf. Heb. 2:14–15). If Jesus, in one way or another, did not die on the cross, God would have failed to fulfil his purpose (Acts 2:23), for 'God was reconciling the world to himself in Christ, not counting men's sins against them' (2 Cor. 5:19).

Thirdly, the resurrection of Jesus was God's seal of approval on the claims Jesus made. As we shall see in the next few chapters, Jesus made claims about himself that no other prophet has done. Was he qualified to make such claims, or did he usurp God's prerogative? God's raising of Jesus from the dead is the answer to the question about who Jesus really is.

Jesus is now in heaven at the right-hand side of God, honoured by God as the Saviour of the world. He reveals himself to people in all sorts of ways. On the road to Damascus, he appeared to one of his fiercest opponents, Saul of Tarsus, and turned him into one of his most dedicated disciples, the apostle Paul (Acts 9:1–22). Another disciple, John, had a vision of Jesus that stood in sharp contrast to the appearance Jesus had when hanging on the cross (cf. John 19:35):

> I turned round to see the voice that was speaking to me. And when I turned I saw seven golden lampstands, and among the lampstands was someone 'like a son of man', dressed in a robe reaching down to his feet and with a golden sash round his chest. His head and hair were white like wool, as white as snow, and his eyes were like blazing fire. His feet were like bronze glowing in a furnace, and his voice was like the sound of rushing waters. In his right hand he held seven stars, and out of his mouth came a sharp double-edged sword. His face was like the sun shining in all its brilliance.
>
> When I saw him, I fell at his feet as though dead. Then he placed his right hand on me and said: 'Do not be afraid. I am the First and the Last. I am the Living One; *I was dead, and behold I am alive for ever and ever! I hold the keys of death and Hades* [i.e. I have authority over death and the world of the dead]' (Rev. 1:12–18; my emphasis).

Notes

[1] K. Cragg, *Jesus and the Muslim: An Exploration*, p. 178.

[2] C. Blomberg, *The Historical Reliability of the Gospels*, pp. 196–197.

[3] One of the most important texts from Josephus reads as follows: 'Now, there was about this time Jesus, a wise man, if it be lawful to call him a man, for he was a doer of wonderful works; a teacher of such men as receive the truth with pleasure. He drew over to him both many of the Jews, and many of the Gentiles. He was [the] Christ; and when Pilate, at the suggestion of the principal men amongst us, had condemned him to the cross, those that loved him at the first did not forsake him; for he appeared to them alive again the third day, as the divine prophets had foretold these and ten thousand other wonderful things concerning him; and the tribe of Christians, so named from him, are not extinct at this day' (translated by W. Whiston, *The Works of Flavius Josephus*, book 18,

ch. 3, par. 3, p. 574). Some historians question the authenticity of this text, suggesting that some of it was edited by a Christian scribe. Since Josephus was not a Christian, it is possible that he would not have written about Jesus being the Messiah or about his resurrection. Most of the passage, however, seems to be authentic (e.g. when referring to Jesus' condemnation to the cross) and is an important ancient non-Christian testimony to Jesus. See Blomberg, *Historical Reliability*, pp. 200–201.

[4] It is worth noting that Muslims who are most open to the idea of redemptive suffering are those who have suffered themselves. Thus each year the commemoration of 'Ashura gives Shi'i Muslims the opportunity to take part in the redemptive suffering of imam Ḥusayn, who was killed at Karbala' in 60/680. Also, militant Arabs, especially Palestinian poets (Samiḥ al-Qasim, Maḥmoud Darwish), have seen in the crucifixion of Jesus a paradigm for their own combat against the injustice done to their people (cf. M. Borrmans, *Jésus et les musulmans d'aujourd'hui*, pp. 192–201). The word used for a Palestinian freedom fighter, *fedayee*, literally means 'the one who sacrifices his life for his people'. It is derived from the same root as *fadi*, the word used by Arab Christians for Christ 'the Redeemer'.

13

The Servant King

At the beginning of chapter 10 we looked at how the Qur'an portrays Jesus. We discovered that his mission, culminating, according to the Christian Scriptures, in his death on the cross and his resurrection from the dead, is viewed in a completely different light in Islam. We shall continue our study, seeking to discern who Jesus Christ really is, and shall do this by looking at Jesus first as a human being, a prophet. In Islamic terms this could be expressed as Jesus being a 'servant of God'. But we need to go on and ask: Is Jesus *only* a human being? Is he *only* a prophet? This chapter and subsequent chapters will attempt to address these questions in detail.

As we have seen, Muslims honour Jesus as one of God's greatest prophets. The Gospels, on the other hand, present us with a paradoxical portrait: Jesus is at the same time God's perfect *Servant* and God's appointed *King*.

God's Servant

In the Gospels the humanity of Jesus is emphasized from the beginning. Matthew and Luke record his birth and situate the newborn child in a family tree going back to Abraham (in Matthew) and Adam (in Luke).[1] Jesus' miraculous conception, to which the Gospels and the Qur'an bear witness, does not in any way detract from the fact of his humanity. He was not, after all, the only man to come into the world in a miraculous way. John the Baptist preceded him in this, as both the Bible and the Qur'an relate. Unlike his cousin, however, Jesus had no biological father.

The Qur'an compares the creation of Jesus to that of Adam: 'God would have you think of Jesus as you think of Adam, created by God from the dust, saying to him "Be" and into being he came' (3:59; cf. 15:29; 32:9; 38:72).

Adam had been created directly by God: he had neither father nor mother.[2] Jesus too was directly created by God in Mary's womb. The Qur'an insists that the virgin birth does not mean that Jesus was of divine origin. However, we must make a distinction between Adam and Jesus. Because Adam was the first human being, his coming into existence *had* to be the result of God's direct creative act, but this was not so with Jesus. Jesus' conception was unique in that he was born of a woman who was a *virgin*. Jesus was born to Mary, who had had no sexual relationship with Joseph (Matt. 1:24–25). The Qur'an does not even mention Joseph.

Arabs are usually named with reference to their father, but Jesus had no father. Therefore, in the Qur'an Jesus is often called the *son of Mary* (thirty-three times), whereas this title occurs only once in the Gospels. Unlike the Qur'an, where it is used to honour Jesus, the Jews used it in a rather derogatory way, because they did not believe that Jesus was God's prophet:

> When the Sabbath came, he [Jesus] began to teach in the synagogue, and many who heard him were amazed.
>
> 'Where did this man get these things?' they asked. 'What's this wisdom that has been given him, that he even does miracles! Isn't this the carpenter? *Isn't this Mary's son* and the brother of James, Joseph, Judas and Simon? Aren't his sisters here with us?' And they took offence at him.
>
> Jesus said to them, 'Only in his home town, among his relatives and in his own house is a prophet without honour.' (Mark 6:2–4; my emphasis)

Razi believes that the title 'son of Mary' indicates that, contrary to what Christians believe, Jesus is *not* the Son of God.[3]

According to the Hadith, Jesus and his mother enjoyed the exceptional blessing of being protected from the devil right from the beginning of their lives: 'There is none born among the offspring of Adam but Satan touches it. A child, therefore, cries loudly at the time of birth because of the touch of Satan, except Mary and her child.'[4]

In the Gospels we read that Jesus, before beginning his ministry, spent

forty days in the desert. After this long period of fasting he was tempted
by the devil. 'If [or, since] you are the Son of God,' the devil said to him,
'tell these stones to become bread … throw yourself down [from the
temple, and God will protect you from harm] … bow down and worship
me [and I will give you all the kingdoms of the world]' (Matt. 4:1–11).

But Jesus refused to take up any of these challenges. He had not come
into the world to test God's faithfulness or to follow the easy route to
fame and fortune; he had come to serve. Faithful to the message preached
by all the prophets, Jesus asserted the oneness of God and God's exclusive right to be worshipped: 'Away from me, Satan! For it is written:
"Worship the Lord your God, and serve him only"' (Matt. 4:10). By
affirming his total submission to God, Jesus took his place among all
monotheistic believers.

Throughout his life in Palestine, Jesus was certainly fully human. Like
all human beings, he experienced tiredness, hunger and thirst (John
4:7–8). He did not disguise his emotions or hide his joys and sorrows.
He wept over the death of his friend Lazarus (John 11:35) and at the
approach of the judgment on Jerusalem (Luke 19:41). Gentle and
humble in heart (Matt. 11:29), he made friends with ordinary people
and even with social outcasts. At first, his relationship with God did not
appear to be unusual, except that he spent whole nights praying. He
stated that God was greater than he was (John 14:28) and he willingly
admitted his ignorance of some of the things that only God knows (Mark
13:32).

Most frequently Jesus referred to himself as the 'Son of Man', a title
that underlined his humanity. This humanity was seen most clearly on
the night before he died, when he was filled with anguish and earnestly
prayed to God to save him, if possible, from the imminent suffering.

> He [Jesus] took Peter, James and John along with him, and he
> began to be deeply distressed and troubled. 'My soul is over-
> whelmed with sorrow to the point of death,' he said to them. 'Stay
> here and keep watch.'
>
> Going a little farther, he fell to the ground and prayed that if
> possible the hour might pass from him. '*Abba*, Father,' he said,
> 'everything is possible for you. Take this cup from me. *Yet not what
> I will, but what you will.*' (Mark 14:33–36; my emphasis)

Jesus was a perfect 'Muslim' in the sense that he was in total submission
to God. As the Qur'an puts it:

Christ will never disdain it as beneath his dignity to be a servant
   to God,
nor indeed do the angels who dwell in the divine presence.
   (4:172)

In another sura, the Qur'an says that Jesus was *only* God's servant:

He was no more than a servant: We granted our favour to him,
And We made him an example to the Children of Israel. (43:59)

But is Jesus a servant of God *in exactly the same sense* as all other people?
In the same sense as the other prophets? Is he *only* the servant of God or
is he far more than that? An examination of his mission as revealed to us
in the Bible will help us answer these questions.

God's King

In the context of the Bible, God's king, who is anointed and commissioned to establish God's kingdom on earth, is known as 'the Messiah'. Because the title had political connotations in his time, Jesus was
reluctant to use it. Instead, he identified himself as 'the Son of Man', a
title he preferred, possibly because of its ambiguity.

Son of Man

At first sight, 'Son of Man' simply means a human being. In the Old
Testament, for example, 'son of man' almost always means just that – a
human being (Ezek. 2:1–3; Ps. 8:4; 144:3). But there is more to it. In the
book of the prophet Daniel the title points to the king God has
appointed to rule over humanity. In one of his visions, Daniel saw this
exceptional king. What he saw he could only express in figurative
language, so the eternal God is described as 'the Ancient of Days':

Thrones were set in place,
   and the Ancient of Days took his seat …
His throne was flaming with fire,
   and its wheels were all ablaze …
The court was seated,
   and the books were opened …

In my vision at night I looked, and there before me was one like a *son of man*, coming with the clouds of heaven. He approached the Ancient of Days and was led into his presence. He was given authority, glory and sovereign power; all peoples, nations and men of every language worshipped him. His dominion is an everlasting dominion that will not pass away, and his kingdom is one that will never be destroyed. (Dan. 7:9–10, 13–14; my emphasis)

The figure of 'the Son of Man' therefore has a deep religious significance, despite the apparent ordinariness of the title. For the Jewish contemporaries of Jesus who knew their Scriptures well, it evoked the majestic vision of God's appointed King. The fact that Jesus identified himself as 'the Son of Man' is extremely meaningful: he was claiming that he was this king – the universal king whose mission is to judge humankind on the Day of Judgment. Here is how Jesus vividly described his role at the end of time:

When the Son of Man comes in his glory, and all the angels with him, he will sit on his throne in heavenly glory. All the nations will be gathered before him, and he will separate the people one from another as a shepherd separates the sheep from the goats ... Then the King will say to those on his right: 'Come, you who are blessed by my Father; take your inheritance, the kingdom prepared for you since the creation of the world ...' (Matt. 25:31–34; cf. Matt. 19:28).

When Jesus was on trial before the Jewish authorities he knew he would be sentenced to death, yet he had no doubt that his condemnation would make no difference to the position God had assigned him. He told his accusers: 'you will see the Son of Man sitting at the right hand of the Mighty One and coming on the clouds of heaven' (Mark 14:62).

So is Jesus God's Servant or God's King? The answer is that he is both: he is the *Servant King*. But he is not king in the way many human kings are. He demonstrates his kingship not by lording it over people, but by serving them. His kingship is that of a servant: 'the Son of Man did not come to be served, but to serve, and to give his life as a ransom for many' (Mark 10:45).

The Servant of the Lord

In the book of the prophet Isaiah we have four portraits known as the

'Servant Songs'. Each of them points to the 'Servant of the Lord'.

The first (Is. 42:1–9) describes the Servant as God's chosen one, the one in whom he delights. Upheld by God and empowered by God's Spirit, his mission is to bring justice to the nations. He carries out his mission peacefully, resolutely and yet with great compassion for those who are weak and faltering. Like Moses, he brings in a new law and a new covenant between God and humankind; however, unlike Moses, he brings light not only to Israel but to all the peoples of the earth.

The second song (Is. 49:1–13) underlines the universal character of the Servant's mission. Called by God from the moment he is born, he enjoys a special relationship with him. Rejected by Israel, he is the initiator of a salvation received by some of the people of Israel along with people from the other nations of the earth. He brings glory to God and is himself glorified by God.

The third song (Is. 50:4–11) depicts the Servant as the perfect disciple: one who listens to God's word and communicates it. Condemned by men, he is vindicated by God. His word is the word of God, comforting those who place their trust in him and judging those who rebel.

The fourth song (Is. 52:13–53:12) shows the Servant as both the sacrificial victim for our sin and the victor over sin. Humiliated by men and put to death by them, he nevertheless prays for them. In fact, his death is an atoning sacrifice for all nations. For having freely given up his life, the Servant is raised to life again, exalted and honoured by God. He is given a multitude of descendants, people who are made righteous by him if they acknowledge what he has done for them.

In defining his mission in terms of service and redemption, Jesus identified himself as this Servant of the Lord: 'It is written: "And he was numbered with the transgressors"; and I tell you that this must be fulfilled in me. Yes, what is written about me is reaching its fulfilment' (Luke 22:37). Jesus was pointing his disciples to the fourth Servant Song, where God declares:

> by his knowledge my righteous servant will justify many,
>   and he will bear their iniquities.
> Therefore I will give him a portion among the great,
>   and he will divide the spoils with the strong,
> because he poured out his life unto death,
>   and was numbered with the transgressors.
> For he bore the sin of many,
>   and made intercession for the transgressors. (Is. 53:11b-12)

So Jesus served both God and humankind; he fulfilled God's will by giving his life as a redeeming sacrifice.

Servant and King

Jesus is God's Servant *par excellence*. Nobody has ever served God in the way he did. He gave his life to save us from eternal death and to restore our fellowship with God. On the eve of his death he gave his disciples a dramatic illustration of what his lordship meant. Having shared with them in a final meal, he got up, took off his outer clothing, wrapped a towel around his waist and washed their feet (John 13:1–13). By taking on the role of a servant he was telling his disciples that he was a *Servant King*.

So did Jesus consider it beneath his dignity to be God's Servant (cf. 4:172)? Of course not! He was God's most dedicated Servant. He considered it his honour to serve God and humankind. He identified so closely with us that he was willing to take upon himself the weight of our sin. And in so doing, he carried out God's will perfectly and showed himself to be more human than all other human beings.

Does the fact that he is God's Servant disqualify Jesus from being God's chosen King? No, quite the opposite: *Because* Jesus served God in such a unique way we know that his relationship with God is unique. And because Jesus exhibited throughout his mission the very character of God, God vindicated him, not by sparing him from death, but by raising him from the dead and establishing him as Lord of all creation:

> [Jesus Christ], being in very nature God,
> did not consider equality with God something to be grasped,
> but made himself nothing,
> *taking the very nature of a servant*,
> being made in human likeness.
> And being found in appearance as a man,
> he humbled himself
> and became obedient to death – even death on a cross!
> *Therefore* God exalted him to the highest place
> and gave him the name that is above every name,
> that at the name of Jesus every knee should bow,
> in heaven and on earth and under the earth,
> and every tongue confess that *Jesus Christ is Lord*,
> to the glory of God the Father. (Phil. 2:6–11; my emphasis)

The way the Scriptures present Jesus' lordship is parallel to a well-known hadith: 'The leader of a people is their servant.'[5] If this is true of human beings, how much more should it be true of God? He is the supreme 'leader' and in him we have the perfect model of leadership. In a sense, we may say paradoxically that only God is able to serve his creatures to perfection. Leading is not only compatible with serving, but if someone is to be a good leader they must have a servant attitude. Perfect service is the mark of unique leadership skills. Through his outstanding service we recognize in Jesus Christ a divinely appointed King. This is the extraordinary revelation of the Gospels: the Lord God is in fact the Servant God!

Notes

[1] The Annunciation of Jesus by the angel in the Qur'an (3:45–47; 19:16–21) is to some degree similar to the account in Luke's Gospel (Luke 1:26–38). But the story of his birth in the Qur'an (19:22–26) is very different (cf. Luke 2:1–7).

[2] Cf. 5:75; Razi, VI:12, pp. 51–52.

[3] Cf. 19:34; Razi, XI:21, p. 185.

[4] Bukhari, *anbiya'* 44:IV, p. 426, no. 641 [3177].

[5] *Sayyidu l-qawmi khadimuhum.* I did not find this saying in the canonical collections of the Hadith. Ibn 'Arabi quotes it the other way round: 'The servant of a people is their leader. The person who through his service demonstrates his lordship is indeed a perfectly dedicated servant' (*al-Futuḥat al-makkiya*, vol. 1, p. 244).

14

Titles for Jesus in the Qur'an and the Bible

We have seen that the Qur'an gives Jesus many titles, which together with his miraculous birth mark him out as a special prophet. He is called an Apostle, a 'Word of God', a 'Spirit from him', and 'the Messiah'. These titles are also found in the Bible. Examining their meaning in both the Islamic and Christian traditions will enable us to gain a better understanding of who Jesus is for Muslims and for Christians.[1]

Jesus is a Prophet and an Apostle

Jesus has an eminent rank among the prophets mentioned in the Qur'an. He is one of the six greatest prophets: Adam, Noah, Abraham, Moses, Jesus and Muhammad. The last three have this in common: each brought a law that was put into writing in a book. As God's prophet and apostle, Jesus received the Gospel, which confirmed the Torah entrusted to Moses. With divine permission he performed miracles that accredited his mission in the eyes of the Israelites. He had the ability to know what people were doing in their homes in secret (3:49).

Throughout his life, Jesus was upheld by the Holy Spirit, *ruh al-qudus* (2:87, 253; 5:113). To safeguard divine unity from being impaired in any way, Muslim commentators identify the Holy Spirit as the angel Gabriel. So according to the Qur'an, Jesus is simply a created human being.

> Christ, the son of Mary was no more than an Apostle;
> many were the apostles that passed away before him. (5:75)

The Gospels also present Jesus as a prophet and apostle of God, but in quite a different sense. Moses had told his people that God would raise up for them a prophet like himself: 'The LORD your God will raise up for you a prophet like me from among your own brothers. You must listen to him' (Deut. 18:15). On the basis of this prophecy, the Jews were waiting for the arrival of a prophet of Moses' stature, a prophet they identified with the Messiah. They were still waiting for this prophet when John the Baptist began preaching in the desert region, calling people to repentance. Some of the people asked him if he was the Prophet (John 1:21), but he firmly denied it and drew his questioners' attention to Jesus (John 1:26–27).

Seeing the miracles Jesus did and hearing his words, many Jews came to the following conclusion: 'Surely this is the Prophet who is to come into the world' (John 6:14; cf. John 7:40). Others thought that Jesus was merely one of the prophets (Matt. 16:14; 21:11; Mark 6:15). God confirmed that Jesus was indeed the Prophet when he testified about him and said, 'This is my Son, whom I love; with him I am well pleased. Listen to him!' (Matt. 17:5). Notice that the words 'Listen to him' echo the promise God had made to Moses (Deut. 18:15). So here, over a thousand years later, God is declaring that Jesus is the Prophet he had promised to send. After Jesus' resurrection, his disciples too announced that their Master was indeed *the* Prophet (Acts 3:20–22), just as they had originally believed (John 1:45).

John's Gospel presents Jesus as the Apostle sent into the world by God, not to condemn the world but to save it (John 3:17). Jesus does what God does (John 10:37); he speaks God's words and is filled with God's Spirit (John 3:34). His mission is to unite his people with God just as intimately as he himself is united with God, so that the world may recognize that God has sent him (John 17:21–23). In fact, knowing God is inseparable from knowing the one he sent: 'Now this is eternal life: that they know you, the only true God, and Jesus Christ, whom you have sent' (John 17:3). This Apostle is not just *sent by* God; he *comes from* God (John 8:42; 17:8) and *returns to* God (John 13:1), having loved his people enough to sacrifice his own life for them (John 15:12–13).

Some Muslims point to Deuteronomy 18:15–18 and the prophecies about the Prophet and apply them to Muhammad rather than to Jesus. We shall return to this issue in chapter 20, 'Do the Scriptures foretell the coming of Muhammad?'

Jesus is the Word of God

The Qur'an calls Jesus a 'Word *of* God', *kalimatuhu* (4:171) and a 'Word *from* God', *kalimatun minhu* (3:39, 45). Muslim commentators consider these to be one title.[2] So how do they understand it?

Razi explains that it should be interpreted in the light of Jesus' miraculous birth. All embryos come into existence, he says, through God's creative word, 'Be'. Since Jesus had no father it was even more appropriate in his case to attribute his existence to God's creative command.[3] According to another interpretation, Jesus is the Word of God because he preached the Word of God with many signs proving the divine origin of his message (3:45).[4]

These explanations of Jesus as 'the Word of God' leave us with some questions. If Jesus is called 'the Word of God' because of the way he was created, which is similar to the way Adam was created according to the Qur'an, why is Adam not called 'the Word of God'? And if it was because Jesus powerfully preached God's Word, why is Muhammad not honoured with this title? The Islamic explanations seek to avoid the risk of undermining the oneness of God, but this does not make them satisfactory.

In order to find the true meaning of the title, we must consider it in the context of the Gospel in which it first appeared (John 1:1–18). The Gospel of John speaks of Jesus in these terms: 'In the beginning was the Word, and the Word was with God, and the Word was God. He was with God in the beginning. Through him all things were made; without him nothing was made that has been made ... The Word became flesh and made his dwelling among us' (John 1:1–3, 14a). Jesus is therefore the Word of God in the sense that he is the incarnation of the *eternal* Word of God, the personified revelation of God. Jesus is God's Word in a way that is, to some degree, similar to the way Muslims consider the Qur'an to be God's word. For Christians, God's eternal Word is revealed in the person of Jesus, whereas for Muslims it is revealed in the Qur'an. However, unlike Jesus who is both human and divine, for Muslims the Qur'an is only divine.[5]

Jesus is a Spirit from God

In sura 4:171, the verse that describes Jesus as God's Word, he is also called 'a Spirit from him', *ruḥun minhu*:

> Christ Jesus the son of Mary was no more than an apostle of God,
> And His Word which He bestowed on Mary,
> And *a Spirit from him*: so believe in God and His apostles.
>   (4:171; my emphasis)

The context indicates that *him* refers to God, but some Muslims explain this title in connection with Gabriel. Razi lists five different interpretations:[6]

(1) People usually describe what is extremely pure and clean by using the word 'spirit'. Because Jesus had no father and was created through Gabriel breathing into Mary, he was pure, hence a 'spirit'. Saying that Jesus is *from him* (Gabriel) amounts to honouring Jesus.

(2) Jesus was instrumental in God's revelation, and this is sometimes described as 'spirit' in the Qur'an: 'We have inspired you a revelation [lit. 'a spirit'] resulting from our command' (42:52; cf. 16:2). So, since Jesus was the agent of God's revelation, he is in a sense a 'spirit from God'.

(3) Jesus is a 'spirit' from God in the sense that he was a 'mercy' from him. God's mercy is referred to as God's spirit: 'God has engraved faith in the hearts of such believers and strengthened them with a spirit from Himself' (58:22). Jesus is a mercy from God because he taught people regarding their lives in this world and in the afterlife.

(4) In Arabic the words for 'spirit', *ruḥ*, and for 'breath', *riḥ*, are very similar. Jesus is 'a spirit' in the sense that he was created through the breathing of Gabriel into Mary. Gabriel is called a 'spirit from God' because he carried out this action with God's command 'We [God] breathed into her [Mary] of Our Spirit [i.e. Gabriel]' (21:91; cf. 66:12).[7]

(5) The purpose of qualifying Jesus as 'spirit' (not *a* spirit) is to exalt him, for he is indeed one of the noble, holy and superior spirits. The words *from him* (God) are meant to magnify, *'aẓẓama*, and honour, *sharrafa*, Jesus.

The fourth of these interpretations identifies the 'spirit' as the angel Gabriel. It is worth noting, however, that the Qur'an makes a distinction between the angels and the spirit (see 70:4; 78:38; 97:4). It was the Holy Spirit who supported Jesus during his mission (2:87, 253; 5:113). It would seem that when Muslim exegetes identify God's Spirit with Gabriel they do so in order to prevent any suggestion that God's Spirit is distinct from God, which would in their opinion undermine God's oneness.

In the New Testament, Jesus is called a 'spirit' in just one verse: '"The first man Adam became a living being"; the last Adam, a life-giving spirit' (1 Cor. 15:45). The context here suggests that the expression 'a life-giving spirit' refers to the risen Christ whose victory over death enables him to grant new life to those who trust in him. The Gospels clearly distinguish between the angel Gabriel and the Holy Spirit. The Holy Spirit was God's agent in the conception of Jesus, whereas the role of Gabriel was simply to tell Mary what would happen and how she would become pregnant (Matt. 1:20; Luke 1:35).

The Holy Spirit is the Spirit of God who descended upon Jesus at his baptism, in the form of a dove (Matt. 3:16). He was active throughout Jesus' ministry (Matt. 12:28; Luke 4:1–2; John 3:34). Just before he died (John 14 – 16) and shortly after his resurrection (Acts 1:8), Jesus promised his disciples that he would send them the Holy Spirit after he had been lifted up to God. This Holy Spirit is 'the Spirit of Truth' whose mission was to give Jesus' disciples full knowledge of Christ and the power to carry his gospel beyond the frontiers of Israel (John 14:15–18; 15:26–27; 16:7–15).

Jesus is the Messiah

The title *al-Masih*, 'Messiah', is given to Jesus eleven times in the Qur'an. For some Muslim exegetes, *al-Masih* is the Arabic word for *māšîah*, which is Jesus' name in Hebrew. The majority of Muslims, however, consider that the word is not a personal name but a title. They differ as to its derivation.

Razi lists ten possible explanations.[8] The first three are based on the active sense of the verb *masaha*, meaning 'to touch', 'to anoint', 'to wipe away', 'to measure up' (a land), or 'to move around' (a place). In other words, Jesus is the subject of the action: 'the one who touches', 'the one who moves around':

1. Ibn 'Abbas thought Jesus is called *al-Masih* because whenever he touched the sick with his hand they were cured.
2. Jesus was a traveller. He used to move all around the country; hence his title, which could be read as *Massih* (an emphatic form of *Masih*) or 'traveller'.
3. Jesus is the Messiah because he often laid his hand on orphans to call God's blessing upon them.

In the passive sense of *masaha*, Jesus is seen as the object of the verb: 'the one who is anointed', 'the one who is touched':

4. He is named *al-Masiḥ* because he was pure, free from sin and evil.
5. A person with flat feet is known (in Arabic) as *mamsuḥ al-qadamayn* (or *amsaḥ*). As this was the case with Jesus he was called *al-Masiḥ*.
6. As a prophet Jesus was anointed with sacred oil.
7. Gabriel touched Jesus with his wing at his birth so as to protect him from the touch of Satan.
8. When Jesus came out of his mother's womb he had sacred oil on him.

The final two interpretations, comments Razi, probably are not based on the derivation of the word but simply aim to praise Jesus:

9. *Al-Masiḥ* means *al-malik*, 'the king'.
10. *Al-Masiḥ* means *al-ṣiddiq*, 'the righteous one'.[9]

Of these interpretations, only the sixth and the ninth come close to the biblical meaning of the word, that is, the anointed king. In the Bible the word 'Messiah' refers to a rite performed in certain circumstances in Israel. It was customary to introduce kings, priests and prophets to their offices by anointing them with sacred oil; hence the meaning later given to the word 'Messiah': the chosen one.

The Messiah is the king God promised he would raise up as one of David's descendants (2 Sam. 7). David's son, Solomon, for all the greatness and prosperity of his kingdom, was only a pale foreshadowing of the king who was to come. This king would enjoy a father–son relationship with God and would make all the peoples of the earth his subjects (Ps. 2). King David called him his Lord (Ps. 110). The prophet Micah spoke about the Messiah too and identified Bethlehem as the place where he would be born, describing his origins as ancient and eternal:

> But you, Bethlehem Ephrathah,
>   though you are small among the clans of Judah,
> out of you will come for me
>   one who will be ruler over Israel,
> whose origins are from of old,
>   from ancient times. (Mic. 5:2)

Isaiah gave him the name Immanuel ('God with us') and predicted that his birth would be miraculous (Is. 7:13–14). This newborn king, announced Isaiah, would preside over an eternal kingdom of peace and justice:

> Of the increase of his government and peace
>   there will be no end.
> He will reign on David's throne
>   and over his kingdom,
> establishing and upholding it
>   with justice and righteousness
>   from that time on and for ever. (Is. 9:7)

In view of all this it is hardly surprising that many people were eagerly awaiting the coming of the Messiah at the time when Jesus was born. However, since the Jews were under the domination of the Romans, their messianic hope had taken on a political emphasis. They were looking for a liberator who would set their nation free from Roman occupation.

The Gospel genealogies present Jesus as the son of David (Matt. 1:1; Luke 3:23–31). The angel Gabriel told Mary that her son would sit on the throne of David, his father: 'Do not be afraid, Mary, you have found favour with God. You will be with child and give birth to a son, and you are to give him the name Jesus. He will be great and will be called the Son of the Most High. The Lord God will give him the throne of his father David, and he will reign over the house of Jacob for ever; his kingdom will never end' (Luke 1:30–33). Jesus was born in Bethlehem, the town of David, as Micah had prophesied (Luke 2:1–7).

Some thirty years later his disciples gradually came to discover that their Master was indeed the Messiah (the Christ) they had been expecting (Matt. 22:41–46; John 4:26). Before setting off for Jerusalem, where he knew he would be crucified, Jesus warned his disciples not to tell anyone of his messianic identity, in order to avoid any popular misunderstanding (Matt. 16:13–20). When interrogated by the religious authorities, he was cautious about using the title. He was not the kind of Messiah the people were expecting – a political king – but he certainly was the Messiah foretold by the prophets (cf. Matt. 26:63–64; Mark 14:60–62; Luke 22:66–70; cf. Dan. 7:13–14).

Jesus' resurrection was his enthronement as Messiah, as his disciples boldly proclaimed soon after his ascension to heaven:

> God has raised this Jesus to life, and we are all witnesses of the fact.
> Exalted to the right hand of God, he has received from the Father

the promised Holy Spirit and has poured out what you now see and hear. For David did not ascend to heaven, and yet he said,

> 'The Lord said to my Lord:
> "Sit at my right hand
> until I make your enemies
>   a footstool for your feet."'

Therefore let all Israel be assured of this: God has made this Jesus, whom you crucified, both Lord and Christ. (Acts 2:32–36; cf. 13:32–33).

So Jesus now reigns as Lord of the world, and particularly as Lord of those who confess that he is the Christ. On the day he returns in glory, his lordship will be recognized by all (1 Cor. 15:20–28).

To sum up, then: the various titles the Qur'an gives to Jesus show his prominent position among the prophets. No doubt this explains why he is referred to as 'eminent in this world and in the age to come' (3:45), as Moses was to some degree (33:69). Jesus is honoured not only in this world: like the angels (4:172), he is near to God's throne (3:45). Yet, although God made him one of the greatest prophets (cf. 2:253), Jesus in the Qur'an is essentially as human as any other prophet.

The titles given to Jesus in the Qur'an therefore do not have the same meaning as the same titles in the Gospels. In the Gospels, not only do they indicate that Jesus has a privileged status among the prophets, but they point to the unique position he holds that makes him unlike any other prophet. This claim to a unique position is something we shall need to examine more closely.

Notes

[1] A good survey on how contemporary Muslim writers view Jesus Christ is available in Arabic in M. Khawwam, *al-Masih fi l-fikri l-islami l-hadith wa fi l-masihiyya*, pp. 197–229.

[2] In general, Muslim commentators do not differentiate between Jesus' being a 'Word of God' and his being a 'Word from God'. They tend to emphasize 'from God' since it is less liable to be misunderstood by non-Muslims who say that Jesus is divine because he is God's Word.

[3] Cf. Bukhari, *anbiya'* 47:IV, p. 428 (Introduction to ch. 47).

[4] Razi, IV:8, pp. 42–43.

[5] This comparison refers to the Ash'ari understanding of God's Word. Mu'tazili theologians do not consider the Qur'an as God's eternal and uncreated Word.

[6] Razi, VI:11, p. 91.

[7] Cf. Bukhari, *anbiya'* 47:IV, p. 428 (Introduction to ch. 47).

[8] Sura 3:45; Razi, IV:8, pp. 43–44.

[9] Cf. Bukhari, *anbiya'* 46:IV, p. 427 (Introduction to ch. 46). Razi goes on to explain what *al-Masih al-Dajjal*, the Antichrist, means. He was given the name *al-Masih* either because, according to the Hadith (Bukhari, *anbiya'* 48:IV, p. 432, no. 649 [3184]), he is blind in one eye, *mamsuh ahadu l-'aynayn*, or because he will go all around the world at high speed, *masaha*. As for *Dajjal*, the word refers either to the one who goes all around the world (according to one meaning of the verb *dajjala*), or to the liar, the impostor.

15

Is Jesus the Son of God?

Here we reach the most sensitive point in the debate between Christians and Muslims. Christians believe that God's revelation reached its climax in Jesus: that God himself came into our world through his Son. Muslims categorically reject this belief as the most serious threat to the oneness of God.

Before dealing with this difficult issue we need to remember something of the background to the Qur'anic denial of Jesus' divinity. The Prophet's mission was to preach God's oneness to the Arabs who used to associate many gods with the supreme God. He preached that since there is only one Creator God, people should worship him and him alone; they must submit to his will and obey his commands (72:18, 20).

The 'associationism' of the Arabs was such that they believed God to have relations:

- a wife or wives (72:3);
- sons (2:116; 6:100–101; 10:68; 17:111; 18:4; 19:91–92; 21:26; 25:2);
- daughters (6:100; 16:57; 17:40; 37:149–153; 43:19; 53:27).

The Qur'an also records the names of the three principal goddesses who were worshipped in pre-Islamic religion (53:19–20). In the face of such beliefs, Muhammad's strong attack upon Arab polytheism was intended to uphold God's transcendence and majesty. It was to prevent any deification of his creatures, who would have become a part of God himself (43:15).

They say: 'The Most Gracious has taken a son!'
Indeed they have put forth a thing most monstrous!
At it the skies are ready to burst, the earth to split asunder,
and the mountains to fall down in utter ruin,
That they should invoke a son for The Most Gracious.
For it is not consonant with the majesty of The Most Gracious
that He should take a son. (19:88–92)

As we saw in chapter 7, the unforgivable sin according to the Qur'an is to include created beings in the worship due to the unique Creator alone (4:48, 116).

It is against this background – the intense struggle against Arab polytheism – that we must understand the criticisms that were aimed at the Christians, for Christian beliefs too were seen as a kind of 'associationism'. With anti-polytheistic energy and zeal, Muhammad preached the Qur'anic message, denouncing the claim that Christ is the Son of God (9:30) and that God is Christ (5:17, 72). With even greater justification he refuted the allegation that God is a member of a triad composed of God, Mary and Jesus:

People of the Book, do not go to unwarranted lengths in your religion and get involved in false utterances relating to God. Truly, Jesus, Mary's son, was the messenger of God and His Word – the word which He imparted to Mary – and a spirit from Him.

Believe, then, in God and His apostles and do not talk of three (gods). You are well advised to abandon such ideas. Truly God is one God. Glory be to Him, He is above having a son, to Him belong all things in the heavens and the earth, and He is the one and only guardian. (4:171)

Surely they are unbelievers who allege that God is the third of three (gods)! There is no god but One. If they do not cease saying such a thing these unbelievers will most surely be seized with a painful retribution. (5:73)

Muslims have interpreted these texts in three ways, as Razi explains in his commentary:[1]

(1) Some Muslims consider that the texts deny what they see as the Christian doctrine of the Trinity, that is, three gods: God, Mary and Jesus. They back their interpretation with sura 5:116, where God

186 Faith to faith

questions Jesus about what he taught: 'Did you ever say to men, 'Adopt me and my mother as two gods in disregard of God Himself'?'

(2) Other Muslims (who probably know that Christians do not believe in a trinity of God, Mary, and Jesus) think that Christians are instructed not even to mention Mary and Jesus alongside God. This interpretation is based on the fact that the word 'gods' does not appear in the texts. (The texts literally say 'three' rather than 'three gods'.) Mentioning the three names together may indeed be misleading, as it suggests that Jesus and Mary are two gods in addition to God. A parallel to this misleading use of language is found in the Qur'an. In the story about the 'Companions of the Cave', the way people talked about their number was rather confusing: 'Three [people], it was said, and four with the dog' (18:22).

(3) Razi is well aware that the Christian doctrine is about 'God who is one in essence, three in persons'.[2] He believes that the Qur'an repudiates the biblical doctrine of the Trinity, which he explains as follows: 'One essence in three persons: Father, Son and Holy Spirit; these three are One just as the Sun is disc, light and heat. They [Christians] refer to the Father as the Substance, to the Son as the Word and to the Spirit as the Life. They claim that the Father is God, the Son is God and the Spirit is God and all are one God.'

This third explanation is a fair description of the Christian doctrine of the Trinity. The only area where we disagree with Razi is how he defines the Christian doctrine of the incarnation. He says that the Word mixed with Jesus' body in the way water mixes with wine or milk. We cannot blame Razi for this definition of the incarnation, which was in fact that of the *monophysite* Christians.[3]

In any case, the Christian doctrine does not make sense to Razi, and he utterly rejects it purely on rationalistic grounds: the three cannot be one, nor the one three. Therefore, he concludes, there is no doctrine more corrupt or untrue than the Christian doctrine of the Trinity.

If God had a son

Razi rejects the Christian doctrine because he sees it as irrational. This rationalistic approach to faith, however, is hardly in line with Islamic teaching. Does Islam make the human mind the supreme arbiter in deciding what is true and what is untrue? I think not, for in Islam as well as in Christianity, revelation takes precedence over rationality. This is clearly established through a Qur'anic verse, which, interestingly enough, is about the possibility of God having a son. In this verse the Prophet is summoned by God to admit that divine revelation may be beyond his human understanding:

> Say: 'If the All-Merciful [God] had a son, I would be the very first to worship [him].'
> Glory be to the Lord of the heavens and of the earth, the Lord of the Throne, beyond all the attributes they ascribe. (43:81–82)

What this text indicates is that Muhammad must surrender to God's revelation even when it contradicts human expectations. According to Razi, some Muslims thought that if verse 81 was taken literally it would suggest that God might have a son, but since this is impossible they have resorted to other interpretations:[4]

(1) Some Muslims see the worship as directed towards God and not his son. They take the verse to mean 'Even if God had a son, I would still be the first to worship only God, and not his son.' This is possible, since the Arabic text is literally 'If the All-Merciful had a son, I would be the first worshipper.' Razi considers this interpretation unwarranted. If God really had a son, yet Muhammad denied it, he would persist in his ignorance and in his denial of the truth. As this attitude is not fitting for the Prophet, this interpretation cannot be the right one.

(2) The second interpretation is a variation of the first, but puts the emphasis on the strength of the argument rather than on the objective fact of the son's existence: 'If you were able to prove that God had a son, I would still deny it and worship only God.' This interpretation does not make sense to Razi. It suggests that the Prophet would reject the claim only if it had been substantiated. Muhammad's denial does not depend on whether the case has been made or not.

(3) Others take the verse to mean 'If God had a son, I would still be the first to disown it.' This interpretation is based on a rather unusual meaning of the verb *'abida*. It could mean 'to refuse' or 'to disown', although the most common sense is 'to worship'. The meaning of the verse is still basically the same as in the previous interpretation and Razi rejects it for the same reason.

(4) Yet other Muslims suggest that the Arabic word *in* means not 'if' but 'no', *ma*. Muhammad was commanded to say something like this: 'God has no son, therefore I am the first monotheistic believer in Mecca and I declare that he has no son.' Again, this interpretation is unlikely and Razi disregards it.

Razi suggests that the conditional statement in the verse should be interpreted literally, that is, '*If* God had a son I would be the first to worship this son and to serve him.' What it aims to show is that if Muhammad refuses to believe that God has a son, it is not because he is biased or delights in polemics. He is prepared to recognize that God has a son if this claim is established; yet since God has no son and there is no evidence to prove the existence of such a son, how can he accept that God has a son? Furthermore, says Razi, since there is clear evidence to show that God *does not* have a son, there was no reason at all for Muhammad to admit to his existence, let alone worship him.

This interpretation is fairly convincing, but it does raise some questions. Is there really clear evidence that God has no son? And if the answer is yes, where is this evidence? And what if the case was made that God has a son? Are Muslims prepared, like the Prophet, to worship this son and to serve him?

Generally speaking, both Muslims and Christians agree that God's revelation takes precedence over human rationality. As to who God is, the human mind is a good servant but an unreliable teacher. From a Christian point of view, at least two reasons explain why we are incapable of knowing God with our intellectual resources alone: first, finite creatures cannot possibly comprehend the infinite Creator, and secondly, the human mind is just as sinful as the whole human being. Knowing God, therefore, means trusting him, rather than trusting our own rationality.

Refuting misconceptions

Does the Qur'an provide clear evidence that Jesus is not God's Son? I think not. What the Qur'an rightly repudiates is a *misconception* of the Trinity and of Jesus' sonship:

- The trinitarian monotheism of the Bible has nothing to do with the tritheism denounced by the Qur'an. Christians believe in one God who is Father, Son and Holy Spirit, not in three gods: God, Mary and Jesus.
- Jesus is not the Son of God because he was conceived miraculously in Mary's womb; rather, Jesus was conceived miraculously because he is the Son of God.
- God created Jesus' human nature when he was conceived. This means that Jesus is a human being in the full sense of the word, and his Qur'anic name *Jesus, son of Mary*, is fully justified.

- God cannot be reduced to the person of the Son alone. While it is correct that *Christ is God* (by virtue of his divine nature), it is not true that *God is Christ*, which the Qur'an rightly rejects (cf. 5:17, 72).
- The incarnation of the Son of God does not at all mean making a man into a god. The incarnation is exactly the opposite of the deification of a man. The former refers to the self-abasement of God, whereas the latter is about the elevation of a man to God's rank. Certainly God did not *take* Jesus as his Son, an allegation duly refuted by the Qur'an.
- The divine and the human natures have been united in the one person of Jesus Christ. Christians worship the *person* of Christ, not his divine or human nature. This union does not deify human nature or humanize divine nature: the two natures remain distinct, unconfused and unmixed.[5] Therefore, in no way do Christians associate what is created with the Creator in their worship.

God begets not, nor is he begotten

Now what about the famous sura which says that God 'begets not, nor is He begotten'?

Say: He is God, the One and Only;
God, the Eternal, Absolute;
He begets not, nor is He begotten;
And there is none like unto Him. (112:1–4)

Historically, this Meccan sura was directed not against Christians but against the polytheistic Arabs and their belief in God's sons and daughters. For Razi, however, it has wider implications.[6] It criticizes the Arabs for taking the angels to be God's daughters (cf. 17:40; 37:150; 43:19; 53:27), and also the Jews, who believe that Ezra is God's son and Christians, who consider that Christ is God's Son:

The Jews call 'Uzayr [Ezra] a son of God, and the Christians call Christ the Son of God.
   That is a saying from their mouth; in this they but imitate what the Unbelievers of old used to say. May God fight against them: how they are deluded away from the truth. (9:30)

Razi sees Christians as divided into two groups: those who believe that Jesus is the Son of God in the real sense, *ḥaqiqatan*, and those who believe that God honoured Jesus by taking him as a son, just as he took Abraham as his friend (cf. 4:125). The belief of the second group (which is actually a Christian heresy known as *adoptionism*) is rejected by the Qur'an on the grounds that God is 'the One who is self-sufficient', *ghani*; therefore, he has no need of any helper (10:68; 17:111; cf. 2:116; 19:35, 92; 21:26; 25:2). While this argument may be flawless, the one Razi uses against the first group is much less convincing. The fact that God 'begets not nor is He begotten' is proved rationally, says Razi. God does not beget because he is not 'a [plural] substance', *jism*; that is, a substance made up of parts, *mutaba'id*, and divisible into portions, *munqasim*. Razi develops this argument in his exegesis of a verse from sura 39:

> Had God willed to adopt a son, He could have chosen as He wished from His creation.
> Glory be to Him: He is God, the One, the Invincible. (39:4)

Razi explains that there are three reasons why God cannot have a son.[7] First, to produce a son means that one part (among many others) comes off the father before it is made in his likeness; but since God is one single substance, *fard mutlaq*, he cannot have a son. Secondly, a son necessarily has the same identity, *mahiyya,* with the corresponding defining character, *ta'yin*, as his father. This is impossible for God and his son: God is 'the Necessary Being by his essence', *wajib al-wujud li-dhatihi*, a description that by definition applies only to one being, that is, God. Third, having a son means the existence of a husband and a wife of the same kind, *jins*. If God had a son he would have a wife with the same nature as his; hence he would no longer be one God. The fact that God is described as *qahhar*, the Invincible, also precludes him having a son. A man needs a son to succeed him after his death, but God is not subject to death: he subdues everything and is subdued by nothing.

So has Razi made his case? I suggest he has, where misconceptions about God are concerned, but not concerning the Christian doctrine of God. Christianity insists on the distinction to be made between the *three persons* and the *one essence* of the Godhead. God's essence is indeed one, single and undivided. It is the Father, not the divine essence, who generates the Son. This divine generation does not have the same characteristics as in human experience:

> What the Father is, this very same reality is also the Son, this the Holy Spirit … The Father gives His substance to the Son,

generating him from eternity ... One cannot say that He gave Him a part of His substance and retained a part for Himself, *since the substance of the Father is indivisible, being entirely simple.* Nor can one say that in generating the Father transferred His substance to the Son, as though He gave it to the Son in such a way as not to retain it for Himself, for so He would have ceased to be substance ... *This reality is neither generating nor generated, nor proceeding,* but it is the Father who generates, the Son who is generated and the Holy Spirit who proceeds, so that there be distinctions between the persons but unity in nature.[8]

Thus Jesus' being the Son of God does not mean that God has a partner or that he needs to have a son: 'The Father begets the Son, not by an act of will, nor out of necessity, but by nature.'[9] The everlasting God is, has always been, and will ever be one God, who is Father, Son and Holy Spirit.

God is not begotten, Razi explains, because he is eternal. If God had been begotten at any time, his existence would have started at that time. Again Razi's argument is valid where it repudiates a *temporal* and *physical* conception of divine sonship, but Christianity holds that Jesus is the Son of God in the *spiritual* sense of the word. His generation by the Father is eternal and has nothing to do with his miraculous conception in Mary's womb: '*Without beginning, always and without end,* the Father begets, the Son is born and the Holy Spirit proceeds.'[10] Unlike the divine essence, which is one and unique, human nature is one, but it is not unique, since it is reproduced every time a human being comes into existence.

In short, Christians agree with Razi that it is possible to know rationally that God has no son if this claim is understood in human terms. We endorse the Qur'anic statement that 'God begets not nor is he begotten', if what is meant is that God is the eternal God and he derives his existence from no-one but himself. However, we must not let our rightful rejection of false and human ideas about God blur the truth about the trinitarian God who has made himself known to us in Jesus Christ and through Scripture. Let us consider the scriptural evidence for the Christian teaching about the identity of Jesus and his relationship with God.

Evidence in the Scriptures

God revealed himself as Father, Son and Holy Spirit from the outset of

Jesus' mission. Before he began his public ministry, Jesus gave a dramatic explanation of his mission. He chose to be baptized by John the Baptist, and, in so doing, identified himself with the people he came to save. John had been calling people to repent and to be baptized for the forgiveness of their sins. When he saw Jesus coming towards him, he was troubled. He tried to deter Jesus from lowering himself with such an act. Jesus was sinless; he did not need to be baptized, so why associate himself with sinners? '*I* need to be baptised by you,' John said to Jesus, 'and do *you* come to me?' (Matt. 3:14; my emphasis). But Jesus insisted. 'As soon as Jesus was baptised, he went up out of the water. At that moment heaven was opened, and he saw the Spirit of God descending like a dove and lighting on him. And a voice from heaven said, "This is my Son, whom I love; with him I am well pleased"' (Matt. 3:16–17).

Although God had given this testimony to Jesus publicly, Jesus did not often draw people's attention to his identity as the Son of God. There are two reasons for his attitude: first, his humility, and secondly, he did not want to be misunderstood by the crowd, who might think he was undermining God's oneness. With his disciples, however, Jesus was more open. They became aware of his holiness (Luke 5:1–11), and amazed at his power over the forces of nature (Matt. 8:27). Jesus revealed to them his identity as the Son of God (Matt. 11:25–27), and little by little they discovered the real meaning of these words (Matt. 14:33). One day Jesus sensed that his disciples were ready to receive the full revelation about himself. He challenged them:

'Who do you say I am?'
Simon Peter answered, 'You are the Christ, the Son of the living God.'
Jesus replied, 'Blessed are you, Simon son of Jonah, for this was not revealed to you by man, but by my Father in heaven.' (Matt. 16:15–16)

A week later Jesus took three of his closest disciples to the top of a mountain and gave them a new revelation of himself: 'There he was transfigured before them. His face shone like the sun, and his clothes became as white as the light. Just then there appeared before them Moses and Elijah, talking with Jesus … While he was still speaking, a bright cloud enveloped them, and a voice from the cloud said, "This is my Son, whom I love; with him I am well pleased. Listen to him!"' (Matt. 17:2–5). This overwhelming experience, combined with the solemn testimony from God the Father regarding Jesus' identity, must have had a great impact on the disciples. Peter refers to this experience in one of his letters to give historical evidence for the sonship of Jesus:

> We did not follow cleverly invented stories when we told you about the power and coming of our Lord Jesus Christ, but we were eye-witnesses of his majesty. For he received honour and glory from God the Father when the voice came to him from the Majestic Glory, saying, 'This is my Son, whom I love; with him I am well pleased.' We ourselves heard this voice that came from heaven when we were with him on the sacred mountain. (2 Pet. 1:16–18)

As God's Son, Jesus is above all the prophets, including Moses and Elijah, who were held in high esteem by the Jews. When speaking to the Jewish leaders, Jesus described the prophets as God's servants, whereas he referred to himself as God's Son (Matt. 21:33–46). He challenged them to prove him guilty (John 8:46), and they realized he was claiming to be God (cf. John 5:18; 10:33). From that day on they tried to find an opportunity to arrest him (John 10:39; 11:53), but were cautious, afraid of how his crowds of followers would react to his arrest (Matt. 21:46; John 12:19). When they eventually seized him, they subjected him to an interrogation and accused him of claiming to be God's Son (John 19:7). Jesus did not deny what he had said, but pointed out that this was in line with divine revelation and in no way undermined the oneness of God.

> The high priest said to him [Jesus], 'I charge you under oath by the living God: Tell us if you are the Christ, the Son of God.'
>
> 'Yes, it is as you say,' Jesus replied. 'But I say to all of you: In the future you will see the Son of Man sitting at the right hand of the Mighty One and coming on the clouds of heaven.'
>
> Then the high priest tore his clothes and said, 'He has spoken blasphemy! Why do we need any more witnesses? Look, now you have heard the blasphemy. What do you think?'
>
> 'He is worthy of death,' they answered. (Matt. 26:63–66; cf. Mark 14:61–64; Luke 22:70–71)

So Jesus was condemned as a blasphemer for having claimed to be the Messiah and the Son of God. Such claims were cited as the main reason for his crucifixion.

Before ascending to heaven, Jesus appeared to his disciples and entrusted to them his final instructions. Those who had already realized that he was far more than a prophet worshipped him; others were not so sure (Matt. 28:17). Jesus commissioned his disciples to spread his message in all the world. He called them to baptize those who responded to the gospel. This baptism would signify a person's faith in the trinitarian God who had revealed himself through Jesus Christ: 'All authority in heaven and on earth has been given to me. Therefore go and make disciples of all nations, baptising them *in the name of the Father and of the Son and of the Holy Spirit*, and teaching them to obey everything I have commanded you. And surely I am with you always, to the very end of the age' (Matt. 28:18–20; my emphasis).

Jesus promised his disciples that he would be with them as they carried out their mission. This mission was, and still is, to preach the good news of the risen Christ, the one to whom God has exclusively committed the power to rule the universe.

Notes

[1] Razi, VI:11, p. 92 and VI:12, p. 51.

[2] *Inna llaha waḥidun bi-l-jawhar thalathatun bi-l-aqanim.* Razi's familiarity with the Christian doctrine comes from his own debates with Christians. A written record of such debates is found in his *Munaẓara fi l-radd ʿala l-Naṣara.* He is less familiar with the Christian Scriptures, as we find no quotations from the Bible in his writings.

[3] *Monophysite* Christians (represented today by the Coptic Church in Egypt and the Syriac Orthodox Church in Syria) believed that Jesus had one nature, which was more divine than human. On the other hand, *Nestorian* Christians (represented today by the Assyrian Church in Iraq and Syria) believed that Jesus had two natures, which were associated but not united: Jesus had a human nature and the Christ had a divine nature. In northern Arabia in the seventh century, many Arab tribes were Christians: the Ghassanides (in the north-west) were monophysites, and the Lakhmides (in the north-east) were Nestorians. These Arab Christians were seen as heretical by the Byzantine Empire, whose doctrine was defined by the church councils; that is, Christ is one person (against the Nestorians) with two natures (against the monophysites). Christ's human and divine natures are united without confusion and change (against the monophysites), and without division or separation (against the Nestorians).

[4] Razi, XIV:27, pp. 196–198.

[5] The Symbol of Chalcedon (451) states, 'We confess that one and the same Lord Jesus Christ, the only-begotten Son, must be acknowledged in two natures, without confusion or change, without division or separation. The distinction between the natures was never abolished by their union but rather the character proper to each of the two natures was preserved as they came together in one person and one hypostasis.' See J. Neuner and J. Dupuis (eds.), *The Christian Faith in the Documents of the Catholic Church*, par. 615, p. 166.

[6] Razi, XVI:32, pp. 168–169.

[7] Ibid., XIII:26; pp. 211–212.

[8] These definitions are from the Symbol of Lateran, which goes back to the Fourth Lateran Council in 1215 (Neuner and Dupuis, *Christian Faith*, pars. 318–319, p. 116; my emphasis).

[9] From 'The Faith of Damasus' (fifth century; Neuner and Dupuis, *Christian Faith*, par. 14, p. 10).

[10] From the Symbol of Lateran (Neuner and Dupuis, *Christian Faith*, par. 19, p. 14; my emphasis).

16

Jesus' claims in the Gospels

In chapter 2 we considered Razi's understanding of the Scriptures. His view was that the text of the Torah and the Gospels had *not* been corrupted. How then does he account for the fact that, relying on the Gospels, Christians believe that Jesus Christ is the Son of God?

Razi gives his answer to this important question in his exegesis of sura 9:30 ('The Christians call Christ the Son of God'). He acknowledges that the Christian teaching about the divinity of Christ poses a major problem, *ishkalun kabirun*. Christ, who is one of God's greatest prophets, says Razi, never taught this doctrine, nor did his companions. So why was this corrupt teaching invented? And how was it possible to ascribe it to Christ?

Before he gives his own answer, Razi refers to an explanation given by Abu l-Ḥasan al-Waḥidi (468/1075), which has become fairly popular among Muslim writers today. According to al-Waḥidi, the person responsible for corrupting the teaching of Christ was a valiant (*shuja'*) man named Paul. The theory goes as follows: Paul persecuted the Christians for a while, but soon realized that they might be right and the Jews wrong, in which case the Christians would go to paradise and the Jews to hell. So he plotted with the Jews to defeat the Christians by deception rather than persecution. He pretended that he had converted to Christianity and was subsequently admitted as one of the church leaders. With his new role he succeeded in infiltrating the Christian community. He propagated his false teaching and convinced Christians to accept it as if it were Christ's teaching.

Razi does not endorse this conspiracy theory, which seems inconsistent even with Islamic teaching. It is unlikely that God would have stopped the Jews from killing Jesus (according to the Islamic understanding) only to let a courageous but deceitful and hateful Jew thwart Jesus' mission by corrupting his message. Razi favours another explanation. He explains that the word 'son' in the Gospel was given to Jesus so as to honour him, just as Abraham is described as God's friend (4:124; cf. Is. 41:8; Jas. 2:23). It is also possible, adds Razi, that Christians wanted to oppose the Jews' hostility towards Jesus with an equally groundless teaching where the sonship of Christ is interpreted in terms of real sonship, *bunuwwa ḥaqiqiyya*.[1] Razi's argument is that the sonship of Christ of which the Gospels speak should be interpreted not *literally* but *metaphorically*. This would mean that he is not truly the Son of God and that Christians have been misguided in believing that he is.

In order to find out whether Christians have been mistaken we need to go back to the Gospels to examine the claims Jesus made about himself. And as we do that, let us take note that the Gospels present Jesus as the *one and only* Son of God – not *one among many* (John 1:14, 18; 3:16, 18; cf. Matt. 11:27; Rom. 8:3, 32). His uniqueness among God's prophets is shown especially through his claims, of which we consider seven.

(1) *Jesus' word is God's word.* As one of God's prophets, Jesus preached the word of God, but went further than a prophet would dare to go. He said that the eternal word of God was *his* word. He claimed that God's message (the gospel) was *his* message, and that *his* word was eternal, just as God's word is eternal (see Matt. 5:17–18): 'Heaven and earth will pass away, but *my* words will never pass away' (Matt. 24:35; my emphasis). No other prophets had ever referred to God's word as their own. Their task was to proclaim 'This is what the LORD says …'; 'Hear the word of the LORD …' (cf. Exod. 8:1; 1 Kgs. 20:13; Is. 28:14; Jer. 19:15). But Jesus was different.

(2) *Jesus has the authority to forgive sins.* One day a paralysed man, lying on a mat, was carried before Jesus. Everyone expected Jesus to heal him, but instead Jesus said to the man, 'Son, your sins are forgiven.'

The teachers of the Law were indignant: 'Why does this fellow talk like that? He's blaspheming! Who can forgive sins but God alone?' (Mark 2:5–6).

It is true that no-one has the right to forgive people their sins; no-one, that is, except God. This belief is shared by Jews and Christians as well as Muslims (cf. 3:135). Yet, in order to convince his critics that he had the power to forgive sins, Jesus turned to the sick man and said, 'Get up, take your mat and go home.' And he did! To the amazement of the crowd, the man got up, took his mat and walked out in front of them (Mark 2:1–12). Would God have given Jesus the power to accomplish this miracle if he had no right to forgive the sick man his sins?

This was not the only time Jesus told someone, 'Your sins are forgiven' (see Luke 7:36–50; John 8:1–11). In Luke 7:49, after hearing such a statement from Jesus, the people muttered among themselves, 'Who is this who even forgives sins?'

(3) *Jesus' authority is above God's law.* One Sabbath day, Jesus was walking through fields of corn with his disciples. The disciples began to pluck ears of corn along the way. The Pharisees who were watching went up to Jesus and asked him, 'Look, why are they doing what is unlawful on the Sabbath?' (Mark 2:23–24).

The law of Moses did indeed forbid the Jews to work on that day. But far from being intimidated by his opponents, Jesus answered them: 'The Sabbath was made for man, not man for the Sabbath. So the Son of Man is Lord even of the Sabbath' (Mark 2:27–28).

Although the text does not tell us how the Pharisees received this answer, it is very likely that they scorned it. There are not many things more shocking to people known for their strict obedience to God's law than to hear someone affirm that his authority is superior to this law.

(4) *The risen Christ is God's new temple.* Jesus was in the temple of Jerusalem on the eve of the Passover feast. Those selling animals and the money-changers had installed themselves in the temple's outer court to sell their merchandise to the crowds of pilgrims. Appalled by this trading inside the house of God, Jesus vehemently turned everyone out. The Jews were furious and demanded that he explain his actions: 'What miraculous sign can you show us to prove your authority to do all this?' Jesus' response was enigmatic: 'Destroy this temple, and I will raise it again in three days' (John 2:18–19).

How daring, how insulting these words were when one remembers that the temple of Jerusalem was the most sacred place for the Jews! And later, when Jesus appeared before the Sanhedrin, the highest religious authority in Israel, one of the main charges levelled against him was an exact repetition of the words he had spoken that day (Matt. 26:61). Even his disciples did not really understand the meaning of his reply. Only after Jesus rose from the dead did they understand that 'the temple he had spoken of was his [resurrected] body' (John 2:21).

(5) *Jesus is the judge on the Day of Judgment.* We saw in chapter 13 that, as the Son of Man, Jesus claimed to be the King on the Day of Judgment (Matt. 25:31–34). In the Qur'an it is *God* who is described as

'the King of the Day of Judgment' (1:4). The fact that Jesus identifies himself as the one who will call people to give account for their lives is most significant: 'Not everyone who says *to me,* "Lord, Lord" will enter the kingdom of heaven, but only he who does the will of my Father who is in heaven. Many will say *to me* on that day: "Lord, Lord, did we not prophesy in your name, and in your name drive out demons and perform many miracles?" Then *I* will tell them plainly, "I never knew you. Away from me, you evildoers!"' (Matt. 7:21–23; my emphasis).

Jesus was fully aware of his twofold mission as God's appointed saviour and judge:

'I tell you the truth, whoever hears my word and believes him who sent me has eternal life and will not be condemned; he has crossed over from death to life. I tell you the truth, a time is coming and has now come when the dead will hear the voice of the Son of God and those who hear will live. For as the Father has life in himself, so he has granted the Son to have life in himself. And he has given him authority to judge because he is the Son of Man.' (John 5:24–27; cf. Matt. 7:21–23; 25:31–46)

(6) *Jesus is 'the way, the truth and the life'.* The prophets called their people to follow God's way. They urged them to believe in God – the One who is the truth – and promised them eternal life. But unlike the prophets, Jesus pointed people not only to God but to himself: 'I am the resurrection and the life. He who believes in me will live, even though he dies; and whoever lives and believes in me will never die' (John 11:25–26). Jesus' very person, and not just his message, is God's way, truth and life. Furthermore, Jesus claims he is the *only* way anyone can find the supreme knowledge of who God is. He is the only way anyone can know God as their heavenly *Father*: 'I am the way and the truth and the life. No-one comes to the Father except through me' (John 14:6). In John's Gospel, Jesus often refers to himself using the words 'I am': 'Before Abraham was born, I am!' (John 8:58; cf. 6:35, 48; 8:12; 10:14; 11:25). In the Jewish context these words had a very special significance. When God revealed himself to Moses he used similar words:

Moses said to God, 'Suppose I go to the Israelites and say to them: "The God of your fathers has sent me to you," and they ask me, "What is his name?" Then what shall I tell them?'

God said to Moses, 'I AM WHO I AM. This is what you are to say
to the Israelites: "I AM has sent me to you"' (Exod. 3:13–14).

Jesus could hardly have been more specific about who he was, which is
why the Jewish leaders found his claim utterly outrageous. No other
prophet had ever spoken of himself in such a way.

Al-Ḥallaj, the great Muslim mystic (309/922), described his relationship with God in terms of complete union, so much so that he dared to
say, '*Ana al-ḥaqq*', 'I am the truth [or, I am God]'. The religious leaders
of the time condemned al-Ḥallaj to death for blasphemy.[2] However, God
did not vindicate al-Ḥallaj by raising him from the dead, as he raised
Jesus!

(7) *Jesus is one with God the Father*. Jesus spent a long time revealing
who he was until he led his disciples to the final point of recognition. At
first he was careful not to say who he was, so as not to let the Jews think
he was calling into question the oneness of God. Nevertheless, as we have
seen, he gave many clues to his identity. At one of the main Jewish
festivals the Jewish leaders decided to test Jesus. They gathered around
him and asked:

'How long will you keep us in suspense? If you are the Christ
[Messiah], tell us plainly.'
   Jesus answered, 'I did tell you, but you do not believe. The
miracles I do in my Father's name speak for me ... I and the Father
are one.' (John 10:24–25, 30)

Those who heard Jesus' words were enraged. They wanted to stone
him, and explained that they were stoning him not for any of his great
miracles, 'but for blasphemy, because you, a mere man, claim to be God'
(John 10:33).

This violent reaction brings us back to the Qur'an, which, as we have
seen, considers Jesus to be a great prophet, but when the question of his
divinity is raised, states categorically:

Jesus was none other than a servant on whom We bestowed grace
and whom We made to be an example to the Children of Israel.
(43:59)

If Muhammad had made the same claims as Jesus

In order to understand why Christians believe that Jesus is far more than a prophet, we need to weigh up carefully his claims in the Gospels. He was a man of integrity and highly respected by his followers. When he spoke they listened, and, as we have seen, his words were not always what they expected to hear from a prophet. He made incredible claims about himself, claims they had to think long and hard about. And because of who he was they could not simply dismiss what he said just because it did not fit their initial expectations.

Muslims and Christians must be prepared to put themselves in each other's shoes if they want to understand each other's faith better. So, without wanting to be in any way disrespectful, let us just suppose for a moment that Jesus' words were uttered instead by the Prophet Muhammad. How would his companions have reacted? If the Prophet had claimed that God's word, the Qur'an, was his own message, if he had granted to some men and women forgiveness of their sins, would the first Muslims have immediately accused him of usurping a divine right? Would they have immediately called into question his moral integrity? Or would they rather have trusted him enough to find out whether, as well as his prophetic mission, a greater mission had been entrusted to him?

Let us pursue our questioning and ask what the attitude of the first Muslims would have been if they had heard the Prophet declare that his personal authority was greater than that of God's law. Would they have immediately accused him of blasphemy? Instead, would they not have considered that this astonishing statement deserved a careful hearing because of the known integrity of the speaker? Would they not have envisaged the possibility that this man could be the unexpected author of the law in question? What would the Prophet's companions have thought if they had heard him announce that the Ka'aba would be destroyed and replaced by a new temple founded by himself in three days? Would they not have tried to understand this enigmatic prediction? And if, against all expectation, the Prophet had come back to life, having been put to death by his enemies, how would his followers have reacted? If they had seen him alive many times before he was taken up to paradise, would they not have sought to interpret everything they had seen and heard in the light of this unprecedented event in history: the resurrection of a prophet?

How would Muslims have understood Muhammad if he had claimed that he would be the judge on the Day of Judgment? How would they have responded if he had claimed that he was the truth and that he was one with God? Would they not have asked themselves whether this exceptional Prophet did not after all enjoy a unique relationship with God? Would they, should they not, have acknowledged that, as he himself was commanded to say, 'If the All-Merciful had a son, I would be the very first to worship him' (43:81)?

Of course, in reality we know that Muhammad did not make anything like the same claims as Jesus. But how should we respond to Jesus' claims? What if the evidence compels us to see Jesus as far more than a prophet? What if the Gospels cannot be interpreted in any other way? Should we not be among those who worship him?

Notes

1 Razi, VIII:16, p. 28.
2 Cf. L. Massignon, *Hallaj: Mystic and Martyr*, pp. 64–71.

17

Islamic interpretation of Jesus' claims

Muslim thinkers who have read the Gospels or who have come into contact with orthodox Christians realize that the sonship of Jesus rejected by the Qur'an is not the same thing as the biblical doctrine. Their rejection of Jesus' divinity is certainly motivated by Qur'anic monotheism, which has profoundly shaped their thinking, but it cannot be based directly on the Qur'an.

Those, such as Razi and Baqillani, who have accused Christians of falsifying the *meaning* of the Scriptures (rather than the *text*) have tried to interpret the Bible in a way that fits the image of the Christ they have derived from the Qur'an. Ghazali's apologetic treatise *The Excellent Refutation of the Divinity of Jesus from the Plain Sense of the Gospel* is a perfect example of this. His work has been described as 'the high water mark of knowledge of Christianity in Islam at the end of the 11th century, though not representative of the general knowledge of Muslims'.[1]

Ghazali deliberately chose to base his arguments on the Gospel of John. It is this Gospel Christians especially point to when speaking about Jesus' divinity. Not that the doctrine is absent in the other Gospels (as shown from some of the texts we considered in chapter 16), but John himself points to this subject as one of his main purposes for writing: 'Jesus did many other miraculous signs in the presence of his disciples, which are not recorded in this book. But these are written *that you may believe that Jesus is the Christ, the Son of God*, and that by believing you may have life in his name' (John 20:30–31; my emphasis). By addressing the key texts, Ghazali seeks to refute the doctrine of Jesus' divinity by showing how the texts can be interpreted differently. We shall consider his objections to the Christian reading of the Gospels in three areas.

'Jesus' miracles are not unique'

First, Ghazali points out that Jesus was not the only prophet to have performed miracles. He argues that because of this, Jesus' miracles do not prove that he was more than a human being.[2]

Ghazali is certainly right to stress that *in themselves* the miracles do not distinguish Jesus from God's other messengers. But Christians do not found their belief in Jesus' divinity on his miracles alone. The evidence for his divinity is first and foremost in his claims. As we saw in the last chapter, the Gospel accounts show Jesus acting in a way in which only God is entitled to act (e.g. forgiving people's sins) and ascribing to himself qualities that are God's alone (e.g. judging people on the Day of Judgment). These claims, unique to Jesus, make his miracles significant.

Both Christians and Muslims believe that God enabled his messengers to work miracles so as to accredit their mission. In sura 3 of the Qur'an we are given a list of some of Jesus' miracles:

And I heal those born blind, and the lepers,
And I quicken the dead, by God's leave;
And I declare to you what you eat, and what you store in your
    houses.
Surely therein is a Sign for you if you did believe. (3:49)

The significance of these miracles is that they represent God's seal of approval on Jesus' unparalleled claims. They were signs confirming the truth of his words. For example, Jesus' healing of the blind was an enactment of what he said about himself: 'I am the light of the world. Whoever follows me will never walk in darkness, but will have the light of life' (John 8:12; cf. John 9:5). When Jesus healed the lepers he was showing that God cares for everyone, including outcasts like the lepers, who were ostracized because they were seen as 'impure': 'whoever comes to me I will never drive away' (John 6:37; cf. Matt. 8:1–4; Luke 17:11–19). And Jesus' raising of the dead pointed to his claim to be the life-giver, the one who gives eternal life and the one without whom there is no resurrection: 'I am the resurrection and the life. He who believes in me will live, even though he dies' (John 11:25).

Jesus' miracles, therefore, did not come by themselves; they were accompanied by his words and bore witness to his claims, verifying the truth of who he said he was and why he said he had come.

'The texts about Jesus' divinity are metaphorical'

Secondly, although Ghazali acknowledges that Jesus is the only prophet to have claimed to be 'Son of God', 'Lord' and 'God', he says that all these expressions must be taken metaphorically, and he justifies Jesus' right to use such language by the fact that he was the founder of a law. But why, in that case, was this privilege not granted to Muhammad, who, from an Islamic perspective, was the last and greatest prophet? Muhammad was given the task of setting up a law that Muslims consider to be, unlike the Jewish and the Christian laws, the perfect and definitive law.

Referring to those texts that present Jesus as God (*ilah*), and Lord (*rabb*), Ghazali argues that they must be taken in a broad sense, otherwise they would blatantly contradict reason. The first title, he says, is used to honour Jesus; and the second must be taken in the sense of 'master' or 'proprietor'.[3] Did God not tell Moses that he would be like God to his brother Aaron (Exod. 4:16; 7:1)? And did God not call people 'gods' (Ps. 82:6)?

Ghazali interprets the fatherhood of God and the sonship of Jesus in a similar way.[4] Thus to call God 'Father', he explains, is a way of reminding ourselves of God's care, mercy and kindness towards humankind (cf. Ps. 103:13). And to call oneself the Son of God is just a way of stating one's respect for God and one's submission to his will. To speak of the Spirit of God is to refer to the grace, blessings and protection with which God surrounds his creatures. Thus, according to Ghazali, Jesus is called the Son of God in a way similar to Adam (Luke 3:38), the angels (Job 1:6), Israel (Exod. 4:22–23), Solomon (2 Sam. 7:14) and Jesus' own disciples (Luke 6:35–36).

John 10

When referring to John 10, Ghazali again argues that Jesus' claims about his divinity must be understood metaphorically:[5]

> Again the Jews picked up stones to stone him, but Jesus said to them, 'I have shown you many great miracles from the Father. For which of these do you stone me?'

'We are not stoning you for any of these,' replied the Jews, 'but for blasphemy, because you, a mere man, claim to be God.'

Jesus answered them, 'Is it not written in your Law, "I have said you are gods"? If he called them "gods", to whom the word of God came – and the Scripture cannot be broken – what about the one whom the Father set apart as his very own and sent into the world? Why then do you accuse me of blasphemy because I said, "I am God's Son"? Do not believe me unless I do what my Father does. But if I do it, even though you do not believe me, believe the miracles, that you may know and understand that the Father is in me, and I in the Father.' Again they tried to seize him, but he escaped their grasp. (John 10:31–39)

If humans could be called 'gods' (Ps. 82:6), how much more so the man whom God had set apart? As a prophet, Jesus was god in a sense, says Ghazali, and being a prophet means much more than being someone to whom God's word is sent. Ghazali concludes that the Jews must have misunderstood the implication of Jesus' words when they accused him of blasphemy.

Ghazali's interpretation of this text identifies the general direction of Jesus' teaching, but does not grasp its full implication. Jesus is denouncing the antithesis between the Creator and the creature by which the Jews drew a sharp distinction between God and humanity. From the fact that people are called 'gods' in Psalm 82, Jesus was arguing that the incarnation of the Son of God is theologically consistent: it perfectly accomplishes God's declared intention to reveal himself to his creatures. But Jesus is not merely identifying himself with the people to whom God's word was addressed. He is not merely the one sent by God, but is pointing out that as the eternal Son of God he is superior; he came to introduce people to his Father so that they too could become God's children – by adoption: 'Yet to all who received him, to those who believed in his name, he gave the right to become children of God – children born not of natural descent, nor of human decision or a husband's will, but born of God' (John 1:12–13). In this connection it is noteworthy that Jesus never associates himself with his disciples in calling God 'Our Father'. He always says either 'my Father' or 'your Father' or simply 'the Father'. The prayer, known as the Lord's Prayer, which Jesus taught his disciples, begins with the words 'Our Father in heaven'. It was not a prayer Jesus himself is recorded as praying, but is rather a model prayer for his disciples to pray. When they asked him, 'Lord, teach us to pray,' he replied, 'When *you* pray, say ...' (Luke 11:1–4; Matt. 6:9–13; my emphasis).

If the Jewish leaders had misunderstood Jesus' claims, why did he not make an effort to clear up the misunderstanding in their minds when they sentenced him for blasphemy? When he appeared before the Jewish court, we find him repeating his earlier claims to be the Son of God, which is why he was condemned and executed (Mark 14:60–64). Thus Jesus maintained that he was the Son of God, not in the metaphorical sense but in the real and spiritual sense of the word.

John 17

Another chapter Ghazali discusses is John 17, where Jesus is praying for his disciples and for all believers. Jesus prays that they would be united to God in a way that mirrors the way he is united to his Father (cf. 1 John 4:12–15; 1 Cor. 6:17):

> My prayer is not for them alone. I pray also for those who will believe in me through their message, that all of them may be one, Father, just as you are in me and I am in you. May they also be in us so that the world may believe that you have sent me. I have given them the glory that you gave me, *that they may be one as we are one*: I in them and you in me. May they be brought to complete unity to let the world know that you sent me and have loved them even as you have loved me. (John 17:20–23; my emphasis)

Ghazali comments that if this union implies the divinity of Jesus, then it also implies the deification of his disciples.[6] As Ghazali quite rightly points out, Jesus' disciples spoke of their union with God without ever claiming divinity for themselves. Yet their writings testify to Jesus' humanity as well as his divinity (Rom. 1:3–4; 8:3, 29, 32; 9:5; 1 John 2:22–24; 3:8, 23; 4:9, 10, 14, 15; 5:9–13, 20). In fact, Christ's union with his Father is the model for his disciples' union with God. The latter does not entail deifying the disciples any more than Jesus' human nature is deified by its union with his divine nature. The union between Jesus' disciples and God, brought about by the presence of the Holy Spirit within them, is like the union of Christ's two natures: God is not humanized, or the disciples deified.

John 8

Ghazali also examines Jesus' arguments with the Jews, in the course of which he said that he existed before Abraham:

> Jesus replied, 'If I glorify myself, my glory means nothing. My Father, whom you claim as your God, is the one who glorifies me. Though you do not know him, I know him. If I said I did not, I would be a liar like you, but I do know him and keep his word. Your father Abraham rejoiced at the thought of seeing my day; he saw it and was glad.'
>
> 'You are not yet fifty years old,' the Jews said to him, 'and you have seen Abraham!'
>
> 'I tell you the truth,' Jesus answered, 'before Abraham was born, I am!'
>
> At this, they picked up stones to stone him, but Jesus hid himself, slipping away from the temple grounds. (John 8:54–59)

We must agree with Ghazali that the patriarch Abraham received a revelation concerning the coming of Jesus; but we can hardly go along with him when he interprets Jesus' existence before Abraham as meaning merely that God had decreed in eternity that he would send his messenger.[7] This explanation ignores the real meaning of Jesus' words 'Before Abraham was born, I am!' As I have already pointed out, here, as elsewhere in the Gospels, Jesus calls himself by the very name of God revealed to Moses (John 8:24, 28, 58; 13:19; 18:5; cf. Exod. 3:14–16).

John 14

Similarly, Ghazali discusses Jesus' reply to Philip in John 14:

> Jesus answered, 'I am the way and the truth and the life. No-one comes to the Father except through me. If you really knew me, you would know my Father as well. From now on, you do know him and have seen him.'
>
> Philip said, 'Lord, show us the Father and that will be enough for us.'
>
> Jesus answered, 'Don't you know me, Philip, even after I have been among you such a long time? *Anyone who has seen me has seen*

the Father. How can you say, "Show us the Father"? Don't you believe that I am in the Father, and that the Father is in me? The words I say to you are not just my own. Rather, it is the Father, living in me, who is doing his work. Believe me when I say that I am in the Father and the Father is in me; or at least believe on the evidence of the miracles themselves.' (John 14:6–11; my emphasis)

When Jesus says, 'Anyone who has seen me has seen the Father', Ghazali takes it to mean that Jesus was simply God's representative.[8] But Jesus' statement goes much further than that. He had been teaching that he was greater than the prophets because they were God's servants, whereas he was God's Son and heir (Matt. 21:33–45). In his reply to Philip, Jesus declared his perfect identity with the Father who had sent him. He said that after he had returned to the Father, the Holy Spirit would be given to his disciples and would enable them to extend the Christian community to all the peoples of the world. In so doing, they would do greater deeds than his own, because while he was on earth the Christian community was limited to the people of Israel.

'The texts are clear about Jesus' humanness'

Thirdly, Ghazali carefully selects a large number of verses that point to Jesus' humanity: his hunger and limited knowledge (Mark 11:12–13); his ignorance of when the last hour will come (Mark 11:32); his being sent by God (John 17:1–3); his plain acknowledgment that he is a man (John 8:39–40).[9] The writer underlines Jesus' words on the cross: 'My God, my God, why have you forsaken me?' (Mark 15:34). He then sets these texts against Christian doctrine and concludes that God cannot possibly have been subjected to the conditions of human life and especially not to death, which is the greatest of life's miseries.

Christians, of course, are aware of these verses, from which they recognize that Jesus Christ is not only truly God but also truly human. By becoming a man, the Son of God took on the human condition so completely that he gave up his divine privileges in order to identify with us fully. He experienced our limitations as well as our needs and weaknesses. And because temptation is part of human experience, he was even tempted by the devil (Matt. 4:1–11). But, unlike all of us, he never gave in and never committed sin (John 8:46; 14:30). As both Son of God and human being, Jesus was in complete submission to God the Father. He was entrusted with a mission, and, when he was about to complete this, he said, 'I am going to the Father, for the Father is greater than I' (John 14:28).

The main thrust of Ghazali's argument is to show how the divinity of Jesus leads to an insoluble problem, namely the suffering, death and burial of God. He knows that Christians do not claim to have an explanation for everything relating to who God is, but as far as he is concerned this is further proof that their faith is inconsistent. It is worth pointing out, however, that it was not Christ's *nature* that died but his *person*. For both Christians and Muslims, death is not extinction, but is the passing away of a person from this life to the next.

Jesus feared death all the more because, as the Son of God, he was the source of life. And because of the unique character of his death, he was forsaken by the Father at the terrible moment when he was atoning for the sin of the world. So it was not God, as such, who died, but his Son in the person of Jesus Christ: 'The character proper to each of the two natures which come together in one person being therefore preserved, lowliness was taken on by majesty, weakness by strength, mortality by eternity ... The Lord of all things hid His immeasurable majesty to take on the form of a servant. The impassible God has not disdained to be a man subject to suffering nor the Immortal to submit to the law of death.'[10]

Motives for Ghazali's interpretation

Ghazali's interpretation of Jesus' claims is undoubtedly reductionist. It aims at reducing Jesus' union with God to a mere moral level. Two motives explain Ghazali's reading of the Gospels. First, his interpretation is thoroughly *rationalistic*. This rationalism, which appears throughout his treatise, is all the more surprising coming from a Sunni theologian. Sunni Muslims, who, as we have seen, represent orthodox and mainstream Islam, consider that God's revelation takes precedence over human reason. Therefore, the Qur'an is not to be submitted to the judgment of human rationality. If this is true of the Qur'an, it is even more so of the Gospels, where God himself, and not just his will, is revealed to us through his Son. This revelation is not irrational but suprarational.

Secondly, Ghazali's reading of the Gospels is based on *theological assumptions* specific to Islamic teaching. The absolute transcendence of God, so central in Islam, makes it impossible to conceive that God could become incarnate in human form. His immutability is such that he cannot experience human reality without ceasing to be God. His majesty and sovereignty are felt to be seriously threatened if he identifies himself with his human creatures, let alone bears the consequences of our sin.

Christian theology bases the incarnation of the Son of God on God's unfailing love for the highest of his creatures. The fact that, unlike all other creatures, humans have been created in God's own image (Gen. 1:26–27) makes it ontologically possible for God to identify with his human creatures. God's love proved boundless in redeeming humankind through the death of Christ. He displayed his sovereignty over evil by raising Jesus from the dead. He demonstrated his uncompromising justice in punishing sin, yet saving the sinner. In achieving the salvation of humankind through Jesus Christ, God revealed himself as the Servant King. Divine transcendence means that, without ever ceasing to be the sovereign Lord of his human creatures, God has become our redeeming Servant!

Just a good prophet and teacher?

Some Muslims today do acknowledge that the Qur'anic portrait of Jesus makes him a very special prophet, indeed an outstanding prophet. Ali Merad, an Algerian scholar, for example, admits that Jesus' miraculous birth together with the titles he is given – in particular 'word and spirit of God' – have far-reaching implications. He encourages Muslims to investigate further the significance of Jesus as an exceptional being whose creation symbolizes the spiritual crowning achievement for humankind. 'It would be presumptuous for Muslims', he says, 'to believe that they know not only the truth but the full truth about Jesus, and to refuse to pursue the way opened by the Qur'an in seeking other witnesses.'[11]

Let us consider one final episode in the Gospels often quoted by Muslims who want to prove that Jesus denied he was God. It is about a young man, a very religious and rich man who had a high idea of Jesus as a teacher. He ran up to Jesus, fell on his knees before him, and asked him a straightforward question: 'Good teacher, what must I do to inherit eternal life?' Jesus answered him with another question: 'Why do you call me good? No-one is good – except God alone' (Mark 10:17–18).

Some Muslims take Jesus' reply to mean, 'God alone is good; you know that I am not God, therefore you shouldn't call me good.' But this interpretation misses the very point Jesus made in his reply. He wanted to challenge the man first on his view of human goodness, and secondly on his understanding of who Jesus is. Jesus did not say to him, 'You must not call me good', but asks him, '*Why* do you call me good?' As this man was apparently a God-fearing and law-abiding person, he should have known from the Torah that no human being is really good (Ps. 14:3; 51:5). Therefore, what Jesus is asking this well-meaning but rather superficial man is this: 'Do you really mean what you say? Who am I to you? If you think I am just a religious teacher, do not say I am good; but if you really consider that I am good, then do you realize who I am?'

Jesus' question, therefore, represents a twofold challenge not only to this man but also to Islamic thinking. First, we have seen that Islam has a rather optimistic outlook on human nature, not seeing it as morally corrupt. Jesus' words urge Muslims to reconsider such optimism. Secondly, Jesus is seen in Islam as a highly respected prophet, but no more than a prophet. The Qur'an does not ascribe any sin to him, which singles him out from among God's prophets, Muhammad included (cf. 40:55; 47:19; 48:2; 80:1–10; 94:1–3). Jesus himself challenged his hearers about the significance of his sinlessness: 'Can any of you prove me guilty of sin? If I am telling the truth, why don't you believe me?' (John 8:46). If all human beings, except Jesus, are sinful, is it adequate to consider that Jesus is a mere man?

Unitarian monotheism or trinitarian monotheism?

Monotheism speaks of the sovereignty of God as well as the total dependence of the universe on him. The monotheistic understanding of creation means that the universe is distinct from the Creator. Islamic monotheism is *unitarian* in the sense that Islam rejects the existence of personal relationships within the Godhead. Christian monotheism, which teaches that God is the Father, the Son and the Holy Spirit, is *trinitarian*.

Trinitarian monotheism means that God is a relational God. Before creating the universe, God was already enjoying a relational life. Within the Godhead the Father related to the Son, the Son to the Father, the Father and the Son to the Holy Spirit, and so on. Because God is relational by definition, he chose to create the world. He created men and women in his image to relate to him in a way modelled on the relationship between the Father and the Son. Thus the relationship God has with his people both reflects and is based on the relationship he has with himself. In other words, what God does reflects who he is.

The reality of a personal relationship between God and his human creatures can more easily be undermined if it is not founded on the reality of God's personal relationship with himself. In this sense unitarian

monotheism does not provide a solid foundation for a personal relationship between God and human beings, especially since Islam does not
see humans as being created in God's image. The personal aspect of this
relationship is weakened when one side overrides the other. Man
predominates in the relationship when there is *legalism* (which reflects a
lack of trust in God's mercy) or the *politicization of religion* (which
reflects a lack of trust in God's sovereignty). Human personhood is stifled
when there is *fatalism* (which disregards human responsibility) or
impersonal spirituality (which ignores the selfhood God gives to human
creatures). Thus unitarian monotheism is open to these four dangers:

(1) *Legalism.* Is it possible for the human creature to enter fully
into a personal relationship with the Creator if such a relationship is not
based on God's eternal relationship with himself? Unitarian monotheism
makes the concept of any personal relationship with God extremely
fragile. The danger of a legalistic relationship with God exists in all religions, but this danger is even more real in a law-based religion such as
Islam.

(2) *Impersonal spirituality.* This is to some extent a reaction to
legalism. Dissatisfied with a formal relationship with God, Muslim
mystics have sought an intimate communion with the Creator. Many of
them (e.g. Ḥallaj) have removed the dividing line between God and
humanity, thus undermining divine transcendence. The Sufi ideal
consists in losing one's identity and merging with God. In the case of Ibn
'Arabi, monotheism turns into monism, *waḥdat al-wujud* (oneness of
being), where the radical difference between the Creator and his creation
disappears. The world is seen no longer as created by God, but as
emanating from God.

(3) *Fatalism.* Unitarian monotheism exalts God as the all-powerful
Lord of the universe. Such an emphasis on God's sovereignty runs the
risk of denying people the full exercise of their God-given freedom and
personal responsibility. Ash'ari (320/930), the most representative of
Sunni Islam, takes the view that all human actions, good or evil, are
created and willed by God (cf. 6:102; 13:16).[12] This often turns into
fatalism in Islam because humans are seen primarily as God's servants.

(4) *Politicization of religion.* This is to some extent a reaction to
fatalism. Muslim reformers have often resorted to an Islamic form of
liberation theology to mobilize their people and overcome their resigna-
tion: 'God does not change a people's state of affairs unless they change
what is in themselves' (13:11). Muslim fundamentalism is based on a
political and military interpretation of the Qur'an and the Hadith, with

its ideology relying primarily on the resolve to fight those who are seen as God's enemies. Fatalism and fundamentalism are two contrasting dangers threatening a Muslim's faith. The history of many Muslim peoples is punctuated by leaps and bounds after long periods of intellectual and spiritual lethargy.

Trinitarian monotheism provides a consistent basis for a clear distinction between the Creator and the creature, conferring on humans a genuine identity and an inherent existence. The plurality of persons in the Godhead is mirrored in people standing before God as free and responsible creatures. God is not just the Lord to be obeyed but the loving Father to be loved. He expects his adopted children to respond to his love and to love each other.

The incarnate Son of God, Jesus Christ, true God and true man, is the model for our union with our Creator. This union does not alter the character proper either to God or to humans. Human deeds are the fruit, both of God's Spirit – the total and primary cause – and of human power – the total but secondary cause. Human responsibility, therefore, does not conflict with God's sovereignty, nor is it confused with it. Human freedom is paradoxical: it is real yet enslaved to evil that deeply troubles our relationship with God. Evil, the result of the absence of good, does not originate with God, and we are fully responsible when we commit sin.

In his unfathomable wisdom, God has allowed evil to exist and has gloriously overcome it through the death and resurrection of Jesus Christ. Thus God has restored to us the freedom we lost because of our disobedience. The fact that he has personally intervened in the history of humankind and has already defeated evil provides Christians with a solid basis for social action. We are called to be God's co-workers, committed to extend his kingdom on earth. At the same time, we look forward to the day when Jesus comes back as God's appointed King. Then the kingdom of God will be fully established and 'the earth will be full of the knowledge of the LORD as the waters cover the sea' (Is. 11:9).

Trinitarian monotheism is, of course, also exposed to dangers. A *weakened sense of God's oneness* is one of them. This danger is real, as shown by the heresy of *tritheism* (the belief that the Father, Son and Holy Spirit are three gods), attached to the name of John Philoponus (490–570). The *deification of human beings*, which is the undue result of the gospel's calling people to enjoy a deep and filial relationship with God, represents another danger. Some Christian mystics have encountered this danger; for instance Meister Eckhart (1260–1328), whose teaching often seems to breach the boundary marking the essential difference between God the Creator and his human creatures. Finally, there is the danger of *irrationalism*: the doctrine of the trinitarian God, which is beyond but not against human understanding, may unnecessarily lead some Christians to believe that the Christian faith is irrational.

Islam is constantly challenging Christians to be alert to these dangers, which threaten to distort God's self-disclosure to humanity through the person and mission of Jesus Christ.

Notes

[1] J. W. Sweetman, *Islam and Christian Theology*, part 2, vol. 1, 1955, p. 23, as quoted in H. Goddard, *Muslim Perceptions of Christianity*, p. 30.

[2] Ghazali, *al-Radd al-jamil li-ilahiyyat 'Isa bi-ṣariḥi l-Injil*, pp. 4–6. Razi uses the same argument. The miracles Jesus performed do not prove that he is God's son. The angels have greater power and knowledge than Jesus, yet they are God's servants just as he is. See Razi's exegesis of 4:172, VI:11, p. 92.

[3] Ghazali, *al-Radd*, pp. 38–40.

[4] Ibid., pp. 40–43.

[5] Ibid., pp. 9–12.

[6] Ibid., pp. 13–17.

[7] Ibid., pp. 52–55.

[8] Ibid., pp. 55–57.

[9] Ibid., pp. 18–25.

[10] From 'The Tome of Leo' (a letter sent by Pope Leo the great to Flavian, Patriarch of Constantinople, dated 13 June 449) (Neuner and Dupuis, *Christian Faith*, pars. 611–612, pp. 164–165).

[11] A. Merad, 'Le Christ selon le Coran' as quoted in M. Borrmans, *Jésus et les musulmans d'aujourd'hui*, p. 231. In a similar vein, M. Ayoub writes about what Christ means for him and for many other Shi'i Muslims: 'Like the Christ of Christian faith and hope, the Jesus of the Qur'an and later Muslim piety is much more than a mere human being, or even simply the messenger of a Book. While the Jesus of Islam is not the Christ of Christianity, the Christ of the Gospel often speaks through the austere, human Jesus of Muslim piety. Indeed, the free spirits of Islamic mysticism found in the man Jesus not only the example of piety, love and asceticism which they sought to emulate, but also the Christ who exemplifies fulfilled humanity, a humanity illuminated by the light of

God' ('Towards an Islamic Christology: An image of Jesus in Early Shi'i Muslim Literature', p. 187).

[12] A thorough exposition of Ash'ari's teaching and the objections that Mu'tazili theologians raised against it is found in D. Gimaret, *La Doctrine d'al-Ash'ari*. His understanding of God's will is treated on pp. 291–307; and his theory about the status of human action on pp. 369–399.

Part 4
Muhammad

18

Proof of Muhammad's prophethood: the Qur'an and other miracles

To many Muslims, the Christian attitude to Muhammad seems unjust, incomprehensible, and even sectarian: 'We Muslims believe in Jesus and in all God's prophets. We make no difference between them at all.[1] So why don't you Christians believe in Muhammad as God's Prophet?'

I have often been challenged in this way, yet put in these terms the question is not entirely fair. It suggests that Muslims believe in Jesus the way Christians do, which of course is not the case. Jesus is certainly seen as one of the greatest prophets of Islam and is revered by all Muslims; but for Christians, as we have seen, Jesus is much more than a great prophet. He is *the* Prophet. Not only did he *preach* the word of God; he is *himself* the eternal Word of God.

So to say that Muslims believe in Jesus but that Christians do not believe in Muhammad is an oversimplification. We must ask what it means to 'believe', and why we believe what we believe. The Muslim attitude towards Christ is dictated by the teaching of the Qur'an, and the Christian attitude towards Muhammad is determined by the teaching of the Bible. While this is quite understandable, Christians should be prepared to consider seriously the challenge of the Qur'an, and Muslims should be prepared to consider seriously the challenge of the Bible. Having considered Jesus' claims in the Gospels, we now turn to the claims of the Qur'an about Muhammad and his mission.

For Muslims, Muhammad is not an ordinary prophet: he is 'the Seal of the Prophets' (33:40). He is God's greatest Prophet and the final Prophet; he confirms the message of former prophets and he brings to completion God's revelation.

220 Faith to faith

The prophetic credentials of Muhammad

Muslims refer to several criteria as evidence for Muhammad's prophetic claims. Razi summarizes some of these in his exegesis of sura 9:32–33.[2] Here the leaders of the Jewish and Christian communities are accused of seeking to conceal the evidence for Muhammad's prophethood: 'They seek to extinguish the very Light of God with their mouths. But God will not allow but that His Light should be perfected, however hateful the unbelievers find it' (9:32).

Razi explains that the 'Light of God' refers to the proofs, *dala'il*, establishing the truthfulness of Muhammad. Just as light illuminates what is right, *al-sawab*, so too these proofs illuminate what is right in the matter of religion. There are many proofs of Muhammad's prophethood, contends Razi. He mentions four:

(1) The *outstanding miracles*, *al-mu'jizat al-qahira*, Muhammad performed. Either miracles authenticate the truth or they do not, says Razi. If they do, then Muhammad's truthfulness is established; if Muhammad's miracles do not prove that he is God's Prophet, then Moses and Jesus must also be rejected as prophets.

(2) The *glorious Qur'an* Muhammad brought. Given that the Prophet was illiterate, the Qur'an is one of his greatest miracles.

(3) The main content, *hasil*, of *Islamic law* that Muhammad transmitted. This law exalts God, calling people to submit to him, to turn away from the pleasures of this life and to seek the bliss of the afterlife. Razi argues that it has been proved rationally that there is no other way to God.

(4) The *flawless message* Muhammad preached. Nothing unworthy of God is found in it – a message all about calling people to God and to God alone.

The evidence that Muhammad is God's Prophet is such, writes Razi, that all efforts to thwart it on the part of the Jewish and Christian leaders are futile; it is like trying to extinguish the sun's light! Not only are these efforts fruitless, he says, but God has promised Muhammad a greater triumph and a higher honour than other prophets in spite of the hostility of those who oppose his message.

The above proofs of Muhammad's prophethood fall into two categories: his *miracles* and his *message*. In his exegesis of sura 9:33, Razi speaks of a third category of proof. In this verse God speaks of how he will fulfil his promise to Muhammad, bringing his light to perfection: 'It is He who has sent His Apostle with Guidance and the Religion of Truth, that He may cause it to prevail over all religion, however hateful the associators find it' (9:33). Perfect prophethood, Razi explains, is therefore the sum of three elements:

(1) The occurrence of numerous signs and miracles (see 1 and 2 above). This is the 'Guidance' (*huda*) with which Muhammad was sent.

(2) The fact that the religion he brought is characterized – as is evident for everyone to see – by rightness (*sawab*), righteousness (*salah*), wisdom (*hikma*) and usefulness (*manfa'a*) in this world and in the next (see 3 and 4 above). This is what is meant by 'the Religion of Truth' (*din al-haqq*).

(3) The ascendancy of Muhammad's religion over all other religions – the meaning of the words 'that He may cause it to prevail over all religion'.

These, then, are the main proofs establishing Muhammad's credentials as God's Prophet. To some degree they correspond to the biblical criteria for prophethood, and so make the comparison between the Qur'anic and biblical perspectives all the more challenging.

The miracle of the Qur'an

The greatest of Muhammad's miracles is said to be the Qur'an. Its miraculous character, *i'jaz al-Qur'an*, is founded on its literary perfection, its content and Muhammad's illiteracy.

The literary form of the Qur'an

When Muhammad started preaching the Qur'an in Mecca, he had little success. His following was small. He was mocked (22:47; 38:16) and accused of being possessed by the devil (*majnun*; 37:36; 51:52), of being a soothsayer (*kahin*; 52:29; 69:42), a sorcerer (*sahir*) and a liar (*kadhdhab*; 38:4; 51:39). In other words, Muhammad was accused of having produced the Qur'an himself. God's response to Muhammad's critics was to challenge them to produce ten suras (11:13) or even just one sura (2:23; 10:38) comparable to the Qur'an. The fact that they were unable to take up this challenge reveals its supernatural quality: 'Were humans and jinns to join their forces to bring about the like of this Qur'an they would never produce anything comparable' (17:88; cf. 52:34).

At other times Muhammad's opponents claimed that he had learned the Qur'an from a human being. The answer to this charge was that Muhammad's teacher was not a native Arabic speaker:

We know well what they are saying, namely: 'It is a man that teaches him.'

The language of the one they are alluding to is a foreign tongue, whereas this Qur'an is in clear Arabic ...

Falsehood is fabricated by those who do not believe in God's revelations: It is they who lie. (16:103, 105)

Razi cites the names of five people – three Jewish converts to Islam, one non-Arab Christian and one Muslim from a Zoroastrian background – who some claim were Muhammad's teachers.[3] Yet given the Qur'an's outstanding eloquence, *faṣaḥa*, none of these people, whose first language was not Arabic, could possibly have taught it to Muhammad.

Razi argues that the claim that Muhammad had a teacher is ground-less on three accounts: first, it comes from people who are disqualified because of their overt hostility towards the Prophet; second, it implies a long-standing and secretive relationship between Muhammad and his alleged teacher; and, third, because this teacher would have been an exceptionally learned man he could not have remained unknown.

There is another Qur'anic text that contains a similar charge against Muhammad:

The unbelievers say: 'This is nothing but a lie which he has forged, and others have helped him at it.'

In truth it is they who have put forward an iniquity and a falsehood.

And they say: 'Legends of the ancient peoples, which he has caused to be written: and they are dictated before him morning and evening.' (25:4–5)

Muhammad is accused by his enemies of having forged the Qur'an with the aid of other people and that the Qur'an contained nothing but 'legends of the ancient peoples'. If Muhammad had really produced the Qur'an with the help of others, Razi observes, his opponents should have been able to take up the challenge and construct a comparable set of teaching using the skills of educated people.

The content of the Qur'an

Razi explains that the Qur'an is miraculous because in addition to its eloquence it reveals things that were unknown to any ordinary human being, and especially to an illiterate man such as Muhammad.[4] Information about things that were previously unknown, *al-ikhbar 'ani l-ghuyub*, is the second aspect of the Qur'anic miracle: 'Such are some of the stories of the unseen, *anba'u l-ghayb*, which We have revealed to you, unknown before this both to you and to your people. Be patient: the end will be in favour of those who truly fear God' (11:49).

It is said that the Qur'an is miraculous in the sense that it reveals some events that took place long ago (cf. 20:133) and others that are still to come. Speaking of past events that God made known to Muhammad through the Qur'an, Ibn Taymiyya writes, 'He disclosed the past, like the stories of Adam, Noah, Abraham, Moses, Christ, Hud, Shu'ayb, Salih, and others. There was no scholar in Mecca from whom he learned ... He was not accustomed to correspond nor to read any written book.'[5]

As for the prediction of future events, Ibn Taymiyya mentions the victory of the Byzantine army over the Persian army in 624 (cf. 30:2–5) and the victory of the growing Muslim community over the polytheistic Meccans in 630 (cf. 54:45). The Qur'an's divine authorship is also said to be proved through the foretelling of eschatological events, for example the resurrection, the final judgment, hell and paradise.

Was Muhammad illiterate?

Muhammad's supposed illiteracy rests on one main Qur'anic text that describes him as the *ummi* Prophet. In this text God promises to be merciful to all who believe in him, including those Jews and Christians who follow the Prophet:

> Those who follow the Apostle, the *ummi* Prophet, whom they find mentioned in their own (Scriptures) – in the Torah and the Gospel ...
> Say, 'People, I am the Apostle of God to you all ... So then, believe in God and in His Apostle, the *ummi* Prophet who believes in God and in His word. Follow him and so find guidance.' (7:157–158)

The word *ummi* is derived either from *ummiyya*, 'illiteracy', or from *umma*, 'nation'. The question is: does *ummi* have the first or the second of these meanings? And in the case of the first meaning, what sort of illiteracy is being referred to? Was Muhammad illiterate in the sense of not being able to read or write? Or illiterate in the sense of being 'religiously illiterate', that is, ignorant of the Jewish and Christian Scriptures? And in the case of the second meaning, was Muhammad an *ummi* prophet because, being an Arab, he was from 'the Nations' as opposed to 'Israel'?

From an exegetical point of view, it is wise to seek the meaning of *ummi* in the light of its Qur'anic context. The word occurs in four other verses. In each of these it appears in its plural form, *ummiyyun*.

Sura 2:78

And there are among them [the Jews] *ummiyyun*, who know not the Book, but see therein their own desire, and they do nothing but make conjectures. (2:78)

Razi explains that the word *ummiyyun* can mean either those who have no Scripture or prophets, or otherwise those who are unable to read or write properly. Since the Jews do have Scriptures and prophets, Razi considers the second meaning to be the right one. He gives another reason why the latter interpretation is to be preferred, citing a hadith where the Prophet describes his people: 'We are an illiterate, *ummi*, nation; we neither write, nor know accounts.'[6] Now this hadith speaks of the Arab people, whereas the Qur'anic verse is about the Jews. So is it legitimate to apply the meaning of *ummi* in this hadith to the Jews? And does the same word necessarily have the same meaning for Arabs as it does for Jews?

I suggest that the word *ummiyyun* should be interpreted in its immediate context. The words 'who know not the Book' in the same verse explain what *ummiyyun* means. They specify what sort of illiteracy the Jews were guilty of. They had the Torah but they failed to understand its message; hence they were 'scripturally' (or religiously) illiterate.

Sura 3:20

If they argue with you, say: 'I have submitted my whole being to God and so have those who follow me.' And say to those who have been given the Scripture and to the *ummiyyun*: 'Do you submit yourselves [to God]?'

If they do, they are rightly guided, but if they turn away, your only task is to deliver the word. (3:20)

According to Razi this verse refers to all non-Muslims, who can be divided into two groups. The first group includes those who claim they have received Scripture, whether this claim is justified (as with the Jews and Christians), or not (as with the Zoroastrians). The second group are those who do not have Scriptures at all, that is, the idolaters.

The Arab associators[7] are described as *ummiyyun*, explains Razi, because they had no Scripture and were therefore compared to those who could not read or write. This comparison is based on the fact that, at the time, most Arabs were not able to write.

Razi concludes that this verse calls Muhammad to argue with all unbelievers, whoever they may be; with those who claim to have Scripture, described as *those who have been given the Scripture*, and with those who have no Scripture, described as *ummiyyun*.[8]

Sura 3:75

> There are those among the people of the Book who, if you entrust them with much treasure, will pay it back to you and there are others who, if you entrust them with a mere dinar, will not repay it until you stand over them all the while. This springs from their saying: 'We are under no obligation to the *ummiyyun*', thus deliberately attributing a false thing to God. (3:75)

In his commentary on this verse Razi mentions two ways of understanding the word *ummi*, neither of which he appears to endorse. For some this word derives from *umm*, meaning 'the origin of something'; so the Prophet was *ummi* in the sense that, not having had any education, he stayed as he initially was, that is, an unlearned person. For others, the word *ummi* derives from Mecca, Muhammad's native city, which is known in the Qur'an as *umm al-qura*, 'the mother of the cities' (6:92; 42:7).[9]

It is worth noting in this verse that the Arabs are called *ummiyyun* by the Jews and from a Jewish perspective. This could only mean, in my view, that Arabs are part of 'the Nations' (*gôyîm* in Hebrew), that is, they do not share in the God-given blessings to Israel of which the Scriptures are among the most significant.

Sura 62:2

It is He [God] who has sent the *ummiyyun* an Apostle from among them to rehearse to them His revelations, to sanctify them and to teach them the Book and Wisdom, for they had indeed gone astray in former times. (62:2)

This verse describes the Arab people, including Muhammad himself, as *ummiyyun*. Here Razi gives us his own interpretation. The word *ummi*, he says, refers to the Nation of the Arabs. They are called this, first, because they are an *ummi* nation without a Scripture, and secondly, because they do not read or write. Razi quotes Ibn 'Abbas, an authority in Qur'anic exegesis and one of Muhammad's companions, as having said about this verse, 'The *ummiyyun* are those who have no Scripture and to whom no prophet had been sent.'[10] Thus only the first part of Razi's interpretation is backed up by the prestigious authority of Ibn 'Abbas.

Un-Scriptured or illiterate?

Having reviewed all the Qur'anic occurrences of *ummi* it appears that, when applied to the Arab nation of which Muhammad was the most eminent representative, the word refers to their religious identity and not primarily to their illiteracy. Thus sura 7:157–158 is best understood by describing Muhammad as 'the un-Scriptured Prophet' rather than as 'the illiterate Prophet'.[11] As an Arab Prophet, Muhammad was from the 'Nations' (or 'the Gentiles') who had no Scripture. Unlike the 'People of the Book', the Arab people (and more generally the 'Nations') had not been given a written revelation from God until the Qur'an was revealed to Muhammad. Thus Muhammad is the *ummi* Prophet in the sense that he is 'the Gentile Prophet'.

Today there are some Muslim scholars who hold that Muhammad is the *ummi* Prophet in the sense that he is 'the Gentile Prophet'. Thus the French translation of the Qur'an by Muḥammad Ḥamidullah has 'the Gentile Prophet' in 7:157–158 (and 'the Gentiles' in 3:20, 75; 62:2). In a footnote the translator explicitly compares the Prophet Muhammad with the other 'Gentile Apostle', Paul.[12] Indeed, the distinction between the nation that received Holy Scriptures (Israel, the Jews) and the nations without the Scriptures (the Gentiles, the Nations, the Greeks) goes back to the Bible (Rom. 1:16; 15:8–9). Although he was from a Jewish background, Paul considered himself as an apostle sent primarily to the Gentiles (Rom. 15:15–18; Gal. 2:8). It is also worth noting that the text of Isaiah which the Hadith applies to Muhammad speaks about the Prophet sent to 'the Nations' (or 'the Gentiles'), or, in Arabic, the *ummiyyun* (Is. 42:1, 6).[13]

If sura 7 cannot be used as evidence that Muhammad was illiterate, the question remains: was Muhammad illiterate or not? Some Muslims look to another Qur'anic text as proof of his illiteracy. In the following text, God reveals the significance of choosing Muhammad to be his Prophet:

> We have, in this way, sent down to you the Book ... Prior to this you did not recite (*tala*) any Book nor set down any scripture in writing by your own hand (*khatta*). Had you done either, those bent on discredit would have their suspicions. (29:47–48)

These verses are seen by Muslims as clear evidence that Muhammad could not read or write. Razi explains that given the supernatural character of the Qur'an, no-one, not even the most educated, could have been able to produce it. However, if Muhammad had been a learned man, the people who denigrated the Qur'an could have suspected it of being the product of Muhammad himself. Thus the illiteracy of the Prophet enhances the evidence for the divine origin of the Qur'an.[14]

The thrust of Razi's argument would still be valid if we understand Muhammad's illiteracy in a religious sense: Muhammad was not a Jewish scribe or a Christian scholar. Unlike the People of the Book he was not familiar with the Scriptures, yet he came with a Book comparable to the Torah and the Gospel, which proves that the Qur'an is God's Word. Thus the above text (29:47–48) can be interpreted in terms of Muhammad's 'religious illiteracy'. The verb *tala* refers not to a mundane reading but to a religious proclamation. Likewise, the verb *khatta* is used in connection with a religious writing. In others words, prior to the preaching of the Qur'an, Muhammad was not 'a man of the Book'. As a Gentile Prophet he was not versed in any of the Scriptures. Therefore, the Qur'an can only be from God.

Taking this evidence into account, one may wonder why, when applied to the Prophet, the word *ummi* has traditionally been understood as meaning 'illiterate', yet when applied to the Arab people it is understood as 'the Gentiles'. Is it not to enhance the miraculous character of the Qur'an? And on the issue of the Qur'an's literary perfection, one could ask: is it appropriate to use literary criteria as evidence of a religious claim, namely that Muhammad is God's Prophet and the Qur'an is God's Word?

Muhammad's other miracles

The Qur'an is seen as Muhammad's greatest miracle, but it is not the only one cited to prove he is God's Prophet. Unlike the Qur'an, Islamic tradition attributes many miracles to him. According to Ibn Taymiyya, 'his miracles were in excess of a thousand – such as the splitting of the moon and other signs like the miraculous Qur'an, the foretelling of him by the People of the Book and his prediction by the prophets, the sorcerers and invisible voices making him known'.[15]

The splitting of the moon is often quoted by Muslims to accredit Muhammad's prophethood. The polytheistic Arabs demanded that Muhammad show them a miracle. In response the Prophet pointed to the moon, which was split in two. Unlike other wonders, this supernatural event is alluded to in the Qur'an. According to Islamic tradition, God produced this miracle as a sign pointing both to Muhammad's mission and to the final judgment:

> The Hour draws near: the moon is split in two.
> Seeing a sign they turn away, saying: 'Still the same old sorcery!'
> They have denied the truth and followed their own whims.
>   (54:1–3)

Ibn Taymiyya explains that Muhammad's contemporaries 'saw and witnessed with their own eyes the splitting of the moon, and information on that has been successively transmitted'.[16] Indeed, in Bukhari's compilation of the Hadith we find three very short reports by Muhammad's companions on this sign. Ibn Mas'ud, for example, said: 'During the lifetime of the Prophet the moon split into two parts and at that the Prophet said, "Bear witness (to this)."'[17]

Other miracles reported in the Hadith include the springing forth of water from between Muhammad's fingers when his companions were thirsty and had no water to make their ritual ablutions before prayer; the multiplication of food when they were hungry; and the moaning of a palm tree trunk after it was replaced by a proper pulpit to be used by the Prophet.[18]

Muhammad is also said to have been identified by various people as

God's Prophet. Such stories are not found in the Qur'an or the Hadith but in other Islamic literature, such as the *Sira* (Muhammad's biographies). According to one story, Muhammad was still a boy when a soothsayer predicted that he would have 'a great future'. Another story has it that Muhammad was a teenager when he went to Syria with his merchant uncle, Abu Ṭalib. When the caravan reached Baṣra, they met a Christian monk, by the name of Baḥira. The monk discerned in the boy a would-be prophet of God and gave his uncle this advice: 'Take your nephew back to his country and guard him carefully against the Jews, for by God! If they see him and know about him what I know, they will do him evil; a great future lies before this nephew of yours, so take him home quickly.'[19] In the popular literature about Muhammad we find many accounts like these, involving people as well as evil spirits. Their historicity, however, is extremely difficult to establish.

Notes

[1] Cf. Qur'an 2:136, 285; 3:84; 4:150, 152.

[2] Razi, VIII:16, pp. 31–33.

[3] Ibid., X:20: pp. 94–96.

[4] Ibid., XII: 24, pp. 44–46.

[5] Ibn Taymiyya, *al-Jawab al-ṣaḥiḥ liman baddala dina l-Masiḥ*, p. 174.

[6] Cf. Bukhari, *ṣawm* 13:III, p. 75, no. 137 [1780]. Razi, II:3, p. 127.

[7] The Arab idolaters are described in the Qur'an as *mushrikun*, literally meaning 'associators', because they 'associate' other gods with God in their worship.

[8] Razi, IV:7, p. 185.

[9] Ibid., IV:8, p. 90.

[10] Ibid., XV:30, p. 4.

[11] Some English translations of the Qur'an, e.g. 'A. Yusuf 'Ali, use the term 'Unlettered Prophet'. The translation 'unlettered' is ambiguous since it is not clear what type of illiteracy it is referring to. It may refer to ignorance of the Holy Letters (scriptural illiteracy) or to ignorance of the letters of the alphabet (illiteracy in terms of not being able to read or write).

[12] See also M. Shaḥrur who understands the *ummi* Prophet as 'the Gentile Prophet' in *al-Kitab wa-l-Qur'an* (The Bible and the Qur'an), pp. 139–143.

[13] Bukhari, *buyu'* 50:III, p. 189, no. 335 [1981]; *tafsir* 48:3:VI, p. 345, no. 362 [4461]. This hadith is quoted in chapter 20.

14 Razi, XIII:25, p. 68.
15 Ibn Taymiyya, *al-Jawab*, p. 173.
16 Ibid., p. 178.
17 Bukhari, *manaqib* 27:IV, p. 533, no. 830 [3364].
18 Cf. Bukhari, *manaqib* 25:IV, pp. 496–507, nos. 771–785 [3306–3320].
19 Cf. A. Guillaume, *The Life of Muhammad: A Translation of Ibn Ishaq's Sirat rasul Allah*, pp. 79–81; see also pp. 90–95.

19

Proof of Muhammad's prophethood: perfect law and political success

Having considered Muhammad's miracles, and especially that of the Qur'an, we now move on and look at his message and political success. What is it about his message that should make us recognize him as God's Prophet? And how do his political and military victories prove that Islam is God's perfect religion?

The perfection of Islamic law

Muslim theologians often compare Judaism, Christianity and Islam, and argue that Islam is by far the best of the three. Although they describe each of these religions as God-given, *adyan samawiyya*, Islam is seen as the last religion, the one with the perfect law, centred on God and his glory. The Muslim community is described as *ummatun wasatun* (2:143). Razi reports how Muslims have understood this expression. The Muslim community is seen as a community that is just, fair, respectable, well balanced, doing good and holding the middle ground between Judaism and Christianity.[1]

Ibn Taymiyya argues along these lines in his treatise against Christians: *Correct Answer to Those who Changed the Religion of Christ*. Looking at the areas of religious, moral and penal law, he seeks to explain how Islamic law is superior to Jewish law and Christian doctrine.[2] To understand his position better, we shall follow some of his arguments. As we do so, it is worth noting that in many areas he appears to have seriously misunderstood the teaching of the Torah and the Gospel. Rather than commenting on each point as it comes, I shall leave my response until the end of the section and give a more detailed response in chapter 21.

The religious law

Christians, says Ibn Taymiyya, claim that justice characterizes Judaism and that grace distinguishes Christianity. But in the religion of the Qur'an, he says, justice and grace are inseparable and perfectly united. Thus Islam is the religion 'which combines grace and law by prescribing justice and exhorting [people] to goodness'.[3] God is a God of justice and mercy, and so too is Islam: 'The Law of the Torah is primarily severity while that of the Gospel is leniency. The Law of the Qur'an is moderate, combining both of these qualities.'[4] Muhammad is said to reflect God's attributes: 'He described himself as the prophet of mercy and pardon, but also as the prophet of slaughter who laughs at fighting.'[5] In this he is seen as perfect, unlike some Jewish prophets, who were ruthless in their fight against their enemies, and unlike Jesus, who was apparently too lenient with his enemies. Similarly, the Muslim community is said to hold the middle ground: 'God describes His community as acting with mercy and in humility towards believers, but with severity and sternness towards unbelievers.'[6]

Islamic Law is said to get the balance right between a focus on this life and a focus on the afterlife. The Torah – by which Muslims understand the law of Moses – is seen as a worldly law dealing mainly with life on earth. Islamic law, however, is seen as far more comprehensive: 'In the Qur'an there is mention of the afterlife. It sets proofs for it and describes it; there are descriptions of the Garden and the Fire which have no parallel in the Torah.'[7] While the Torah is accused of being too centred on 'this world', Muslims see the Gospel as having gone to the opposite extreme. It is seen as too spiritual in the sense that it has little concern for this world, being centred on the next.

The Jews killed many prophets and most refused to believe in Jesus as God's prophet sent to them. On the other hand, Christians claim that Jesus is the Son of God. Ibn Taymiyya argues that Muslims stand between these two extremes. They recognize that Jesus is one of God's greatest prophets, Islam preserves the oneness of God, and Muslims believe in all prophets without distinction.

The moral law

For Ibn Taymiyya, the moral code for the Jewish community is not strict enough. Divorce, for instance, is lawful and no restriction is cited on polygamy. The Christian code, on the other hand, is too strict, where divorce and polygamy are unlawful. Islamic law, however, is viewed as neither too harsh nor too lax: 'By it God made it easy for mankind to follow Him in a way which was not easy for those before Muhammad.'[8] As far as Muslims are concerned, God did not impose regulations too difficult to observe (22:78); divorce is lawful but highly inadvisable, polygamy is restricted to four wives and is conditional: the husband must treat all of his wives fairly (4:3).

Ibn Taymiyya argues that the Gospel has a major weakness, for 'there is no independent *shari'a* in it'.[9] The teaching is too idealistic, he says, with Jesus calling people 'to goodness, to pardoning offences, to bearing injuries, and to asceticism in this life'.[10] And the Christian community has gone well beyond the teaching of its founder, distorting Christ's teaching and turning what was meant to be leniency into weakness and laxity:

> God sent Christ with pardon and tenderness, with forgiveness to evildoers and bearing with their wrongdoing in order to moderate their morals and put an end to the pride and harshness in them. However, these Christians have gone to excess in laxity so that they have failed to command the good and prohibit what is forbidden. They have failed to do *jihad* [holy war] in the way of God, and to judge justly between people. Instead of establishing firm punishment [for crimes], their worshippers have become solitary monks.[11]

Islamic law is said to contain Christian virtues to a greater extent, and because the *shari'a* is both a moral and a criminal law, people are deterred from abusing these virtues. Offenders face the penal law in all its severity: 'In the law of Muhammad there is leniency, pardon, forgiveness, and noble qualities of character greater than what is in the Gospel. There is in it, moreover, severity, *jihad*, and setting punishments for unbelievers and hypocrites greater than what is found in the Torah. All of this is to the limit of perfection.'[12]

The penal law

Islamic penal law is superior to Jewish law, explains Ibn Taymiyya, in that it allows more leniency when dealing with murderers. The criminal law in the Torah, on the other hand, is exclusively based on justice, and retaliation is the only rule for any offence (Exod. 21:24). While maintaining the principle of justice, Islamic law allows for offenders to be forgiven by those they have wronged. If criminals are forgiven, they have to pay compensation to the victims or their families:

> O you who believe!
> The law of equality is prescribed to you in cases of murder:
> The free for the free, the slave for the slave, the woman for the woman.
> But if any remission is made by the brother of the slain, then grant any reasonable demand, and compensate him with handsome gratitude. (2:178)

Ibn Taymiyya observes that 'in the law of the Qur'an the acceptance of indemnity (*diya*) is accepted, but that is not legislated in the Torah'.[13] Forgiving a murderer, for instance, is a good deed, one for which God will reward the person (5:45). Thus the payment of blood money will benefit both the offender and the victim (or his or her family). The law of the Torah is said to be too strict on another account: it prescribes capital punishment in too many cases, whereas Islamic law requires the death penalty only for apostasy, murder and sexual immorality.

How, then, does Christianity compare with Islam? For Ibn Taymiyya, the fact that there is no criminal law expounded in the Gospel makes Islamic law appear far more comprehensive and equitable. From his perspective, writing in the fourteenth century, he certainly prefers Islamic justice to secular justice and perceives another major weakness in Christianity: 'The legal system among them [Christians] is double. There is the judgement of the church, but in this there is no protection for the oppressed from the oppressor. The second is the administration of justice by their kings; this, however, is not a revealed law, but operates according to the opinions of the rulers.'[14]

So why was the Christian community not able to protect the rights of the oppressed against the oppressor? According to Ibn Taymiyya, it is because Christians think that 'the Law of the Gospel demands that people abandon their rights and that it does not establish the rights of the oppressed against his oppressor'.[15] In holding such views Christians are said to have misinterpreted the teaching of Christ, a teaching that has been restored by Islamic law. Ibn Taymiyya contends that it is not possible to believe, as Christians do, that God has ordained forgiveness instead of justice; otherwise the law of the jungle would take over: 'there would be no deterrent to restrain evildoers, and the strong would oppress the weak and cause corruption on the earth (2:251)'.[16] Therefore, God prescribes justice yet encourages people to forgive (cf. 3:134; 4:92; 16:126; 42:43). Justice and forgiveness are combined in Islamic law; the former is a command whereas the latter is only a good deed: 'A revealed law must include a legal system which is just, and must at the same time exhort people to pardon and to act with kindness. The Law of Islam has done this.'[17] For Muslims, the Islamic law is perfect in every respect; it is the ultimate expression of God's will, and combines the best in Jewish law and the best in Christian doctrine. The perfection of Islamic law is therefore seen as evidence that Muhammad is God's greatest Prophet. Conversely, the fact that Muhammad is said to be the *final* Prophet implies that Islamic law must be spotless, for if it had not been perfect there would be need for yet another prophet to bring God's law to perfection.[18]

Ibn Taymiyya's comparison of Islam with Jewish law and Christian doctrine is summarized in the table below.

Jewish law	Islamic law *'the perfect religion'*	Christian doctrine
Characterized by justice.	Justice and grace perfectly united.	Characterized by grace.
Jewish prophets were ruthless against their enemies.	Muhammad showed firmness and mercy	Jesus was too lenient on his enemies
Too worldly: focus on this life.	Well balanced: focus on both this life and the afterlife.	Too spiritual: focus on afterlife.
Refuse to believe in Jesus.	Recognize Jesus as one of the greatest prophets.	Claim that Jesus is the Son of God.
Divorce allowed. Polygamy unrestricted.	Divorce lawful, but inadvisable. Polygamy restricted.	Divorce and polygamy are unlawful.
Harsh criminal law: no forgiveness.	Justice and forgiveness.	No criminal law.

It goes without saying that Christians would want to challenge much of this analysis, especially in the description of the Torah and the Gospel. We shall take another look at some of these issues in chapter 21, but for now let us take note of the following:

(1) While the Gospel does not lay down specific penal laws, it does emphasize the importance of maintaining justice and punishing criminals, a responsibility in the hands of the State – 'Everyone must submit himself to the governing authorities, for there is no authority except that which God has established … [The one in authority] is God's servant, an agent of wrath to bring punishment on the wrongdoer' (Rom. 13:1–4).

(2) Jesus did not come to abolish the Torah, but to fulfil it (Matt. 5:17–20). The moral and civil law of the Torah gives us vital guidance as to God's values and priorities for every society. In chapter 24, for example, we shall see how the teaching of the Torah on how to treat non-Israelites in the community has lost none of its relevance in our twenty-first-century world. Christians who take the Scriptures seriously find not only a focus on the life to come but a wealth of teaching on how to live in this life.

(3) Was Jesus too lenient on his enemies? True, he spoke words of love and forgiveness and did not fight as a political Messiah, but he had stern words for those who distorted God's truth and refused to believe in him (Luke 11:37–52). And most of all, in his death and resurrection he triumphed over the greatest of enemies – sin, death and evil (Col. 2:13–15).

(4) A careful examination of the Torah will reveal that, as well as being a God of justice, the Israelites knew the Lord to be a 'compassionate and gracious God, slow to anger, abounding in love and faithfulness' (Exod. 34:6; Num. 14:18; Neh. 9:17). In fact, it is hard to miss this repeated emphasis in the law, especially when we remember that the Israelites so often turned away from God.

(5) The grace of God is indeed the focus of the gospel. But this is not to the neglect of his justice. As we saw in chapter 8, the cross of Jesus Christ is the supreme illustration of this – where God's grace and justice are revealed together, demonstrating that he is both 'just and the one who justifies' (Rom. 3:26).

Christians would be among the first to admit that when Ibn Taymiyya wrote at the beginning of the fourteenth century, the church was not in the best of health. Nevertheless, it is worth emphasizing again that whenever we engage in Christian–Muslim dialogue, it is best not to compare what is an ideal on one side with what is a poor example on the other.

Perhaps this survey of Ibn Taymiyya's thinking also serves as an illustration of the way in which many Muslims throughout the centuries have argued against a *misconception* of the gospel, rather than against the *true message* of Jesus Christ. For Muslims and Christians alike it is another call to careful study and genuine dialogue.

The political success of Islam

We have noted that Razi considers the ascendancy of Islam over other religions to be an indisputable proof of Muhammad's prophethood; that through the political supremacy of the Muslim community, God demonstrated that Muhammad was his Prophet.[19]

The verse about Islam's superiority (9:33) is repeated twice in the Qur'an (48:28; 61:9): 'It is He who has sent His Apostle with Guidance and the Religion of Truth, that He may cause it to prevail over all religion, however hateful the associators find it' (61:9). According to Razi, there are three means by which this superiority can be achieved: through arguing and demonstration, *bi l-ḥijja wa l-bayan*; through numerical growth and prosperity, *bi l-kathra wa l-wufur*; and through victory and conquest, *bi l-ghalaba wa l-istila'*.

For Razi, the *rational supremacy* of Islam has always been well established; therefore the promise made to Muhammad can only refer to the forthcoming *political victory* of Islam. But what if someone objects and says that Islam is still far from being the prevailing religion in many nations of the world: India and China, for example? Razi quotes several responses to this objection. These include the fact that Islam has prevailed over all of the Arabian Peninsula; or that Islam has triumphed over Judaism in Arabia, over Christianity in Syria, and over Zoroastrianism in Persia; or that Islam will indeed rule over all other religions but only after Jesus has come back from heaven to implement Islamic law.

Like Razi, Ibn Taymiyya considers that the political ascendancy of the Muslim community demonstrates that Muhammad is truly God's Prophet. There is nothing unusual about this conclusion, he writes, for God granted victory to the prophets who came before Muhammad and punished their enemies (cf. 54:15–45); and God did the same for Muhammad and his community to an even greater degree:

God supported him greatly with the support He gave only to prophets. He did not support any one of the prophets as He supported him, just as it was he who brought the finest of books to the finest of communities with the finest of laws. God made him master (*sayyid*) of the children of Adam ... God's customary pattern of behaviour (*sunnat Allah*) is to grant victory to His messengers and to those who believe both in this world and on the Day of Witnesses, and this is the case.[20]

From an Islamic perspective, God's faithfulness to his prophets and his people means that he gives them the power to overcome their enemies (cf. 3:12; 24:55; 40:51; 37:171–173). The God-given success of the Muslim community is seen to be both religious and political, for 'He made it conquer with proof and clear argument, and He has made it conquer by power and spear.'[21]

The community of the final Prophet is said to enjoy God's blessing on earth like no other religious community has ever done. Ibn Taymiyya compares Judaism, Christianity and Islam in terms of their political success. The predicament of Jewish religion is rather bleak, he says: 'One should say to the Jews that they are the lowliest of all peoples. Even if it were supposed that what they hold is the unchanged religion of God, it is, nevertheless, overcome and conquered throughout the world.'[22] As for the Jewish people, Ibn Taymiyya links their obedience to the law with their welfare. Their subsequent disobedience resulted in the loss of their nationhood:

> When they were following the religion of Moses and living according to guidance and the religion of truth, they were victorious. After that, innovations multiplied among them, as they know (5:59–60). The People of the Book [Christians] admit that the Jews worshiped idols and killed the prophets. God said that it was for this reason they were destroyed twice (17:4–8). The first destruction occurred when Nebuchadnezzar carried them off to Babylon, and that destruction lasted seventy years. The second destruction occurred about seventy years after Christ.[23]

And what about Christianity? Ibn Taymiyya's analysis here is slightly different but his conclusion is the same. Christianity, he writes, achieved some political success, but only when it was too late; Christian doctrine had already been corrupted. In other words, despite a measure of political achievement by the Christian community, there was still the need for a greater and uncorrupted religion: 'To Christians one can say that they were continually conquered, overcome, and scattered throughout the earth until Constantine was victorious and established the religion of the Christians by the sword, killing those Jews and pagans who opposed him. However, the religion he made victorious was changed and corrupted and not the religion of Christ.'[24]

As one would expect, Ibn Taymiyya contends that with the coming of Muhammad, God's kingdom on earth was established to a degree never achieved before. In 630 the Prophet returned to Mecca with the Muslim army and definitively overcame his enemies. The city surrendered peacefully and the Ka'aba was purged of its idols. The Arabs began to join the new religion in great numbers. When Muhammad died two years later, Islam had conquered virtually the whole of Arabia. This victory was the first step towards Islam's conquest of many other peoples: 'When God sent Muhammad, the absolute oneness of God and His service alone with no rivals made such a conquest as no people had ever known, nor had any prophet ever accomplished ... Most of the people of the earth are with Muhammad ... [He and his people] made the religion of the Lord conquer from the eastern part of the world to the west by word and deed.'[25]

Thus the political success of Islam, a historical fact, is seen to carry important theological significance. Muslims believe that its success demonstrates that Muhammad is God's greatest Prophet, that Islam is God's perfect religion and that the Muslim community is the best religious community in the world.

> You are the best of Peoples, evolved for mankind,
> Enjoining what is right, forbidding what is wrong, and believing
>   in God. (3:110)

Bearing this evidence in mind, the question we must ask is this: is political and military success necessarily proof of God's approval? And is God's view of success always the same as ours?

We shall return to many of these issues in chapter 21. But first we need to consider another area often presented as proof of Muhammad's prophethood – texts in the Christian and Jewish Scriptures claimed to point to Muhammad.

Notes

[1] See Razi's exegesis on sura 2:143, in II:IV, pp. 88–97.
[2] Ibn Taymiyya, *al-Jawab al-ṣaḥiḥ liman baddala dina l-Masiḥ* (1984),

pp. 350–369.
[3] Ibid., p. 351.
[4] Ibid., p. 357.
[5] Ibid.
[6] Ibid.; cf. Qur'an 5:57; 48:29.
[7] Ibn Tamiyya, *al-Jawab*, p. 354.
[8] Ibid.
[9] Ibid., p. 355.
[10] Ibid.
[11] Ibid., p. 358–359.
[12] Ibid., p. 358.
[13] Ibid., p. 355.
[14] Ibid., p. 366.
[15] Ibid.
[16] Ibid.
[17] Ibid.
[18] Cf. Razi's exegesis of sura 33:40, in XIII:25, p. 185.
[19] Cf. Razi's exegesis of sura 9:33, in VIII:16, pp. 32–33.
[20] Ibn Taymiyya, *al-Jawab*, p. 177.
[21] Ibid., p. 163.
[22] Ibid., p. 360.
[23] Ibid., p. 361.
[24] Ibid., p. 362.
[25] Ibid., pp. 362–363.

Do the Scriptures foretell the coming of Muhammad?

The Qur'an asserts that God's prophets spoke about Muhammad long before he came. Muslims see this as another miracle giving evidence for his prophethood. Their argument is based on two texts. In sura 7:157 Muhammad is described as being written about in the Torah and the Gospel. And more specifically, in sura 61:6, Jesus is said to have announced the coming of *Aḥmad* after him, this name being one of several names given to the Prophet:[1]

> And Jesus, the son of Mary, said:
> 'People of Israel! I am the Apostle of God to you, confirming the truth of the Torah which you have already and giving you glad word of an Apostle who will come after me, whose name is Aḥmad.' (61:6)

Razi does not include the prophecy about Muhammad in his list of Muhammad's credentials for prophethood. Ibn Taymiyya does, yet like many other theologians he does not quote any text from the Bible to prove his point. Does this fact indicate that early Muslim theologians had limited access to the Scriptures?

Contemporary Muslim writers use such arguments to a much greater extent. They contend that the Scriptures really do point to Muhammad but that Christians and Jews have misinterpreted them. The texts they often refer to are in the books of Isaiah (Is. 42:1–9), Deuteronomy (Deut. 18:18), and the Gospel of John (John 14 – 16).[2] Some also refer to the *Gospel of Barnabas*, which is not part of the Christian Scriptures.

The Servant of the Lord

One of Muhammad's companions was once asked how the Torah described the Prophet. His answer is recorded in Bukhari's compilation of the Hadith:

[Muhammad] is described in the Torah with some of the qualities attributed to him in the Qur'an as follows:

O Prophet! We have sent you as a witness and a giver of good tidings and a warner and guardian of the illiterates.[3] You are My slave and My messenger. I have named you *al-Mutawakkil* (he who depends on God). You are neither discourteous, harsh nor one who makes noise in the markets, and you do not do evil to those who do evil to you, but you deal with them with forgiveness and pardon. God will not let him die till he makes straight the crooked people by making them say: 'No-one has the right to be worshipped but God,' which will open blind eyes and deaf ears and enveloped hearts.[4]

These words are a distant echo of the prophet Isaiah's first Servant Song (Is. 42:1–9), where the Servant of the Lord is described as the one whom God has chosen, the one who will not shout or raise his voice in the streets, and the one who will bring justice to the nations. So was Isaiah referring to Muhammad? This seems highly unlikely when we take a closer look at the text. A careful reading of Isaiah 42 is bound to bring out the contrast between the Servant's peaceful mission and Muhammad's mission, which was marked by a series of wars. Moreover, the Gospel writer Matthew quotes this prophecy of Isaiah, convinced that it had been fulfilled in Jesus:

Many followed him [Jesus], and he healed all their sick, warning them not to tell who he was. This was to fulfil what was spoken through the prophet Isaiah:

'Here is my servant whom I have chosen,
    the one I love, in whom I delight:
I will put my spirit on him,
    and he will proclaim justice to the nations.

He will not quarrel or cry out;
   no-one will hear his voice in the streets.
A bruised reed he will not break,
   and a smouldering wick he will not snuff out,
till he leads justice to victory.
   In his name the nations will put their hope.'
   (Matt. 12:15–21; cf. Is. 42:1–4)

Throughout his ministry, Jesus demonstrated true humility. He had come to serve and did not want to take advantage of his miracles for his own glory. The other Servant Songs in Isaiah, especially the fourth, which describes the Servant's sufferings with incomparable beauty (Is. 52:13–53:12), are sufficient proof, if such were needed, that these prophecies can refer only to Jesus (cf. Matt. 8:16–17):

He was despised and rejected by men,
   a man of sorrows, and familiar with suffering.
Like one from whom men hide their faces
   he was despised, and we esteemed him not.
Surely he took up our infirmities
   and carried our sorrows,
yet we considered him stricken by God,
   smitten by him, and afflicted.
But he was pierced for our transgressions,
   he was crushed for our iniquities;
the punishment that brought us peace was upon him,
   and by his wounds we are healed.
We all, like sheep, have gone astray,
   each of us has turned to his own way;
and the LORD has laid on him the iniquity of us all. (Is. 53:3–6)

The 'New Moses'

Muḥammad 'Abduh wrote, without giving specific details, that Moses and Isaiah prophesied about the coming of Muhammad. As for Isaiah, the Egyptian scholar most likely had in mind the above text (Is. 42), but what about Moses? Today many Muslims quote from the book of Deuteronomy. In this text, which I referred to in chapter 14, Moses tells the Israelites about the coming of a prophet *like him*. It is therefore known as the prophecy about 'the New Moses':

The LORD your God will raise up for you a prophet like me from among your own brothers. You must listen to him ...

The LORD said to me: '... I will raise up for them a prophet like you from among their brothers; I will put my words in his mouth, and he will tell them everything I command him.' (Deut. 18:15, 17–18)

Muslims who take this prophecy as being fulfilled in Muhammad present a threefold argument:

(1) The Bible refers to the Israelites as the brothers of the Ishmaelites, that is, the Arabs (e.g. Gen. 16:12; Gen. 25:18). Jesus himself was an Israelite, whereas, as an Arab, Muhammad was a brother to the Israelites.

(2) The similarity between Moses and Muhammad is far greater than that between Moses and Jesus. Unlike Jesus, Moses and Muhammad were born in the usual manner. They were both married and had children. They died of natural causes and were buried. Jesus was only a prophet, but they were also political and military leaders. Unlike Jesus, they defeated their enemies. After initial resistance and scepticism their people accepted them, whereas Jesus, with the exception of a few followers, was rejected by the Israelites. As for the revelations entrusted to them, unlike Jesus, Moses and Muhammad brought a law which – it is claimed – was written down in their lifetime.

(3) Like Moses, God's words were dictated to and 'repeated by Prophet Muhammad exactly as he had heard them. Muhammad's own thinking or authorship were not involved in any way in what he uttered.'[5]

So was Moses speaking about the coming of Muhammad? Was Muhammad the great Prophet the Jews were told to expect? Again, it is highly unlikely, for when considering Deuteronomy 18:17–18 we need to bear in mind the following:

(1) In the context of the people of Israel, the 'brothers' can only mean fellow Israelites (cf. Lev. 10:6; 1 Kgs. 12:24; Mic. 5:2–3). See, for example, the previous chapter of Deuteronomy, where the people are told, 'When you enter the land the LORD your God is giving you and have taken possession of it and settled in it, and you say, "Let us set a king over us like all the nations around us," be sure to appoint over you the king the LORD your God chooses. He must be from *among your own brothers. Do not place a foreigner over you, one who is not a brother Israelite.*' (Deut. 17:14–15; my emphasis).

(2) Since Abraham remarried after the death of Sarah, Isaac had

several other brothers in addition to Ishmael (Gen. 25:1–4), yet only Isaac was the 'son of the promise' (Gen. 18:10–14). God made his covenant with Isaac, not with any of his brothers (Gen. 17:15–22). Fully aware of God's unique relationship with Isaac, Abraham made him his heir: 'Abraham left everything he owned to Isaac. But while he was still living, he gave gifts to the sons of his concubines and sent them away from his son Isaac to the land of the east' (Gen. 25:5–6). It is noteworthy that when referring to God, Jesus always speaks of 'the God of Abraham, Isaac and Jacob' without ever mentioning Isaac's brothers (cf. Matt. 8:11; Matt. 22:32).

(3) Jesus knew that Moses' prophecy was pointing to himself. He told the Jewish leaders, 'If you believed Moses, you would believe me, for he wrote about me' (John 5:46). Jesus' disciples were convinced that he was 'the New Moses' and quoted the text from Deuteronomy as being fulfilled in him (John 1:45; Acts 3:20–22).

So in what sense was Jesus like Moses? Many aspects of Moses' ministry were fully expressed in Jesus' mission. Moses foreshadowed Jesus in that just as Moses delivered his people from slavery in Egypt, Jesus delivered his people from slavery to sin and death.

> [Moses] gave to Israel the foundational theological and ethical con-stitution that undergirded the message of centuries of later prophets. He was faithful in intercession and passionate concern for the good of his people, as well as in declaring God's specific judgements. He suffered with and for his people and finally died without seeing the full fruition of his life's mission. In these respects he not only set a model for subsequent true prophets, but, given that *no* OT [Old Testament] prophet was really 'like' him (cf. Deut. 34:10–12), he also prefigured the one prophet who was not only like him (cf. Acts 3:22ff.) but indeed surpassed him as a son surpasses a servant (cf. Heb. 3:2–6).[6]

As far as God's revelation is concerned, Jesus is much greater than Moses. He is not only *God's prophet* to whom God spoke face to face; he is *God's Word*. He is not only *God's messenger*; he is *God's message*, powerfully expressed through his teaching and miracles and supremely demonstrated in his death and resurrection.

> In the past God spoke to our forefathers through the prophets at many times and in various ways, but in these last days he has

spoken to us by his Son, whom he appointed heir of all things, and through whom he made the universe. (Heb. 1:1–2)

Jesus has been found worthy of greater honour than Moses, just as the builder of a house has greater honour than the house itself. For every house is built by someone, but God is the builder of everything. Moses was faithful as a servant in all God's house, testifying to what would be said in the future. But Christ is faithful as a son over God's house. (Heb. 3:3–6)

The 'Paraclete'

The Gospel of John records Jesus' dialogue with his disciples at the end of the Last Supper and before his arrest (John 14 – 16). Before he left, Jesus spoke about the coming of the 'Paraclete', a word since translated as the 'Counsellor', 'Helper', 'Comforter' or 'Advocate':

And I will ask the Father, and he will give you another Counsellor to be with you for ever – the Spirit of truth. (John 14:16–17)

But the Counsellor, the Holy Spirit, whom the Father will send in my name, will teach you all things and will remind you of everything I have said to you. (John 14:26)

When the Counsellor comes, whom I will send to you from the Father, the Spirit of truth who goes out from the Father, he will testify about me. (John 15:26)

But I tell you the truth: It is for your good that I am going away. Unless I go away, the Counsellor will not come to you; but if I go, I will send him to you. (John 16:7)

I have much more to say to you, more than you can now bear. But when he, the Spirit of truth, comes, he will guide you into all truth. He will not speak on his own; he will speak only what he hears, and he will tell you what is yet to come. (John 16:12–13)

Some Muslims today claim that Muhammad is the 'Paraclete' whose coming was foretold by Jesus. Maurice Bucaille takes this view.[7] His main argument is that the two Greek verbs 'to hear' and 'to speak' 'define concrete actions which can be applied only to a being with hearing and speech organs. 'It is impossible', he says, 'to apply them to the Holy Spirit.'[8] Bucaille therefore suggests that 'the presence of the term "Holy Spirit" in today's text could easily have come from a later addition made quite deliberately. It may have been intended to change the original meaning which predicted the advent of a prophet subsequent to Jesus and was therefore in contradiction with the teachings of the Christian churches at the time of their formation; these teachings maintained that Jesus was the last of the prophets.'[9]

It has also been suggested that the Greek word *paraklētos* was not the original word. Some argue that it has been substituted for a similar-sounding word, *periklytos,* meaning 'the praiseworthy one', an equivalent of the Arabic *Muhammad.*[10]

The problem with these suggestions is that there is no textual evidence to support them. None of the manuscripts we have today contains such variant readings. Moreover, Jesus identifies 'the Paraclete' as 'the Spirit of truth' (John 14:17; 15:26; 16:13). Bucaille's difficulty could easily have been removed if attention had been paid to the fact that Jesus told his disciples that he was speaking figuratively (John 16:25). There is no need to take his words literally by saying that the Holy Spirit is unable to hear or speak as a human being does. For, after all, is it not God who communicates his word through his Spirit?

How, then, was Jesus' prophecy fulfilled? In the book of Acts we are told that just before he ascended to heaven, Jesus reminded his disciples of his promise to send them the Holy Spirit: 'Do not leave Jerusalem, but wait for the gift my Father promised, which you have heard me speak about. For John baptised with water, but in a few days you will be baptised with the Holy Spirit' (Acts 1:4–5). Jesus told his disciples that the coming of the Holy Spirit would take place *in Jerusalem* and *shortly after his departure.* Indeed, ten days after Jesus left his disciples, on the day of Pentecost, the Holy Spirit came upon them. This day was a turning point in the life of the disciples. Boldly, they began preaching the gospel to the gathered crowds – crowds of Jews from many nations who had come on pilgrimage to Jerusalem for the festival of Pentecost (Acts 2:1–41).

What about the *Gospel of Barnabas?*

Some well-meaning Muslims, including scholars, claim that the only authentic gospel is the *Gospel of Barnabas.* This gospel, it is alleged, contains the real teaching of Jesus. Here is how M. 'Ata ur-Rahim presents this writing and its author:[11]

> The Gospel of Barnabas is the only known surviving Gospel written by a disciple of Jesus, that is, by a man who spent most of his time in the actual company of Jesus during the three years in which he was delivering his message. He therefore had direct experience and knowledge of Jesus' teaching, unlike all the authors of the four accepted Gospels. It is not known when he wrote down what he remembered of Jesus and his guidance ... It is possible that he did not write down anything until he returned to Cyprus with John Mark. The two made this journey some time after Jesus had left the earth, after parting company with Paul of Tarsus, who had refused to make any further journeys with Barnabas on which Mark was also present.[12]

In the *Gospel of Barnabas* it is claimed that Jesus announced the coming of Muhammad after him. This prediction occurs twelve times.[13] In some of these predictions Jesus denies that he is the Messiah, and tells people that the Messiah is still to come:

> Said the woman, 'O Lord, perchance thou art the Messiah.'
> Jesus answered, 'I am indeed sent to the house of Israel as a prophet of salvation; but after me shall come the Messiah, sent of God to all the world; for whom God hath made the world. And then through all the world will God be worshipped, and mercy received, insomuch that the year of jubilee, which now cometh every hundred years, shall by the Messiah be reduced to every year in every place.'[14]

So, if the Messiah is not Jesus, then who will he be? Jesus declares that the expected Messiah will be called Muhammad:

> Then said the priest, 'How shall the Messiah be called, and what sign shall reveal his coming?'
> Jesus answered, 'The name of the Messiah is admirable, for God himself gave him the name when he had created his soul, and placed it in a celestial splendour. God said, "Wait Mohammed; for thy sake I will create paradise, the world, and a great multitude of creatures, whereof I make thee a present, insomuch that whoso

shall bless thee shall be blessed, and whoso shall curse thee shall be accursed. When I shall send thee into the world I shall send thee as my messenger of salvation, and thy word shall be true, insomuch that heaven and earth shall fail, but thy faith shall never fail." Mohammed is his blessed name.'

Then the crowd lifted up their voices, saying, 'O God, send us thy messenger: O Mohammed, come quickly for the salvation of the world!'[15]

So what are the facts of the case? Is the *Gospel of Barnabas* the most authentic gospel? First, we must take note that the *only extant manuscript* of the *Gospel of Barnabas* is in Italian, a language not spoken in Jesus' time. According to the experts who have studied it, the manuscript (preserved in a library in Vienna) can be no older than the sixteenth century. It therefore has nothing to do with the *Epistle of Barnabas*, which dates from the second century.

Secondly, the *authorship* of this gospel is highly doubtful. Unlike the four Gospels, the author says explicitly that he, Barnabas, wrote the gospel and his name replaces that of Thomas in the list of Jesus' twelve apostles. All the historical records we have, however, indicate that Barnabas was not one of Jesus' disciples. He was one of Paul's closest friends, and introduced him to the church leaders in Jerusalem shortly after Paul's conversion on the road to Damascus (Acts 9:26–28). Later, he was with Paul among the prominent church leaders in Antioch, Syria (Acts 11:25–30). He was Paul's fellow worker (with Mark) on their first missionary journey (Acts 13 – 14). Later, Paul and Barnabas had a disagreement and parted company, but since their disagreement had nothing to do with theological issues (Acts 15:36–41), it is highly unlikely that Barnabas would have written a gospel in sharp contradiction to Paul's teaching. The three men (Paul, Barnabas and Mark) remained on good terms with each other, as Paul's letter to the Colossians shows (Col. 4:10). Rather than being a disciple of Jesus, the author of the *Gospel of Barnabas* is more likely to have been an Italian convert to Islam.

Thirdly, and most importantly, we need to consider the *content* of the *Gospel of Barnabas*. It is to a large extent in line with Islamic teaching. Jesus, for example, denies that he is the Son of God and even sends his disciples to correct those who thought him to be God. He is not crucified, but Judas his betrayer, transformed by God into Jesus' likeness, is mistaken for him and is crucified in his place. Jesus' disciples come during the night, steal the body (of Judas) and claim that Jesus had risen from the dead. Jesus had been carried up by three angels into the third heaven before he could be arrested. Then he comes back for a short while, escorted by these same angels, to comfort Mary and his disciples. He is now in heaven and will return before the end of time to correct what Christians have taught about him. He will then die and be raised on the last day.

This picture of Jesus is so close to the traditional Islamic teaching that it leaves us in no doubt as to the author's apologetic intent. The author, however, makes some significant mistakes, sometimes making claims incompatible with Islamic teaching.[16] In his excessive zeal he has Jesus say that he is not the Messiah, but that he is the forerunner to the Messiah who will be descended from Abraham via his son Ishmael. This of course contradicts the Qur'an, which, as we have seen, describes Jesus as *al-Masiḥ* several times (3:45; 4:157, 171–172; 5:17, 72, 75; 9:30–31). According to the *Gospel of Barnabas*, Mary gave birth to Jesus without pain, which is again contrary to the Qur'an (19:23). In line with the canonical Gospels to some extent, the portrait of Jesus is not Islamic in many respects. The miracle of Jesus' turning water into wine at a wedding where many people had already drunk more than enough would shock many Muslim readers. Moreover, the author does not seem to know much about the geography of Palestine, as he places the town of Nazareth on the shores of the Sea of Galilee (even though it is in fact more than ten miles away).

In short, since distance, time and language separate the writer from Jesus, his apocryphal writing can hardly give us an accurate account of Jesus' life and message.[17]

Notes

[1] See chapter 2, n. 1.

[2] Other passages quoted less frequently include Ps. 45:3–5. This text describes God's messenger as a political and military leader, a role fully part of Muhammad's mission but not of Jesus' mission. The Christian response is that Jesus is, as we have seen, God's appointed king, and everyone will submit to him when he comes again in glory. Another verse Muslims point to is Song 5:16, where the Hebrew word for 'lovely' is *maḥᵃmuddîm*.

[3] The Arabic word for 'illiterates' is *ummiyyun*. In chapter 18 we noted that this word could be translated either 'the Nations' (from *umma*, 'nation') or 'the illiterates' (from *ummiyya*, 'illiteracy'). As this hadith

refs to Is. 42:1–9, which speaks in vv. 1 and 6 of 'the nations' or 'the Gentiles' (Heb. *gôyîm*), the first option is to preferred.

4 Bukhari, *buyu'* 50:III, p. 189, no. 335 [1981]; *tafsir* 48:3:VI, p. 345, no. 362 [4461].

5 J. Badawi, *Muhammad in the Bible*, pp. 25–47. See also A. Deedat, *What the Bible Says about Muhammad*, pp. 5–15.

6 C. Wright, *Deuteronomy*, pp. 217–218.

7 M. Bucaille, *The Bible, the Qur'an and the Science: The Holy Scriptures Examined in the Light of Modern Knowledge.* For a response to this book from a Christian perspective see W. Campbell, *The Qur'an and the Bible in the Light of History and Science.*

8 Bucaille, *Bible, Qur'an*, p. 105.

9 Ibid., p. 106.

10 See, e.g., 'A. Yusuf 'Ali's note 5438 on sura 61:6. He explains that '"*Aḥmad*" or "*Muḥammad*", the Praised One, is almost a translation of the Greek word *Periclytos*. In the present Gospel of John, 14:16, 15:26, and 16:7, the word 'Comforter' in the English version is for the Greek word *'Paracletos'*, which means 'Advocate', 'one called to the help of another, a kind friend', rather than 'Comforter'. Our doctors contend that Paracletos is a corrupt reading for Periclytos, and that in their original saying of Jesus there was a prophecy of our holy Prophet *Aḥmad* by name. Even if we read Paraclete, it would apply to the holy Prophet, who is 'a Mercy for all creatures' (21:107) and 'most kind and merciful to the Believers' (9:128)' (*The Holy Qur'an: Translation and Commentary*).

11 M. 'Ata ur-Rahim, *Jesus, a Prophet of Islam.*

12 Ibid., p. 39.

13 Ch. 17, p. 18; ch. 36, p. 46; ch. 43, p. 56; ch. 72, p. 91; ch. 97, p. 123; ch. 112, p. 142; ch. 163, p. 211; ch. 212, p. 260; ch. 220, p. 271. These references are based on the *Gospel of Barnabas*, tr. L. and L. Ragg.

14 Ibid., ch. 82, p. 104; cf. ch. 42, p. 54; ch. 96, p. 122; ch. 112, p. 142.

15 *Gospel of Barnabas*, ch. 97, pp. 123–124; cf. ch. 163, p. 212; ch. 220, p. 271.

16 Some may ask, 'If the *Gospel of Barnabas* was written by a Muslim, why does it contradict the Qur'an?' It was possibly written with the eager enthusiasm of a recent convert who had not yet fully grasped all the teachings of the Qur'an, partly because he did not know Arabic.

17 A thorough study of this writing is found in D. Sox, *The Gospel of Barnabas.* For a good introduction see N. Anderson's *Islam in the Modern World: A Christian Perspective*, pp. 223–234; J. Slomp, 'The Gospel in Dispute'.

21

Is Muhammad God's Prophet?

When Jesus began his mission, many Jews were eagerly awaiting the coming of the Messiah. Some people had already come falsely claiming to be the Messiah, but none of them enjoyed much success (Acts 5:36–37). It is not surprising, therefore, that Jesus warned his disciples that more false prophets would come after him claiming to be messengers sent from God (Matt. 24:5). He even predicted that some would enjoy a great deal of success, but that in the end their deeds would testify against them: 'Watch out for false prophets. They come to you in sheep's clothing, but inwardly they are ferocious wolves. By their fruit you will recognize them' (Matt. 7:15–16). These predictions soon proved astonishingly accurate, coming true within the lifetime of the apostles. Men who were well informed about the Christian faith, and who had even been members of the churches founded by Jesus' apostles, began spreading doctrines alien to the Gospel. As a result, the apostles had to urge the early Christians to resist such teachings firmly and to expose them as heretical (1 John 2:18–23; 4:1–6). The Christians were also faced with spiritual phenomena for which they were not prepared. The apostles told them to examine things carefully, to hold on to what was good and to avoid every kind of evil (1 Thess. 5:19–22).

But what about Islam, which appeared some six centuries after Christianity in an area where Christianity was scarcely present and where it was poorly represented? The teaching of the Bible is still relevant when assessing the position of anyone who claims to be a prophet. We need to take another look at Muhammad and his mission, and as we do so we must ask: what does the Bible say about the role of a prophet's miracles?

What does the Bible say about the content of the prophet's message? And what does it say about the meaning of victory and success?

The role of miracles

When God sent prophets to Israel, some were accompanied by signs authenticating their mission. God accredited Jesus in this way, yet many refused to believe in him (Matt. 11:20–24). Jesus confronted those who denied that God had sent him and pointed them to the fact of his miracles:

> The Jews gathered around him, saying, 'How long will you keep us in suspense? If you are the Christ [Messiah], tell us plainly.'
>
> Jesus answered, 'I did tell you, but you do not believe. The miracles I do in my Father's name speak for me, but you do not believe because you are not my sheep … Do not believe me unless I do what my Father does. But if I do it, even though you do not believe me, believe the miracles, that you may know and understand that the Father is in me, and I in the Father.' (John 10:24–26, 37–38)

Jesus' decisive miracle, which he gave to those who continued to reject his apostleship, was that of his resurrection. Long before his death he spoke about it, saying that he would die and be raised to life on the third day (Matt. 12:38–40). There is certainly no greater miracle than this: it is not just unprecedented, but unique. No-one can come back to life of his or her own accord; hence God's raising of Jesus from the dead is a powerful demonstration of his identity as God's messenger. It confirms the truth of his teaching and of his claims.

Muhammad too is said to have worked miracles. But how do his miracles compare with those of Jesus? And is there compelling evidence for them?

Are Muhammad's miracles proven beyond doubt?

(1) *Muhammad's illiteracy.* As we saw in chapter 18, the 'miracle of the Qur'an', *i'jaz al-Qur'an*, is based to a large degree on the assumption that Muhammad was illiterate, according to a traditional interpretation of sura 7:157–158. We investigated the possible meanings of the word *ummi*, and concluded that in the Qur'anic context it could refer to

Muhammad as 'the Gentile Prophet' just as much as 'the illiterate Prophet'. Thus the illiteracy of Muhammad is a theory far from being proven. If Muhammad was not illiterate, the eloquence of the Qur'an becomes far less miraculous.

(2) *The literary quality of the Qur'an.* While the Qur'an may well represent a masterpiece in Arabic literature, I am not convinced that it is unique. It is comparable with other pieces in Arabic literature; for example, some outstanding poems from pre-Islamic Arabic literature known as *al-mu'allaqat.* The problem with analysing the Qur'an's literary quality, however, is that the discussion soon becomes rather subjective. Literary criteria are not universally acknowledged and our judgment is easily biased when faith issues are involved. Yet even if we concede that the literary style of the Qur'an is miraculous, we cannot base our conclusions on its language alone. It is far more important for us to consider its message; only then will we know for sure whether it is from God.

(3) *The content of the Qur'an.* Razi explained that the Qur'an is miraculous because in addition to its eloquence it reveals things that were unknown to an ordinary human being. But to what extent is this true? The information about former prophets and the prediction of events at the end of time was easily accessible through the Jews who lived in Arabia. And as for the apparent prediction of the Byzantines' victory over the Persians (624) and that of the Muslims over the Meccans (630), their prophetic character is not guaranteed. The predictions are not very specific and the dating of the relevant texts remains uncertain. One may also observe that for predictions to be proven as genuine prophecies, without any possible doubt, they need to be fulfilled a long time after they are uttered. Otherwise they might be regarded simply as the product of a person's understanding of how things would be in the near future. The prophecies about Jesus were fulfilled hundreds of years after they had been put into writing.

(4) *Muhammad's other miracles.* And what about Muhammad's other miracles? It is worth noting that with one exception these miracles are not mentioned in the Qur'an. The Hadith relates several miracles but the authenticity of these accounts cannot be established beyond reasonable doubt. Muslim scholars agree that many hadiths have been made up and attributed to the Prophet. The most famous of these miracles, the splitting of the moon, is referred to in the Qur'an (54:1–3). But should this text be interpreted literally, as Muslims have traditionally understood it? Some Muslims have given this passage a metaphorical interpretation.

Like the splitting of the heavens mentioned in the Qur'an (55:37; 69:16; 84:1), they take the splitting of the moon to be 'a sign of the Hour', that is, it is understood allegorically as referring to the end of time.[1]

(5) *Predictions in the Torah and the Gospel.* We have seen that another 'miracle' put forward by Ibn Taymiyya concerns Muhammad's being predicted in the Bible. The Qur'an states that Muhammad's coming was prophesied in the Torah and the Gospel (7:157), and that Muhammad was announced by Jesus himself (61:6). However, it does not refer to any specific biblical text. We have examined those texts most often quoted by Muslims: Jesus fulfilled the prophecy about the Prophet 'like Moses' (Deut. 18:18) and the one describing 'the Servant of the Lord' (Is. 42:1–9). As for the coming of the *Paraklētos*, the Comforter, Jesus' promise was fulfilled ten days after he ascended to heaven, when the Holy Spirit was sent to the disciples in Jerusalem (John 14:16, 26; 15:26; 16:12–13; Acts 1:8; 2:1–4).

Are miracles sufficient evidence of prophethood?

If someone performs miracles, are we to assume automatically that this person is a prophet sent from God? In other words, are miracles sufficient evidence of prophethood? The Torah asserts that the answer to this is no. And why? Because miracles can be performed by people who are not sent by God (see Exod. 7:11–12; Matt. 24:24). False prophets and false teachers, for instance, can often work miracles. We can be certain that God allows them to do so, not in order to plunge us into confusion, but possibly to test our motivation. He wants us to love him more than anything else, to serve him and to live in obedience to his commands:

> If a prophet, or one who foretells by dreams, appears among you and announces to you a miraculous sign or wonder, and *if the sign or wonder of which he has spoken takes place*, and he says, 'Let us follow other gods' (gods you have not known) 'and let us worship them', you must not listen to the words of that prophet or dreamer. The LORD your God is testing you to find out whether you love him with all your heart and with all your soul. It is the LORD your God you must follow, and him you must revere. Keep his commands and obey him; serve him and hold fast to him. (Deut. 13:1–4; my emphasis)

This solemn warning makes it clear that miracles are not sufficient on their own to establish the truthfulness of a prophet. It may be that they bear witness to the trustworthiness of a person, but this is not necessarily the case.

Jesus warned his disciples not to let themselves be deceived by miracles: 'False Christs [messiahs] and false prophets will appear and perform great signs and miracles to deceive even the elect – if that were possible' (Matt. 24:24). Miracles, then, are a possible evidence of prophethood, but they are not essential. John the Baptist, for example, described by Jesus as the greatest prophet, did not work any miracles (Matt. 11:11; John 10:41).

So if miracles are not conclusive, how can we know whether or not someone is God's messenger? The above text from Deuteronomy teaches that it is the *content of the message* that matters most of all. Does the message call for the worship of the one God? If it does, then who is this God? Is he the saving God who revealed himself to the people of Israel, 'who brought [them] out of Egypt and redeemed [them] from the land of slavery'? (Deut. 13:5). It is crucial that the prophet's message be examined so as to determine whether God has really sent this person.

Even if Muhammad is shown to have performed miracles, they are not in themselves sufficient evidence of his prophethood. The decisive test will be to examine the *message* he brought. His miracles will enforce his credentials as Prophet *if and only if* his message is shown to be a message from God.

The content of the message

The Qur'an often describes the gospel entrusted to Jesus as confirming the Torah given to Moses (5:46). Similarly, the Qur'an claims that it confirms both the Torah and the Gospel (2:91; 3:3, 81; 4:47). These statements are based on the assumption that God, being one God, would give his prophets basically the same message to bring to their people. In other words, we would expect the messages brought by successive prophets to be consistent with one another.

The unity of God's word explains why the Qur'an calls upon Jews and the Christians to confirm that Muhammad's message was indeed of divine origin (cf. 10:94; 16:43; 21:7). The coherence of God's word in the Qur'an is seen as evidence that God is the author: 'Will they not consider the Qur'an? Had it not been from God they would surely have found in it much contradiction' (4:82). Razi explains that this verse is a response to those who challenged Muhammad's prophethood. He reminds us again of the evidence: the Qur'an is eloquent; it discloses things that were un-known to Muhammad; and there are no discrepancies in it, *salamatuhu mina l-ikhtilaf*.[2] Surely the *internal* coherence of the Qur'anic message is important, but it is not sufficient. Its *external* coherence needs to be established as well; we need to be sure that it is consistent with the Scriptures already revealed, namely the Torah and the Gospel.

Right from the start of his mission, Jesus taught that his message was in line with God's previous revelation: 'Do not think that I have come to abolish the Law or the Prophets; I have not come to abolish them but to fulfil them' (Matt. 5:17). Jesus fulfilled the teaching of the Torah in many ways: he brought its teaching to completion, he brought out the spiritual meaning of the law and showed its full implications, and he did what had been foretold about him. In doing so, like no other prophet, he exposed the sinfulness of human beings and revealed the full extent of God's love for us. And above all, through his death and resurrection, he revealed God as the Saviour of the world (1 John 4:14).

Is Muhammad's message consistent with earlier revelation?

In order to assess Muhammad's prophethood, we must ask how the teaching of the Qur'an compares with the message of the prophets before him. There is no doubt that 'the Seal of the Prophets' (33:40) saw his mission as following directly in the footsteps of his predecessors. Islam was the triumph of monotheism over Arab polytheism and no-one can dispute that the oneness of God is at the very heart of Islamic doctrine. The Qur'an presents a coherent body of beliefs about God, creation, rev-elation, humankind, the general resurrection and the Day of Judgment, to mention only the major themes. Its internal consistency is evident, but its external consistency – its conformity with God's earlier revelations – is simply not there.

Islam is clearly a monotheistic religion, and God's attributes in Islam broadly correspond to what we find in the Bible. However, there is one central attribute missing from the Qur'an: it fails to point to God as the *Saviour*, the God who achieved our salvation through the death and resurrection of Jesus Christ. Because the Qur'an does not know God in this way, it fails to recognize the very nature of Jesus' mission. The way Ibn Taymiyya describes Jesus reflects what the Qur'an says about him and is typical of how Muslims understand his teaching: 'The generality of what distinguished the Gospel from the Torah consisted in noble traits of character, praiseworthy asceticism, and permission of some of what had been forbidden; all of this, however, was in the Qur'an, and in it more perfectly.'³ This is an extremely poor description of the Christian message. The Gospel is not merely a call for 'noble traits of character'; first and foremost it is about God's saving work in Jesus Christ. It is not just a message calling us to lead better lives; it is a call for us to recognize our sinfulness before God and to trust in Christ as our only hope of forgiveness.

The Gospel speaks of how God fulfilled the promise he made to Adam, Abraham, Moses, David and to many other prophets, that he himself would one day save humankind from sin, death and eternal condemnation. He foreshadowed the fulfilment of this promise when he 'brought [his people] out of Egypt and redeemed [them] from the land of slavery' (Deut. 13:5). The Qur'an tells the story of the Israelites' liberation under the leadership of Moses and despite the fierce opposition of Pharaoh (10:75–93), but fails to discern the prophetic dimension of this event and its fulfilment in Jesus Christ. This great omission in Muhammad's message makes it impossible for Christians to see Islam as confirming the Gospel. The Qur'an appears to be missing what is at the very heart of the Gospel: the good news of God's saving love in Jesus Christ.

Is the Gospel teaching inferior to Islamic law?

In chapter 19 we followed Ibn Taymiyya as he argued for the superiority of Islamic law. He was convinced that Christian doctrine fails to reach such heights of perfection. We noted, however, that in several areas he had not fully understood the teaching of the Gospel. So let us take another look at the principles for Christian living.

Just as God's saving love is at the heart of the Gospel message, so too is God's love the basis for Christian living. Love is the driving force in Christian ethics. Loving one's neighbour is not an option as it is in Islamic law; it is a command. Every human being is to be regarded as a neighbour regardless of racial, religious, social or cultural background (Luke 10:25–37). And this command also means loving our enemies (Matt. 5:43–48). Just as divine love is expressed in forgiving those who least deserve it, so God requires that we too express our love in forgiving others (Matt. 18:21–35).

Recall that Ibn Taymiyya described Christianity as being too idealistic. But is Jesus' teaching really as idealistic as Muslims think it is? It is certainly perfect, but it is not unattainable. Humans are indeed weak and sinful, but God is powerful and is able and willing to empower us to live up to his highest standards. This explains why the moral standards in Christianity are different from Islam, and indeed significantly higher.

It is true that we do not find in the Gospel a detailed moral code similar to the Islamic one. This is because Christian ethics are based not on laws and regulations, as in Islam, but on principles and values. Their implementation varies according to who people are and according to their historical and social context. For any legal system to be just it must take on board the changing circumstances of the people for whom it is designed; it must be adaptable and flexible so as to suit every nation on earth.

'God is love' (1 John 4:8, 16). As well as demonstrating his love in Jesus Christ, God has revealed his love in his law. He entrusted the law to Moses in order to establish justice in Israel and more specifically to care for the weak, such as the widow, the fatherless and the non-Israelite living in the land (Deut 10:18–19). These principles have lost none of their relevance for today.

The fact that there is no legal system in the Gospel does not imply that Christianity is not concerned with life on earth. As Christian Aid, the Christian charity, puts it, 'We believe in life *before* death.' Indeed, many Christians worldwide are actively involved in relief and development, in education, in caring for the marginalized in society, and in calling for an end to abuses in human rights.

Modern societies are so different from the Israelite society of Bible times that the literal application of the Mosaic law is impossible, indeed undesirable. Jewish scholars agree that the Torah must be correctly interpreted so as to be relevant for modern Jews. This is obvious in Western societies, which are becoming increasingly secular. Muslim societies face the same challenge, though to a lesser degree. In no Muslim country is Islamic law applied entirely and literally. Thankfully not many Muslims advocate the implementation of Islamic penal law in all its rigour.

The teaching of the Torah and the Gospel is helpful in terms of providing guidelines for civil and penal law. God has also created all humans with a moral law written on our hearts (Rom. 2:14–15). This means that all, believers and non-believers, are to take part in the administration of justice; and all of us are accountable to God as to how we fulfil this responsibility.

In short, Christians have been entrusted with the gospel, a message of good news about God's love and forgiveness. This message cannot be

260 Faith to faith

easily proclaimed if, at the same time, justice is being administered in
God's name. How is it possible to talk about God's love and forgiveness
for the sinner and to prosecute this same person? For the gospel to be free
from any restriction and confusion it has to be dissociated from the
judiciary and the State. Christians do, however, recognize the legitimacy
of the civil authorities and their role (Rom. 13:1–7). These authorities
have the right and the obligation to govern their people and to establish
justice among them. Their task includes punishing evildoers, and in
doing so reflecting God's justice to some degree. Christians therefore
have a responsibility both to bear witness to the gospel and to contribute
to implementing justice in society.

How then does the Qur'anic message brought by Muhammad compare
with the gospel of Jesus Christ? Since the Qur'an fails to point to God as
Saviour and fails to see God's love as the guiding principle for living in
this world, Muslims must ask themselves to what extent they see their
religion to be perfect. If sin is as serious as the Bible says it is, then is it
enough to have a law to guide us? Do we not need a Saviour to rescue
us?

The meaning of success

Razi and Ibn Taymiyya argued that Islam's military and political success
in Muhammad's lifetime and in the years following his death is evidence
for his claim to prophethood. No-one would question this success,
although the political power of the Islamic nations has been on the decline
over the last few centuries. The present State of Israel, founded in 1948,
and its repeated military victories over its Arab neighbours, represents another serious challenge to Islamic supremacy. Nevertheless, Islam remains
one of the world's greatest religions and the Muslim community represents
one-fifth of the world's population. Islam is an established religion, yet
the fact that *only one person in five* is Muslim shows that its success is not
to be overestimated. The same could be said of any of the other major
world religions (Buddhism, Christianity and Hinduism). That none of
these religions is dominant serves as a helpful deterrent against religious
triumphalism and is a much-needed warning that truth is not to be
gauged merely in numerical terms.

In the days of the early church, there was a respected Jewish teacher of
the law named Gamaliel, who taught the apostle Paul before Paul became
a Christian (Acts 22:3). For Gamaliel, historical success was the real test
for any movement that claimed to be from God. When some Christian

leaders were facing fierce opposition from the Jewish authorities, Gamaliel convinced his peers in the Jewish high council not to condemn them to death. Instead, he advised them to wait and see whether or not the Christians would succeed:

> Men of Israel, consider carefully what you intend to do to these men. Some time ago Theudas appeared, claiming to be somebody, and about four hundred men rallied to him. He was killed, all his followers were dispersed, and it all came to nothing. After him, Judas the Galilean appeared in the days of the census and led a band of people in revolt. He too was killed, and all his followers were scattered. Therefore, in the present case I advise you: Leave these men alone! Let them go! For if their purpose or activity is of human origin, it will fail. But if it is from God, you will not be able to stop these men; you will only find yourselves fighting against God. (Acts 5:35–39)

But was Gamaliel right? On the face of it, he appears to have given a wise answer, yet when we look at the experience of history his thesis is shown to rest on shaky ground. Time and again, we find people who have stood for the truth to be in a minority, viewed as failures by the world. We also find leaders who have won incredible victories and commanded immense followings, yet who have advanced cruel and inhumane policies far from God's truth.

Since God is all-powerful, we can be sure that his purpose cannot be defeated by any of his creatures; it is bound to succeed. Yet what success means for God does not necessarily coincide with our expectations. As Gamaliel was a teacher of the Torah he should have known this. The Bible tells us that divine success is not to be judged by human standards.

Hundreds of years before the coming of Jesus, the people of Israel were living under a theocratic regime. The king was God's representative on earth and his army was the Lord's army. In this context Israel's victories over its enemies were seen as God's victories. Yet even in this context, military achievements were critically assessed. Take King David, for example. He conquered Jerusalem and made it the capital of his kingdom (2 Sam. 5:6–12), but when he wanted to build a temple for God he was not allowed to do so. The reason God gave him is highly significant: 'You are not to build a house for my Name, because you are a warrior and have shed blood' (1 Chr. 28:3; cf. 1 Chr. 22:8). The military hero of Israel was not fit to carry out one of God's greatest peacetime achievements!

Even in Israel God's faithful servants often faced hardship, humiliation and persecution. Yet these events are not interpreted in terms of failure and divine disapproval. On the contrary, the servants are commended for the endurance they showed through their suffering in a hostile world described as 'not worthy of them':

> They were stoned; they were sawn in two; they were put to death by the sword. They went about in sheepskins and goatskins, destitute, persecuted and ill-treated – the world was not worthy of them. They wandered in deserts and mountains, and in caves and holes in the ground. These were all commended for their faith, yet none of them received what had been promised. God had planned something better for us so that only together with us would they be made perfect. (Heb. 11:37–40)

Jesus began his public ministry at a time when Palestine was part of the Roman Empire. Among the religious parties struggling to win the Jews' allegiance were the Zealots, who were in favour of armed rebellion against the Romans. Many Jews were waiting for the promised Messiah to set Israel free from the Roman occupation, and some of Jesus' disciples shared in this messianic hope (Matt. 10:4). They were convinced that God's Prophet would restore Israel to its lost glory. However, not only was Israel's independence not on Jesus' agenda; he ended up on a cross – executed like a criminal. Many saw this as a complete failure. With the death of Jesus all nationalistic expectations, which some Jews had tried to keep alive, definitively collapsed. Jesus' disciples were utterly disappointed. They were confused and would have been plunged into deep despair had it not been for the empty tomb. Here again is how two of them described their feelings to the risen Christ before they realized whom they were talking with:

> He was a prophet, powerful in word and deed before God and all the people. The chief priests and our rulers handed him over to be sentenced to death, and they crucified him; *but we had hoped that he was the one who was going to redeem Israel.* And what is more, it is the third day since all this took place. In addition, some of our women amazed us. They went to the tomb early this morning but didn't find his body. They came and told us that they had seen a vision of angels, who said he was alive. Then some of our companions went to the tomb and found it just as the women had said,

but him they did not see. (Luke 24:19–24; my emphasis)

The fact that Jesus did not fulfil the political expectations of his people is extremely significant. His mission was far more important than liberating Israel from the oppression of the Romans; it was to achieve a far greater victory: he came to defeat death, the true enemy of humankind. Jesus' resurrection from the dead powerfully demonstrated that he did triumph over death. He won this decisive victory so that God might freely hold out to us the gift of eternal life.

While Jesus' victory was conclusive, he did not compel people to believe in him. He could have appeared to his enemies, if not to humiliate them, then at least to show them that God had vindicated him. But instead he chose not to use his victory against anyone or to force anyone to believe in him. He appeared to his disciples so as to strengthen their faith and to reinforce what they knew about him. He then commissioned them to take the gospel everywhere and to make disciples of all nations (Matt. 28:16–20). He never promised that they would rule the world with the gospel; if anything, he promised that they would share in his sufferings: 'No servant is greater than his master. If they persecuted me, they will persecute you also' (John 15:20; cf. Matt. 16:24).

Jesus returned to heaven forty days after his resurrection. His ascension marked his enthronement at the right hand of God. His kingship is universal: it is over all the kingdoms of the world. But being a spiritual kingship, it cannot and should not be imposed on anyone. Therefore, it must not be associated with any political power. The gospel is about God's offer of eternal life to everyone. A genuine response to this offer has to be personal and free from any pressure. And this offer will continue to be made until Jesus comes back to earth to establish God's kingdom:

> Look, he is coming with the clouds,
>   and every eye will see him,
> even those who pierced him;
> and all the peoples of the earth will mourn because of him.
>   So shall it be! Amen.

'I am the Alpha and the Omega,' says the Lord God, 'who is, and who was, and who is to come, the Almighty.' (Rev. 1:7–8)

Jesus and Muhammad have both been successful in their missions, but in two very different ways. Muhammad overcame his enemies with the word and the sword. He died having been acclaimed by his people as God's victorious Prophet. His victory brought many peoples to worship the Creator God as the one and only God. Jesus, on the other hand, never fought his enemies. They thought they had defeated him until God raised him from the dead. His supreme victory over death reveals God as the Saviour. Whoever believes in Jesus, recognizing his victory over sin and death, has eternal life: 'if you confess with your mouth, "Jesus is Lord," and believe in your heart that God raised him from the dead, you will be saved' (Rom. 10:9).

So is Muhammad God's Prophet?

Having examined Muhammad's mission from a Christian perspective, we are left with no option but to challenge his credentials as a prophet. If his miracles were proven they would still not represent sufficient evidence. We have seen that this evidence can be provided only if his message is consistent with earlier prophetic messages; and although Islamic law is internally coherent, its conformity with God's previous revelations is only partial. The success of Islam, especially in the first centuries following its rise, does not necessarily point to its divine origin, especially when compared with God's decisive victory through the resurrection of Jesus Christ.

Thus Christians can subscribe wholeheartedly to the first part of the Islamic creed, *ashhadu an la ilaha illa-llah* ('I bear witness that there is no god but God'), but cannot, without dismissing their own faith, endorse the second part, *wa anna muhammadan rasulu-llah* ('and that Muhammad is the Apostle of God').

This position is the logical outcome of a comparative study of Christianity and Islam. It should come as no surprise to well-informed Muslims who know that, in the final analysis, the claims of Christianity and Islam are incompatible. This incompatibility is behind the Islamic assumption that, in one way or another, the Bible has been corrupted. With very few exceptions Christians question neither the historical authenticity of the Qur'an nor the way it has been interpreted by Muslim scholars. They conclude from the discrepancies between the teaching of the Bible and the Qur'an, particularly on what they say about Jesus Christ, that the latter is simply not God's Word.[4]

Notes

[1] Nazzam, a reputed Mu'tazili theologian (c. 231/846), is one of those who suggested an allegorical interpretation of the Qur'anic text about the splitting of the moon (see Shahrastani, *Kitab al-Milal wa l-nihal*, p. 215, n. 70); see also 'A. Yusuf 'Ali's footnote on this verse (n. 5128), which lists three different interpretations Muslims have given to the Qur'anic text: literal, allegorical and eschatological.

[2] Razi, V:10, p. 157.

[3] Ibn Taymiyya, *al-Jawab al-sahih liman baddala dina l-Masih*, p. 355.

[4] Christians have expressed contrasting views about Islam. Some are very negative (e.g. R. Morey, *Islam Unveiled: The True Desert Storm*; G. J. O. Moshay, *Who Is This Allah?*); others are quite positive (D. Kerr, '"He walked in the Path of the Prophets": Toward Christian Theological Recognition of the Prophethood of Muhammad'). Ibn Taymiyya criticizes those Christians who agree that Muhammad was a prophet, but a prophet sent only to the Arabs. If they admit that Muhammad is a prophet, he argues, they should believe in the whole message of the Qur'an. This includes accepting that Muhammad was sent to all peoples and that the religion of the Christians is false (*al-Jawab*, pp. 146–152). Although this argument is quite sound, some well-meaning Christian Islamicists remain unconvinced.

22

Is there revelation in Islam?

Some Christians have a very negative approach to Islam. I myself have often been embarrassed by some of their hasty judgments on Muhammad, whom they consider to be an impostor and even an antichrist. While I cannot accept that the Qur'an is God's Word or that Muhammad is God's Prophet, I nevertheless try to approach Islam as positively as I can. I have no interest in attacking Muslims or in offending them where I can avoid it. On the contrary, many of my friends are Muslims. Certainly I do not want to pretend there is no difference between Islam and Christianity, but neither do I want to dismiss all of Islam carelessly.

So how should Christians respond? Is there truth in Islam we can point to? And has God, in one way or another, shown something of himself to Muslims?

General and special revelation

The Bible teaches that God reveals himself to humankind in many and various ways. Theologians speak of two categories of revelation: (1) *general revelation,* God's revelation that can be known by all people in all the world, whether or not they have the Scriptures; and (2) *special revelation,* God's revelation in the Scriptures and through his Son, Jesus Christ; the specific revelation that point to God as the Saviour and speaks of what he has said and done.

General revelation can be found in at least three areas. First, as human beings we have been created in God's image (Gen. 1:27–28). Although disfigured by sin, this image is not completely annihilated. People still possess a religious sense that enables them to glimpse aspects of the truth without the help of revealed Scripture. God created humankind so that they 'would seek him and perhaps reach out for him and find him, though he is not far from each one of us' (Acts 17:27).

In addition to these partial insights into the truth, which people can find for themselves, God bears witness to himself in the created world:

> The heavens declare the glory of God;
>> the skies proclaim the work of his hands.
> Day after day they pour forth speech;
>> night after night they display knowledge.
> There is no speech or language
>> where their voice is not heard.
> Their voice goes out into all the earth,
>> their words to the ends of the world. (Ps. 19:1–4; cf. Ps. 8:3)

Creation's testimony, though silent, displays some of God's attributes: his goodness, his eternity, his majesty, his power and his glory. Every human being is therefore given a natural knowledge of God independent of any particular revelation on God's part.

Three components of God's general revelation, then, are (1) the creation of human beings – in God's image; (2) the creation of the world – reflecting God's character; and (3) the universal blessings of God – given to all his creatures. General revelation is the basis on which we could reach a genuine knowledge of God if we listen carefully to its testimony. But in reality, sinful as we are, our inclination is to stifle the voice of our conscience and to distort the witness it bears to God. However sincere our religious quest may be, it does not prevent us from some form of idolatry, be it subtly or crudely expressed. So, relying on general revelation alone, our perception of God, however sublime, is consequently limited and indeed corrupted:

> The wrath of God is being revealed from heaven against all the godlessness and wickedness of men who suppress the truth by their wickedness, since what may be known about God is plain to them, because God has made it plain to them. For since the creation of the world God's invisible qualities – his eternal power and divine nature – have been clearly seen, being understood from what has been made, so that men are without excuse.
>
> For although they knew God, they neither glorified him as God

nor gave thanks to him, but their thinking became futile and their foolish hearts were darkened. Although they claimed to be wise, they became fools ... (Rom. 1:18–23)

The truths contained in all religions point to the reality of general revelation, but this does not mean that God approves of these religions as such. Because God's revelation in human religions is partial and often distorted, there is a need for a special revelation whose reliability is guaranteed by God himself.

The truth found in the Qur'an about God and his attributes can in part be accounted for in terms of general revelation. Arabs knew *Allah* as the supreme God and the creator of heaven and earth well before the rise of Islam: 'If you ask them [polytheistic Arabs] who created the heavens and the earth, they would surely say: God'. (31:25; cf. 39:38; 43:9). The very name of Muhammad's father, *'Abdullah*, 'servant of God', testifies to the fact that God was worshipped by Arabs prior to Islam. But what about other related Qur'anic themes such as creation, the prophets, Israel, and the final judgment? The Qur'anic teaching on these topics indicates that Islamic Scripture embraces, in its own way, aspects of both the biblical tradition and the religious tradition of the Arabs. The guiding principle behind this rational synthesis is a powerful monotheism. Thus the Qur'an is influenced by both general and special revelation, which means that Islam is neither a biblical religion nor a religion entirely independent of the biblical tradition.

In so far as they are both monotheistic religions, Christianity and Islam offer to Christians and Muslims a solid common ground on which both communities can meet. Providing that we show a genuine attitude of humility and respect, this meeting can help us to understand, challenge and enrich each other.

General and special grace

To say that the Prophet of Islam does not meet the biblical criteria for prophethood does not necessarily cast doubt on Muhammad's integrity. He was probably the most zealous Arab for God in his generation. His knowledge of the gospel was certainly partial, but we should beware about jumping to conclusions about his motives. I do not believe he was God's prophet, nor do I presume that he was an impostor (deliberately misleading his people for personal gain). It is possible that he was sincere in believing that God called him to be a prophet and in believing that he received the Qur'an from God. As the Qur'an often states, 'only God knows the secrets of the heart' (3:119), and 'he alone is fully aware of what is unknown' (5:116).

Just as I want to avoid making hasty judgments about Muhammad, so too I want to avoid judging individual Muslims. Not recognizing Islam as a God-given religion does not imply a value judgment on a Muslim's religious life. God loves and cares for all he has made; he is at work in the lives of all his human creatures regardless of their religious background. Many Christians do not live up to the teaching of the Gospel any better than Muslims follow the teaching of the Qur'an.

Just as we can speak of God's general and special *revelation*, so too we can speak of God's general and special *grace* – where *grace* refers to the blessings God gives, even though they are completely undeserved.

General grace (or *common grace*) refers to God's blessings given to all people. This aspect of God's grace is universal and experienced by the whole of the human race. He has an ongoing care for his creation, sustaining it, upholding it, and preserving it from chaos; and has given us an awareness of many of his moral standards. Without any discrimination, God lavishes material and spiritual blessings on his human creatures.

> Yet he [God] has not left himself without testimony: He has shown kindness by giving them rain from heaven and crops in their seasons; he provides them with plenty of food and fills your hearts with joy. (Acts 14:17)

> He causes his sun to rise on the evil and the good, and sends rain on the righteous and the unrighteous. (Matt. 5:45)

Special grace (*saving grace*) refers to God's saving work in the lives of his people, resulting in their believing in him as their Saviour, receiving forgiveness and the assurance of eternal life (Eph. 2:8–9).

The reality of God's general revelation and common grace on the one hand, and the consonance of Islamic monotheism with God's special revelation in the Bible on the other, mean that God-fearing Muslims worship the true God even if they do not know him in the fullness of his revelation in Jesus Christ. It also explains why many Muslims lead godly lives and display genuine piety in their daily living. They submit to God, as best as they can, by seeking to keep the moral standards of his law, individually as well as in their relationships with others.

In saying this, I am not saying that God-fearing and pious Muslims have enough of God's revelation. On the contrary, they still need to hear of Jesus Christ as much as anyone else; they still need to respond to the gospel and put their trust in Jesus as their Lord and Saviour.

Take Cornelius, for example (Acts 10:1 – 11:18). He was a Roman centurion in the days of the early church. He is described as 'devout and God-fearing; he gave generously to those in need and prayed to God regularly' (Acts 10:2). Yet he was neither a Jew nor a Christian. God sent an angel to him, not to tell him that all was fine in his life, but rather to get him to invite Peter to explain the gospel to him. Being a God-fearing person was not enough: he needed to respond to Jesus. On hearing the message, Cornelius and his family were the first Gentiles to trust in Christ.

A challenge for Christians

A Christian perspective on Islam is necessarily critical: it involves assessing Islamic doctrine in the light of biblical teaching. This teaching, which is all about God's supreme revelation in Jesus Christ, challenges any revelation that claims to be divine. It also challenges those who claim to be God's people: Jews as well as Christians. Jesus himself did not hesitate to criticize the Jewish leaders (Matt. 23:1–36). He declared that on the Day of Judgment people who have heard but refuse to believe in him will be more severely judged than those who have not heard his message (Matt. 10:15; 11:20–24; 12:41–42). He expressed unreserved admiration for a Roman officer and a Gentile woman, in whom he saw more evidence of faith than he had found in any of the people of Israel (Matt. 8:5–10; 15:21–28).

Jesus' dealing with the Samaritans is even more significant since they were discriminated against by the Jewish people on account of their religious beliefs and racial background. On one occasion Jesus healed ten lepers, but only one, a Samaritan, took the trouble to return to thank him. Jesus did not let this 'coincidence' go unnoticed, but used it to commend the exemplary attitude of the Samaritan: 'Were not all ten cleansed? Where are the other nine? Was no-one found to return and give praise to God except this foreigner?' (Luke 17:17–18).

Jesus' determination to overturn his people's prejudice against the Samaritans appears even more clearly in the famous parable of the good Samaritan, where the hero of the story is not the priest or the teacher of the law but the Samaritan (Luke 10:25–37). It is hard for us to realize how provoking this parable must have been. What could be more outrageous for a teacher of the law than to have someone say, 'Go and do as that Samaritan did if you want to know how to love your neighbour.' To be asked to learn from a Samaritan how to put God's principles into practice was certainly the last thing the teacher of the law would have wanted to hear.

Christians need to be careful not to dismiss any truth in Islam or any evidence of God's grace at work in the life of Muslims. Christians must be prepared to learn from Muslims and, if need be, to have their views about them challenged.[1]

Jesus' call for Christians to be vigilant is twofold: they need to look critically into any non-Christian religion just as much as they need to examine themselves to see if their own lives are in tune with their faith. Believing the right things without the evidence of a changed life is a sure indication that such faith is not genuine at all. If people have faith in Jesus Christ, if they have been saved and forgiven by God, then a changed life must be the visible proof (Jas. 2:14–24). At the final judgment Jesus will show no favouritism to his disciples. They will be judged not according to their words but according to the reality of their Christian living. If they fail this test they will be condemned as surely as those who have made false claims to prophethood:

'Watch out for false prophets. They come to you in sheep's clothing, but inwardly they are ferocious wolves. By their fruit you will recognise them. Do people pick grapes from thornbushes, or figs from thistles? Likewise every good tree bears good fruit, but a bad tree bears bad fruit. A good tree cannot bear bad fruit, and a bad tree cannot bear good fruit. Every tree that does not bear good fruit is cut down and thrown into the fire. Thus, by their fruit you will recognise them.

'Not everyone who says to me, "Lord, Lord," will enter the kingdom of heaven, but only he who does the will of my Father who is in heaven. Many will say to me on that day, "Lord, Lord, did we not prophesy in your name, and in your name drive out demons and perform many miracles?" Then I will tell them plainly, "I never knew you. Away from me, you evildoers!"' (Matt. 7:15–23)

In the final analysis, the touchstone upon which the truthfulness of any faith is to be tested is its teaching about Jesus Christ: who he is and why he came (cf. 1 John 2:22–23; 4:2–3). We must be under no illusion:

our faith is worthless unless our whole life comes under the lordship of Jesus Christ.

Note

[1] Christians must be prepared to be challenged about their beliefs and practices, some of which may be out of line with Jesus' teaching. They should listen carefully to Qur'anic criticisms, which in some cases may be justified (cf. 9:31, 34). Muslims may have a point in some of their arguments. For example, was not Ibn Taymiyya right when he said that 'No prophet was ever found to command the invocation of angels for intercession, nor the calling on dead prophets and holy men to seek their intercession' (*al-Jawab al-ṣaḥiḥ liman baddala dina l-Masiḥ*, p. 355)? Ibn Taymiyya spoke out against this doctrine before many of the Protestant Reformers did!

Part 5
Contemporary issues

23
Israel or Palestine?

As a Christian Arab, two issues have been on my agenda ever since I came to Europe: first, the Arab–Israeli conflict and the rights of the Palestinian people, and secondly, the situation faced by immigrants in Europe. I am convinced that both impact on Christian–Muslim relations.

The majority of immigrants living in Europe are Muslims, yet for centuries Europe has been closely associated with Christianity. So what is the place of Muslims in a non-Muslim country? And how should they be treated? In the next chapter we shall look at how the Torah and the Gospel call us to respond.

In this chapter we shall focus on the issue of Israel or Palestine. Most European countries gave unconditional support to the establishment of the State of Israel in 1948. Many Christians too, and especially evangelicals, continue to give it their backing, claiming that it fulfils biblical prophecies.[1] But is such an endorsement necessarily the right attitude? Is it consistent with God's purpose for the land? And is it compatible with God's justice? Christians cannot escape the questions presented to them by the conflict in the Middle East.[2]

The promise of a land

The theological debate about the land of Israel begins with the promise God made to Abraham:

> Leave your country, your people and your father's household and go to the land I will show you.

> I will make you into a great nation
>   and I will bless you;
> I will make your name great,
>   and you will be a blessing.
> I will bless those who bless you,
>   and whoever curses you I will curse;
> and all peoples on earth
>   will be blessed through you. (Gen. 12:1–3)

This promise is seen by many Zionist Jews and a number of evangelical Christians as the biblical foundation for the eternal right of the Jewish people to have a nation in Palestine. But this is not the only way to understand this promise and its fulfilment. We must remember that the Gospel teaches that Jesus of Nazareth is the Messiah of Israel and that in him God's promises to his people are fulfilled.

First of all, the gift of the land of Canaan to the people of Israel was *temporary*. The coming of the Messiah made obsolete the very concept of a Promised Land. Speaking about the radical changes that the coming of the Messiah would bring about, the prophet Ezekiel announced that the land of Israel would no longer be the exclusive property of the Jews:

> 'You are to distribute this land among yourselves according to the tribes of Israel. You are to allot it as an inheritance for yourselves and for the aliens [non-Israelites] who have settled among you and who have children. You are to consider them as native-born Israelites; along with you they are to be allotted an inheritance among the tribes of Israel. In whatever tribe the alien [non-Israelite] settles, there you are to give him his inheritance,' declares the Sovereign LORD. (Ezek. 47:21–23)

This command to share the land with non-Jews on an equal footing with the Jews is highly significant: it symbolizes that the coming of the Messiah marks *a new order*. God's promises to Israel would be enjoyed by all peoples, for there would be no more discrimination between Israel and the nations.

If this prophecy is taken literally, it demonstrates the irony of the present situation: the State of Israel was established mainly by European Jews at the expense of native Palestinians, many of whom have been dispossessed of their own lands and made refugees in neighbouring countries!

Secondly, the land of Israel stood for the *kingdom of God*. The gospel is all about the kingdom of God Jesus came to establish (Matt. 4:17; Luke 17:21). The only time Jesus alluded to the Promised Land was in the Beatitudes: 'Blessed are the meek, for they will inherit the earth [or the land]' (Matt. 5:5).

Jesus' disciples were convinced that all the promises made to Israel, including the restoration of David's kingdom, had been fulfilled by Jesus, 'the Son of David' (see Acts 15:12–18). After all, Abraham himself, to whom the promise was initially made, 'was looking forward to the city with foundations, whose architect and builder is God' (Heb. 11:10). This city is Jerusalem, not the city in the land of Canaan, but 'the heavenly Jerusalem' (Heb. 12:22; Gal. 4:26). If my interpretation amounts to spiritualizing God's promise to Israel, it has the merit of being based on how Jesus and his disciples interpreted it.

Finally, God's promise to Abraham was *conditional*. In other words, it stipulated that the Israelites would inhabit the land only as long as they obeyed God's laws. Otherwise God would punish them, just as he did with the Canaanites, the former inhabitants of the land (Gen. 15:16; Deut. 18:12). Moses clearly warned his people and spoke of the judgment they would face if they turned away in disobedience: 'Just as it pleased the LORD to make you prosper and increase in number, so it will please him to ruin and destroy you. You will be uprooted from the land you are entering to possess. Then the LORD will scatter you among all nations, from one end of the earth to the other' (Deut. 28:63–64). This warning became reality twice in the history of Israel. In 586 BC Nebuchadnezzar, king of Babylon, invaded Jerusalem, destroyed its temple and deported its people. In AD 70 the Roman army besieged Jerusalem and expelled its inhabitants.

Jesus knew what was going to happen to Jerusalem and wept over the future judgment of the city. Nevertheless, he presented this tragic event as the direct consequence of the people's rejection of him.

> As he approached Jerusalem and saw the city, he wept over it and said, 'If you, even you, had only known on this day what would bring you peace – but now it is hidden from your eyes. The days will come upon you when your enemies will build an embankment against you and encircle you and hem you in on every side. They will dash you to the ground, you and the children within your walls. They will not leave one stone on another, *because you did not recognize the time of God's coming to you.*' (Luke 19:41–44; my emphasis)

Unlike the prophets who foretold that the Israelites would return from Babylon, Jesus did not promise his people that their nation would be restored (Luke 21:20–24).

The present-day State of Israel, therefore, has no theological significance. If anything, Israel is no better or worse than any other nation. Its recent history demonstrates that it is far from God's moral standards.

The ongoing conflict

The establishment of Israel on Arab land was an immense injustice. It was bound to create human tragedy for the historical inhabitants of the land. Indeed, it deprived the Palestinian people of their homeland and forced many into refugee camps. This sense of injustice was deeply felt by Arab peoples throughout the world. Many Palestinians were plunged into despair, especially after Arab governments failed to achieve what they had promised them: to bring them back to their homeland. Palestinian refugees decided to take their destiny into their own hands: the Palestine Liberation Organization (PLO) was born. Although some resorted to terrorism when the world seemed indifferent to their plight, Israel seemed invincible. In June 1967 it conquered new Arab territories, and, as a result, the problems faced by an Arab population living under Israeli occupation increased.

The 1980s witnessed the *intifada* (uprising) of the Palestinian youth in the occupied territories of the West Bank and Gaza Strip. There were demonstrations and stone-throwing attacks on Israeli soldiers and civilians. The government reaction was harsh. This 'stone revolution', well covered by the media, had a dual impact: it showed the world that the Palestinians had not given up their hope for independence and forced many Israelis to ask soul-searching questions about their own identity. Those who for years had considered themselves to be the oppressed were becoming the oppressors. The policy of the Israeli government resulted in an increasing number of Palestinians being imprisoned, deported and tortured. Palestinian lands were confiscated and new Jewish settlements were established. Israel was becoming a country of apartheid.

In the early 1990s both parties came to realize that the only way out was to acknowledge each other's right to exist. In September 1993 Israeli and Palestinian leaders signed the Oslo Agreement – the first step towards peace. People opposed to the peace process nevertheless remained active on both sides. In November 1995 Israeli society was shaken when Prime

Minister Yitzhak Rabin was assassinated: a Jew murdered, not by an Arab, but by another Jew.

In the summer of 2000 the peace process reached a critical stage. The sensitive issue of Jerusalem, which had been left deliberately until this point, was now the focus of the talks. Ever since the Israeli army conquered East Jerusalem in June 1967 all the Israeli leaders had been claiming that 'Jerusalem is the eternal and indivisible capital of Israel'. Thus Israeli negotiators were not prepared to make a serious compromise over Jerusalem. They refused to accept the return of East Jerusalem under Arab sovereignty. As a result, the Palestinians felt that the Israeli government wanted to have peace with them without acknowledging their equal rights to the land, and more specifically their equal rights to Jerusalem, which is cherished not only by Jews but by all the native people of the land. Israel's intransigence, combined with its ongoing policy of establishing new Jewish settlements on Palestinian territories, inflamed the Palestinian people with rage and despair. The response to the failure of this decisive round of the peace talks was the second *intifada*. This uprising, which started in September 2000, in less than twelve months claimed the lives of over eight hundred people, mostly Palestinians. A United Nations resolution blamed the Israeli government for its use of excessive force against Palestinians.

Applying the teaching of Scripture

A few comments need to be made about this conflict, which has placed Israel in opposition to Arabs, Christians and Muslims alike:

First, the Jewish, Christian and Muslim Scriptures teach that *the earth is the Lord's*. He is the ultimate owner of the land, and that includes our homeland. Arabs and Jews both claim ownership of the disputed land, yet it is by no means inherently theirs; it belongs to God (7:128; Ps. 24:1; 1 Cor. 10:26).

Jesus warned his disciples against putting all their hope and energy into gaining this world in a way that would endanger their eternal life: 'Will a person gain anything if he wins the whole world but loses his life? Of course not! There is nothing he can give to regain his life' (see Matt. 16:26, GNB). It is extremely sad that many Jews and Arabs have literally lost their lives in the successive wars against each other. Yet there are even more people who have jeopardized their eternal lives by putting their political commitment first on their agenda. This conflict between Arabs and Jews has exposed the sinfulness of all. No-one can claim to have clean hands. So far, the only victor in this conflict is evil, inflicting so much suffering on both communities.

Secondly, the Scriptures teach that *God is a merciful God.* He calls people to repent and to receive his forgiveness. God not only forgives but exhorts his people to do likewise. The 'Holy Land' has been, in a sense, one of the most unholy places in the world because of all the wars that have taken place there, wars waged by people who supposedly worshipped a merciful God. Arabs and Jews need to go back to their Scriptures and to seek God's mercy and help to enable them to be merciful to each other.

For Christians, God's mercy has been demonstrated in history through the suffering servant, Jesus Christ. Jesus' love led him to suffer to bring us reconciliation with God. Looking to him as the suffering servant can help us make sense of our own suffering.

Thirdly, *the God of peace is also the God of justice.* The initial injustice suffered by Arabs, and especially the Palestinians, needs to be acknowledged and redressed by the international community. In political terms this means that Israel and the Arab nations should no longer be treated with double standards. Will Israel ever be forced to end its occupation of Arab lands and to comply with the United Nations resolutions, as Iraq was forced to withdraw from Kuwait, Indonesia from East Timor, and Serbia from Kosovo? Israel seems to be the only country in the world to defy the UN resolutions without having to face international sanctions.

The cry for 'justice, only justice' of the Palestinian people must be heard.[3] This means recognizing their right to have a credible State in which to recover their dignity and national identity. It means accepting East Jerusalem as their capital, and removing the Jewish settlements in Gaza and the West Bank. Otherwise, in the words of one Israeli, this State would be nothing more than a 'trussed chicken'. The Gaza Strip, for instance, is one of the most densely populated places in the world. This autonomous Palestinian territory, which measures 140 square miles, is inhabited by one and half million people. The Palestinian population live on 65% of the territory. The remaining 35% is occupied by Jewish colonies owned by just six thousand Jewish settlers.

Fourthly, *the concept of a Jewish State is in itself problematic.* History and many contemporary situations indicate that whenever a country is closely associated with one religion or ethnic group, religious and ethnic minorities are likely to be at best discriminated against, and at worst persecuted. A secular, plural and democratic State is more in line with

Jesus' teaching than a religious State, be it Christian, Islamic or Jewish (cf. Matt. 22:21).

How would we react, for example, if the United Kingdom were designed for white Christians only? Few would advocate such a thing, yet the State of Israel was conceived by Zionist ideology as the homeland for the Jews, Jewishness being defined by racial and religious criteria.[4] This ideology is challenged not only by the Arab population living in Israel, but also by 'Messianic' Jews. Are 'Messianic' (Christian) Jews still Jews? While the answer is a definite yes for them, their very existence, especially in Israel, let alone their missionary activity, is seen as a threat to Jewish identity. In no State will the protection of human rights be guaranteed unless its citizens are seen for who they are: human beings, regardless of their ethnic and religious background.

The Middle East conflict therefore raises some fundamental issues: Is it possible for a State to be closely associated with one particular religion or ethnic group without people from other backgrounds becoming second-class citizens? How will a relatively small land accommodate the claims of both the Jewish and Palestinian peoples? Will they ever really accept each other and not merely tolerate each other? Of course, these questions are relevant not only to Israel, but to the other States in the region too. The solution of one secular and democratic State for all, regardless of religious and ethnic identity, may seem idealistic today, but in the long run this option will guarantee peace because it does justice to both Jews and Palestinians, to people with one faith and to those of no faith at all. Unless the structural discrimination of the State of Israel is adequately addressed, it is wishful thinking to believe that Israelis and Palestinians can live alongside each other (cf. Jer. 6:13–15). It is high time for Israel to realize that military power and nuclear weapons represent no guarantee for peace with the Palestinian people. Critical and courageous decisions, including the repudiation of Zionist ideology, need to be made. Only then will justice, peace and reconciliation be given a serious chance to become a meaningful reality in the Middle East.

Do not show partiality

Many Christians in the West naturally sympathize with Israel as God's chosen people and as the victims of the Holocaust. However, the undue and damaging result of this attitude is often a pro-Israeli bias. Combined with prejudice against Arabs and Muslims, this bias has meant that Christians have been unable to make a positive contribution to implementing justice and peace in the Middle East. It also explains, to some degree, why many Arabs and Muslims are suspicious of the West and Western Christianity. People who are understandably concerned about the conflict in the Middle East should therefore examine their attitudes towards Israel and the Arabs to ensure that they are not showing favouritism to one party to the detriment of the other. 'Do not show partiality in judging; hear both small and great alike. Do not be afraid of any man, for judgment belongs to God' (Deut. 1:17).

Notes

[1] See T. Weber, 'How Evangelicals Became the Best Friends of Israel', pp. 38–49; P. Bennis and K. Mansour, '"Praise God and Pass the Ammunition!" The Changing Nature of Israel's US Backers', pp. 16–18, 43. See also periodicals such as *Israel and Christians Today*, and the so-called Christian Embassy in Jerusalem.

[2] One of the outstanding books written on the issue is by C. Chapman: *Whose Promised Land? Israel or Palestine?* See also P. Walker, *Jerusalem: Past and Present in the Purposes of God*; *Jesus and the Holy City: New Testament Perspectives on Jerusalem*; and K. Cragg, *Palestine: The Prize and Price of Zion*.

[3] N. Ateek, *Justice, Only Justice: A Palestinian Theology of Liberation*. See also R. Abu El-Assal, *Caught in Between: The Story of an Arab Palestinian Christian Israeli*; E. Chacour, *Blood Brothers*; and A. Rantisi, *Blessed Are the Peacemakers: The Story of a Palestinian Christian*.

[4] As soon as the State of Israel was created (in 1948), its government sought to rid the land of the remaining Arab population. This policy is evidenced by a well-documented case in which the Israeli government devised a secret transfer scheme designed to encourage the Palestinian population in Galilee to leave the country and settle in Argentina and Brazil. See Nur Masalha, 'A Galilee without Christians? Yosef Weitz and "Operation Yohanan" 1949–1954', in A. O'Mahony (ed.) *Palestinian Christians: Religion, Politics and Society in the Holy Land*, pp. 190–222.

24

Love the immigrant as yourself

The problem Israel faces because of its Arab and Messianic minorities is found in many European countries too. Over the past few decades, and for various reasons, the number of immigrants in Europe has increased dramatically. Most of these immigrants will not return to their home countries; indeed, for some, their second and third generations have been born in Europe and many hold European passports. They represent a significant part of society.

Since the traditions, culture and religion of the immigrant population are often different from those of the host country, many European people feel threatened; they sense that their national identity is in danger. Some have openly pleaded for different legislation to be applied, restricting the immigrants' rights.

Christians are perhaps more sensitive than others to the religious aspects of immigration. Some have even been tempted to support discriminatory policies. Such an attitude, however, is unacceptable; Christians should not tolerate any form of racism. Religious racism can be worse than ordinary racism because it dishonours God and is more difficult to eliminate.

The Bible presents us with a double requirement: first, to hold fast to the truth it reveals, and secondly, to remain unconditionally welcoming to those who do not have the same faith or ethnic background as ourselves. Since it is not possible to examine every aspect of the subject here, we shall focus on outlining some of the guiding principles of the biblical teaching.

Strangers in Israel

Once established in the Promised Land, the people of Israel numbered among them quite a proportion of other people described as 'strangers'.[1] These people were non-Israelites, who nevertheless lived in the same community as the Israelites. There were some who had joined when they left Egypt (Exod. 12:38), and others who had been living in the land of Canaan when the Israelites had entered (2 Chr. 8:8). Later, other strangers, such as Ruth the Moabite, came to live in Israel.

At the time of King Solomon, the number of strangers was approximately 153,600 (2 Chr. 2:17), a fairly high number in relation to the total population of Israel. They provided most of the labour force needed for the building of the temple (1 Chr. 22:2; 2 Chr. 8:7–8).

Because the people of Israel were God's chosen people, they were in danger of despising the non-Israelites living in the land. Hence the law of Moses included very specific teaching on how the Israelites should behave towards them. It highlighted the fact that Israel's election did not in any way mean that God neglects the other nations, who are represented, as it were, by the strangers in Israel. On the contrary, it says that God cares for them and sees to their needs, beginning with the most basic: 'For the LORD ... shows no partiality and accepts no bribes. He defends the cause of the fatherless and the widow, and loves the alien [stranger], giving him food and clothing. And you are to love those who are aliens [strangers], for you yourselves were aliens [strangers] in Egypt' (Deut. 10:17–18; cf. Ps. 146:9).[2]

Regarding food, God commanded the Israelites to allow strangers and Levites (religious people who had no secular job) to benefit from the first-fruits of the earth (Deut. 26:11). He ordered them to leave the surplus from their harvest for the stranger, the poor (Lev. 19:10; 23:22), the orphans and the widows (Deut. 24:19–21). God required the Israelites to share out the three-yearly tithe with the stranger, the Levite, the orphan and the widow (Deut. 14:29).

> And you and the Levites and the strangers among you shall rejoice in all the good things the LORD your God has given to you and your household.
>
> When you have finished setting aside a tenth of all your produce in the third year, the year of the tithe, you shall give it to the Levite, the stranger, the fatherless and the widow, so that they may eat in your towns and be satisfied. (Deut. 26:11–12)

The legal provisions often grouped together the strangers, the Levites, the poor, the widows and the orphans so as to emphasize the precariousness of their lives. Since the situation of all these people was more fragile than that of the ordinary Israelite, the law was especially attentive to their needs and guaranteed them protection.

The general command about loving one's neighbour (Lev. 19:18) had a specific application in the command about loving the stranger. In case the Israelites were tempted to consider that the strangers were not their neighbours, the Torah insists: 'When a stranger lives with you in your land, do not ill-treat him. The stranger living with you must be treated as one of your native-born. *Love him as yourself*, for you were strangers in Egypt. I am the LORD your God' (Lev. 19:33–34; cf. Exod. 22:21; 23:9; my emphasis). Loving strangers meant respecting their basic rights. In general, they were to have the same rights as the Israelites. Here are some we find mentioned in the Torah:

(1) The non-Israelite living in the land was entitled to rest on the same basis as an Israelite. This implied a Sabbath (Exod. 20:10; 23:12; Deut. 5:14) and a sabbatical year during which they too were to enjoy the fruits of the earth (Lev. 25:6).

(2) They were entitled to a fair wage, which had to be paid without delay (Deut. 24:14–15).

(3) They were entitled to the same advantages as the Israelite: if they were poor, they could benefit from interest-free loans (Lev. 25:35); if they were rich, they could acquire slaves from among the Israelites (Lev. 25:47);[3] if they killed someone accidentally, they could protect their lives by taking refuge in one of the towns designated for that purpose – the 'cities of refuge' (Num. 35:15).

(4) They were entitled to impartial justice. If they broke the law, they were not to be punished more severely than an Israelite (Lev. 24:22); if they brought a case against an Israelite, judgment was to be given fairly (Deut. 1:16; 24:17). Giving a judgment detrimental to a defenceless man or woman would be an act so serious that it would call for a particularly severe punishment: 'Cursed is the man who withholds justice from the stranger, the fatherless or the widow' (Deut. 27:19).

Love for strangers included the opportunity for them to participate in Israel's feasts: the Passover (Exod. 12:19, 48, 49; Num. 9:14), Pentecost (Deut. 16:11) and Tabernacles (Deut. 16:14). They could be closely integrated into the community of Israel. The official act solemnizing this integration was their taking part in the covenant between God and Israel and their commitment to respect its laws (Deut. 29:10).

In short, far from discriminating against the non-Israelites who lived in the land, the Torah protected their rights and put the Israelites under the obligation to care for them. The purpose of the law was to create the conditions for their integration into the national community so they could enjoy the same blessings as the Israelites.

Now what about today? Has this teaching of the Torah become invalid in the twenty-first century? Or is it not, on the contrary, astonishingly relevant for every country where communities of different origins live side by side?

This is especially true for Israel. Christians who care for Israel have a responsibility to remind the Jews of the remarkable teaching of their own Scriptures. Is it possible for a people, who in the past suffered greatly in a so-called Christian civilization, not to acknowledge the same right for the Palestinian people to have a homeland? Is it right for Jews to discriminate against non-Jews living in Israel?

Jesus' teaching

In a previous chapter we looked at Jesus' attitude towards the Samaritans, who were the largest non-Jewish community in Israel (Luke 9:51–56; 10:25–37; 17:11–18). We noticed that he used every opportunity to challenge his people on their prejudice. And he went even further by laying claim to total solidarity with the stranger: 'For I was hungry and you gave me something to eat, I was thirsty and you gave me something to drink, I was a stranger and you invited me in' (Matt. 25:35; cf. Matt. 25:31–46). In a sense, Jesus was a stranger among his people, who did not acknowledge him as the promised Messiah (Luke 4:14–30).

Unlike the Torah, Jesus did not give detailed teaching about the stranger. Two reasons may explain this. On the one hand, Jesus simply endorsed the general directives of the law. On the other hand, the new people of God, that is, the church, is made up of citizens of the whole world without any discrimination between nations (see Matt. 8:11–12; 21:43). In fact, according to the perspective opened up by the coming of Jesus Christ, Christians themselves are strangers on the earth (1 Peter 1:1; 2:11). Like Abraham, they are marching towards the real Promised Land, the heavenly city where all of them will be guests of God (Heb. 11:13–16).

Applying the teaching today

The teaching of the Bible, in both the Old and New Testaments, is therefore crystal clear. If any discrimination should exist between nationals and immigrants, it should favour the latter, for immigrants are among 'the underprivileged', together with others such as the unemployed and many single-parent families.

Christians should be among the first to oppose any policy that sets out to discriminate unfairly. 'National preference' policies, for example, give nationals, rather than immigrants, priority regarding job opportunities, national insurance, health care, child benefit and housing. People receive benefits on the basis of nationality rather than needs. Such policies are clearly contrary to the teaching of Scripture; they represent a serious violation of human rights and are bound to create more tensions between nationals and immigrants.

Of course, not all immigrants are economically deprived, but many, if not most, are socially marginalized, emotionally under pressure and alienated from their culture. They often try to make life easier by living close to each other in a micro-society of their own. While this is humanly understandable, it is doubtful that in the long run these ethnic communities help people to integrate into the wider society. Immigrants who settle in Europe must be encouraged not to live apart from the host society. They should play their full part in the life of the larger community, for their own sake, as well as for the sake of their host country.

Europe will become the natural home for immigrants as long as they feel they are contributing to the life of the country, their rights are being protected, and, last but not least, they are being treated fairly. Experience confirms what the Torah says: having good laws is not enough. A fair legislation does not guarantee that immigrants (or indeed anyone else) will not be discriminated against. People must be convinced that immigrants are to be respected, listened to, accepted, appreciated, made welcome, and, whenever needed, helped. In a word, they are to be loved.

Muslim immigrants

Muslims in Western Europe form a large proportion of the immigrant population, and many have become European citizens. The brand image of Islam in the public mind tends to be rather tarnished. There are various reasons for this. The legacy of history still weighs heavily on relationships between Europe and the Muslim world. These relationships, past and present, have often been antagonistic (e.g. the Crusades, colonialism, Western support for Israel, and the Gulf War). Islamic fundamentalism is mistakenly associated with mainstream Islam. Islamic ideologies in some Muslim countries (e.g. Afghanistan, Iran, Saudi Arabia and Sudan) lead many to believe that Islam is a backward, intolerant and oppressive religion. Finally, unlike other religions, Islam explicitly denies the core of the gospel (the lordship of Jesus Christ, his divinity, his death and resurrection).

The first to suffer from this tarnished image are the Muslims themselves, especially those immigrants who are exposed to Western criticism and prejudice against Islam. Christians and Muslims from European backgrounds should serve as bridge-builders between European nationals and Muslim immigrants. Because of their faith they are in a better position to explain Islam to non-Muslims and to help Muslims relate to European culture.

Many Europeans are convinced that peaceful coexistence with Muslims is at best problematic and at worst impossible. They are opposed to anything that may result in Islam becoming more influential. In Britain, for example, many are against any new mosque-building project or government funding of Muslim schools, although there are many Catholic, Protestant and Jewish schools funded by the government. This attitude, clearly discriminatory, produces only a superficial sense of security in people who feel threatened by their Muslim neighbours. If coexistence proves difficult, we should investigate why that is so. It is quite possible that both sides share the blame. If we are not prepared to admit our responsibility, we shall inevitably search for a scapegoat.

Very often these problems of coexistence unveil our prejudice as well as real cultural differences. Social problems are not to be underestimated. In many situations, problems arise from the poor conditions, material and moral, that surround all marginalized members of society, whether they be immigrants or nationals. Education and job opportunities are key to helping such people integrate into the community.[4]

The immigrant population in Europe represents an opportunity for Europeans to re-examine their civilization. Likewise, Muslims living in Europe should consider their situation as an opportunity to look afresh at traditional Islamic teaching. Admittedly, living in a non-Muslim society means making some necessary adjustments. These adjustments need not be perceived as compromise; Islamic jurisprudence is based on various principles including *'urf*, customary law. Among the core values of European culture are religious freedom, tolerance and the primacy of the individual over the community. If Muslims want to live in harmony with other people, they need to accept these values as part of the conditions of living in a pluralistic society. There are two areas where these values are particularly relevant: family and conversion. The extent to which Muslims are willing to be part of European society will be seen, for instance, in their readiness to respect the decision of a Muslim woman to marry a non-Muslim, or of a Muslim man or woman to convert to a religion of their choice. This acceptance is highly significant, since Islamic law rules out both cases. If Muslims are prepared to move in this direction they will prove wrong those who think that Islam is a religion of the past. They will also make a distinctive and much needed contribution to shaping the new face of Europe.

Notes

[1] These people lived alongside the Israelites (Heb. *gēr* or *tôšhāḇ*) as opposed to the non-Israelites who lived in their own countries (*nēḵār* or *zûr*).

[2] The NIV English translation of the Bible, from which most of the quotations in this book come, tends to use the term 'alien' rather than 'stranger'. But since 'aliens' can have outer-space, extraterrestrial connotations nowadays, I shall use the term 'strangers' instead. The GNB uses the expression 'foreigner', or 'the foreigner who lives with you'.

[3] Lev. 25:44–46 allows Israelites to have slaves from among the children of strangers living among them or from the surrounding nations, just as Lev. 25:47–55 authorizes a resident stranger to have slaves from among the Israelites on condition that they are guaranteed the right to be redeemed at any moment and, in any case, to be freed in a Jubilee year.

[4] Many books have been written about the Muslim population in Europe and the questions that both European nations and the Muslim community need to address as a result of their coexistence. See, e.g., C. Chapman, *Islam and the West: Conflict, Co-existence or Conversion*; J. Nielsen, *Muslims in Western Europe*; and L. Newbigin et al., *Faith and Power: Christianity and Islam in 'Secular' Britain*.

Conclusion:
One God, one humanity,
one world

The Gospel calls Christians – and the Qur'an calls Muslims – to be witnesses for God. In each community this means renouncing both ignorance and confrontation. It means making the effort to listen, to explain and to understand.

For God's message to be understood and accepted, the messenger must relate it to the situation of the people. Not only this, but the very nature of the message, which is about a merciful God calling for a free response, determines the way it should be communicated. In other words, if mission (Christian or Islamic) is in God's *name*, it must be carried out in God's *way*. This means dialogue, fairness, respect, and the opportunity to respond freely.

One God

A genuine dialogue will help Christians and Muslims to understand and accept each other better – it will give us a more accurate idea of each other's faith. Dialogue also involves making the most of the heritage common to Christianity and Islam, as well as appreciating the differences, not to mention the contradictions, between the two faiths. The Qur'an appeals to Jews and Christians to agree with Muslims on what lies at the heart of their monotheistic faiths:

> Say: 'You People of the Book: come now to a formula acceptable to each of us, namely that we worship God alone; we do not ascribe any partner to Him; and we take no others as lords beside God.'

If they turn away then say: 'Bear witness that, for our part, we are surrendered [to God; lit. *we are muslims*].' (3:64)

Razi points out that the title 'People of the Book', by which the Qur'an describes Jews and Christians, represents one of the most beautiful names and prestigious titles given to a faith community. It acknowledges that they have been entrusted with the Book of God, *kitabu-llah*.[1] Razi suggests that the appeal in sura 3:64 is directed more specifically towards Christians because it is their doctrine about Jesus Christ that is disputed in the previous verses (3:59–61). The Qur'anic appeal offers a common ground for both Christians and Muslims with its three articles of faith: God alone is to be worshipped, God is not to be associated with anything else, and no human being is to be seen as holding divine authority.

One aim of this book has been to emphasize that Christians are unreservedly monotheistic, but that their monotheism is *trinitarian* whereas Islamic monotheism is *unitarian*. The Christian doctrine about Christ, based on the teaching of the Scriptures, does not make a god of the man Jesus. Instead, it recognizes that God, having freely determined to save his human creatures, has lowered himself and has himself fully identified with us in Christ. The incarnation of God does not undermine his oneness, his transcendence, or indeed any of his attributes. God's self-disclosure in Christ enhances his uniqueness and provides historical evidence for his uncompromising holiness, his sovereign victory over evil and his overwhelming love for humanity.

God's revelation in Christ, as the Servant King, is most amazing. As a result Christians have an even deeper sense of God's greatness and of what divine majesty really means. They wholeheartedly worship God, for only he is worthy to be worshipped and only he has the exclusive right to be Lord. The apostle Paul, who had passionately resisted God's revelation in Christ until Jesus revealed himself to him on the road to Damascus, expressed his sense of awe and wonder:

Oh, the depth of the riches of the wisdom and knowledge of
   God!
How unsearchable his judgments,
   and his paths beyond tracing out!
'Who has known the mind of the Lord?
   Or who has been his counsellor?'
'Who has ever given to God,
   that God should repay him?'

For from him and through him and to him are all things.
To him be the glory for ever! Amen. (Rom. 11:33–36)

Christians fully endorse the threefold statement of faith as expressed in sura 3:64. Yet having said that, one must admit that the reality of Christian practice is sometimes out of line with biblical teaching. Not all who call themselves Christians follow the teaching of the Bible. This, of course, is not specific to Christianity. Muslims too can hardly claim that all of them are faithful to the teaching of their religion, and many so-called Islamic practices have little to do with orthodox Islam. Therefore, in their appreciation of each other's faith, Christians and Muslims need to allow for the fact that neither the Christian nor the Muslim community lives up to the teaching of their Scriptures. Christianity is not necessarily reflected in the lives of those who claim to be Christians; Islam is not always demonstrated in the practice of Muslims. In the final analysis, the only reliable source for Christian doctrine is the Bible, and for Islamic teaching, the Qur'an.

One humanity, one world

In many countries Christians and Muslims live in multi-ethnic and pluralistic societies. They are part of the same society as people of other faiths and of no faith at all. The credibility of their witness depends partly on the quality of their relationships with people outside their own community.

In most European countries Christians and Muslims represent minority groups. They have many of the same concerns about some of the negative aspects of an increasingly secular society: materialism, immorality, violence, individualism, atheism, drugs, alcoholism, and abortion laws. Yet, instead of responding to the challenges that such a society presents to their faith, many are tempted to react by adopting a defensive attitude. This often means allowing a self-centred community life to develop, and in so doing they miss the opportunity to contribute to the social and spiritual welfare of the wider community. Faith then runs the risk of appearing irrelevant to those people without any belief in God. Christians and Muslims therefore need to find in their respective Scriptures the resources to develop a more positive outlook towards society.

The Qur'an stresses the unity of human beings as well as their diversity. The following text highlights both of these aspects and relates the diversity of humankind to the purposeful will of God the Creator:

'Humanity! Truly We have created you from a male and a female and made you to be nations and tribes in order that you might know each other. Truly the most honoured of you in God's sight are those who fear Him most. God knows and observes all' (49:13). This text addresses not only Muslims but people in general, *al-nas*. By referring us to our origins, it urges us, as Razi explains, to show no pride towards or superiority over each other.[2] We have the same father and mother: Adam and Eve. We have been created by God in the same way: through a father and a mother. Consequently, we partake of the same nature, *jins wahid*. Thus humanity is one and all humans are equal. And as far as our humanity is concerned we all enjoy the same God-given dignity: 'We have honoured the sons of Adam' (17:70).

Having underlined the unity of all human beings, the Qur'anic text (49:13) states that God has made people belong to different ethnic groups. Why? Because he wants people to relate to each other and to know each other. This implies that ethnic differentiation has been divinely ordained to facilitate human communication. Thus human diversity corresponds to God's purpose for humankind. He created us not only to worship him (cf. 51:56) but also to have genuine fellowship with each other. The fact that ethnic differentiation has often led to racial discrimination indicates how far we human beings have strayed from the purpose our Creator assigned for us. What was meant to be a bridge between people of different racial backgrounds has become a barrier, and, even worse, a threatening frontier!

Human equality does not override religious identity. God created us so that we may know him and enjoy his blessings. Our faith matters, as does the way we live out our faith. In the words of the Qur'an, 'The most honoured of you in God's sight are those who fear Him most' (49:13; cf. 35:28). This suggests that what matters most is not so much who we claim to be, but rather where we are in our relationship with God. This relationship is characterized by *taqwa*, 'fear', which means acknowledging God's lordship in our life and acting accordingly:

> The fear of the LORD is the beginning of wisdom,
> and knowledge of the Holy One is understanding. (Prov. 9:10)

The teaching of the Bible reinforces what the Qur'an says in sura 49:13 about the oneness of humankind in spite of our ethnic and religious diversity. The dignity of humankind is founded on the fact that all of us have been created in God's image (Gen. 1:27). Sin has seriously distorted this image, but has not erased it (Gen. 9:6; Jas. 3:9). All people, regardless of religious or ethnic background, are called to play a part in making society more just, more caring, more enjoyable, and, in a word, more human. After all, Christians, Muslims, Jews, people of other faiths and of no faith live in one world that is constantly shrinking. We share in the suffering of this world and have many of the same hopes for it. To a large extent, this world will be what we have made it.

If humanity is one, then we are, in a sense, all brothers and sisters. Christians, who believe that God is the loving Father, know what God means by love. Jesus taught his disciples how to love their fellow human beings (Luke 10:25–37). He showed them throughout his mission that true love is not merely a sentiment, but love in action:

> This is how we know what love is: Jesus Christ laid down his life for us. And we ought to lay down our lives for our brothers. If anyone has material possessions and sees his brother in need but has no pity on him, how can the love of God be in him? ... let us not love with words or tongue but with actions and in truth. (1 John 3:16–18)

> For God so loved the world that he gave his one and only Son that whoever believes in him shall not perish but have eternal life. (John 3:16)

A personal response

God's love for all calls for a personal response from all. For me, as a Christian Arab, this has involved looking carefully at the religion of most of the Arabs, having a positive approach to Islam and being prepared to be challenged by the Qur'anic message. I hope that this concern comes across in this book.

Muslims believe that the message of all God's prophets is essentially the same because each has been sent by the same God to the same humanity. It is true that many of God's attributes are found in the Torah, in the New Testament, as well as in the Qur'an. However, the Gospel is unique, for, first, it is primarily about God's love; and secondly, in no other prophet is God's love revealed the way it is in Jesus Christ: a redeeming love that saves humanity from sin, evil and death (see 1 John 4:8–10).

This wonderful message, which I know to be true in my life, explains why I am a Christian. I know that I need God as my Saviour, I know that he is my loving Father – and I know that I cannot find such a message in Islam. This gospel message – this message of good news – is for everyone, including Muslims. Since most Muslims do not have many opportunities to know more about it, I urge the Muslim reader in particular to get a copy of the Bible and to examine seriously the claims of Jesus Christ before responding to this decisive question: is Jesus merely who the Qur'an says he is, or is he really 'the Saviour of the world'?

Notes

[1] Razi, IV:8, pp. 75–77.
[2] Ibid., XIV:28, p. 17.

Muslim theologians and mystics

We have considered the teaching of several Muslim theologians and mystics. Here we take a closer look at nine of the most significant, beginning in the third Islamic century with Ibn Ḥanbal (241/855) and ending nearer the present day with Muḥammad 'Abduh (1323/1905). We shall see how their teachings fit into the history of Islamic thought and to what extent they have been accepted in the Muslim world.

Aḥmad Ibn Ḥanbal (164/780 – 241/855)

Aḥmad b. Muḥammad b. Ḥanbal, known as Ibn Ḥanbal, was born and died in Baghdad. He was a renowned scholar, first studying the Shariʿa under Shafiʿi, the founder of the Shafiʿite school of *fiqh* (Islamic jurisprudence).

Depending on the caliph of the time, Ibn Ḥanbal was either persecuted or honoured by the establishment. He spent several years in prison where he wrote polemical treatises against those Muslims he saw as heretical. His major work, *al-Musnad*, is a collection of the Hadith, containing some 28,000 sayings attributed to the Prophet. These traditions, compiled by Ibn Ḥanbal's son, 'Abdullah, is the largest of the nine canonical compilations.

Ibn Ḥanbal's doctrine was based on a literal interpretation of the Qur'an and the Hadith. He taught that all divine attributes found in these primary sources of the Islamic faith are to be taken at face value. So we must accept anthropomorphic expressions about God (e.g. God's hands, God's smile, God sitting on the throne) as referring to divine realities, even if we are unable to explain how they apply to God. This is what is meant by the famous principle *bila-kayfa* (lit. 'without how'). He taught that because the Qur'an is the Word of the eternal God it is uncreated. And as for faith, it consists of three elements: trusting God, obeying his commands and professing allegiance to God and his Prophet.

After Ibn Ḥanbal's death, his disciples drew upon his teaching and formed the Ḥanbalite school of jurisprudence. Of the four schools of *fiqh* (Shafi'ite, Malikite, Ḥanafite, Ḥanbalite), it is the most conservative, characterized by a strict application of Islamic law and a strong emphasis on tradition. Today the Ḥanbalite school no longer enjoys the prestige it had in the first centuries, now being the least representative of the Muslim community. However, the Wahhabite doctrine is a renewed form of Ḥanbalism. This doctrine, preached by Muḥammad b. 'Abd al-Wahhab in the eighteenth century, represents the theological foundation for the religious and political system of Saudi Arabia.

Abu 'Abdallah al-Ḥusayn b. Mansur al-Ḥallaj (244/858 – 309/922)

Al-Ḥallaj, whose name means 'the wool-carder', was born at Ṭur (in modern-day Iran) and moved with his father to Wasiṭ (in Iraq). As a child he learned the Qur'an by heart and attended the Sufi school founded by Sahl al-Tustari. At the age of twenty he went to Baṣra, where he met another famous Sufi, 'Amr al-Makki, and officially became a Sufi by experiencing *tawba*, conversion to God. He married and had three sons and one daughter. (His son Ḥamd would later put his teaching into writing.) In 264/878 he moved to Baghdad and became the disciple of the celebrated Sufi Junayd.

In 282/895 Ḥallaj performed his first pilgrimage to Mecca, where he remained for a year. He became an itinerant preacher, calling people to find God in their own hearts, a call earning him the title *Ḥallaj al-asrar*, 'the carder of consciences'. He attracted many disciples as well as enemies. In addition to the expected hostility from theologians, many Sufis blamed him for divulging 'the secret of the way'.

In 291/903 Ḥallaj went on his second pilgrimage to Mecca, this time with four hundred disciples. He subsequently undertook a long preaching tour of India and Turkestan, taking his message beyond the frontiers of the Muslim community. He returned to Mecca for his third and final pilgrimage, praying that God would exalt his name through the suffering of his servant.

Ḥallaj returned to Baghdad in 296/909. There he set up a model of the Ka'aba in his house. At night he prayed and by day he preached in the market-place, the streets, the mosques and the graveyards. At the same time he worked all kinds of miracles and people were healed. The focus of his preaching was the overwhelming love of God that filled his heart with joy. He wanted to die as a martyr, killed by his own community for their sake.

In 301/913 Ḥallaj was arrested and put in prison. He was one of the many victims of the repressive regime of the time, but was also charged with heresy and charlatanism. Eight years later he was condemned to death, tortured, exposed on a cross and beheaded, and his body was burnt. He is said to have uttered several sentences before his execution. In one of them he asked God to be merciful and to forgive his enemies.

The mystical experience proposed and modelled by Ḥallaj was that of union in love with God. The first steps of this experience meant complying with God's commands, external obedience being the means, *wasiṭa*, to attain the divine realities, *ḥaqa'iq*. Muslims should not simply submit to the letter of the Shari'a, he said, but need to understand and comply with the *spiritual* meaning of its commands. 'The important thing is to proceed seven times around the Ka'aba of one's heart.' In doing so people would purify themselves of their 'external wrapping' and become one spirit, *ruḥ*, with God. This experience, he said, is epitomized by the cross, whereby the self is fully destroyed so as to make room for the only real existent, *al-Ḥaqq*, that is, God. This is what Ḥallaj meant when he said long before he died, 'I am going to die according to the religion of the Cross.'[1]

Abu-l-Ḥasan 'Ali al-Ash'ari (260/873 – 324/935)

Born in Baṣra (Iraq), Ash'ari died in Baghdad. For more than twenty years he was the disciple of Abu 'Ali al-Jubba'i, the leader of the Mu'tazilite school in Baṣra. He later departed from Mu'tazilism and produced a large number of works of a dogmatic and polemical nature.

Ash'ari is the author of a famous survey of Islamic beliefs called *Maqalat al-islamiyyin*, 'The Doctrines of Muslims'. His writings present us with a comprehensive, systematic and coherent body of teaching. For the sake of consistency and clarity, he is in many ways a radical thinker. For him, God's key attribute, apart from his oneness, is his *sovereign will*. He taught that God predestined some people to paradise and others to hell, and that good and evil have no moral value in themselves, but depend entirely on God's judgment. Thus murder is an evil act only because God declared it as such in his law – whereas he made the same act (of killing people) lawful in some circumstances, such as in holy war. Furthermore, God wants and creates all human acts, including unbelief, sin and evil. For Ash'ari, faith essentially meant trusting God, *al-taṣdiq bi-llah*. Therefore all Muslims who genuinely believe in God and his Prophet are true believers, including non-practising and disobedient Muslims.

Ash'ari founded his teaching on the Qur'an as well as the Hadith, interpreting them in a highly rational, yet not a rationalistic, way. Many Muslims gradually adopted his mainline teaching and formed what came to be known as the Ash'arite school. This school has become the most representative in Sunni Islam. Its prominent theologians include Ghazali, Razi, and before them Baqillani (whose *Kitab al-Tamhid* is a comprehensive treatise of Ash'arite theology), and Juwayni (whose *Kitab al-Irshad* is a précis of an elaborated Ash'arite theology.)[2]

In contrast to the Ash'arite school, the Mu'tazilite school advocates a rationalistic monotheism. It hold that only God is eternal and that his Word, the Qur'an, is created. God's *justice* is seen as his paramount attribute, and faith means obedience to God's law. Thus disobedient Muslims are nominal Muslims; they will suffer eternal punishment in the same way as non-Muslims. People's eternal destiny depends entirely on their compliance with God's law. Human acts are inherently good or bad. The Mu'tazilite school attributes to the Hadith far less authority than to the Qur'an, which must be interpreted metaphorically wherever it contradicts human reason.

Ash'arite school	Mu'tazilite school
Emphasis on God's sovereign will.	Emphasis on God's justice.
God is free to show his mercy to whomever he pleases and to punish whomever he pleases.	God must punish the disobedient, and must forgive the obedient and truly repentant.
Faith basically means trusting God.	Faith basically means obeying God's law.
All Muslims will enter paradise, although disobedient Muslims may first have to spend some time in hell.	Only obedient and repentant Muslims will enter paradise. Sinful Muslims will condemned to eternal punishment.
Qur'an is eternal, uncreated.	Only God is eternal. Qur'an is created.
Qur'an and Hadith.	Qur'an. Hadith has far lesser authority.
Revelation takes precedence over reason.	Revelation is interpreted in rational terms.

Abu Muḥammad 'Ali b. Ḥazm (384/994 – 456/1064)

This Spanish-Arabic scholar, known as Ibn Ḥazm, was a poet, jurist and theologian. He was born in Cordoba to a high official in the Umayyad Empire of Islamic Spain and received a broad education, spending his childhood in the palace of the caliph. As an adult, he was part of the establishment and, as Andalusia was going through political unrest, he was twice taken prisoner (in 412/1022 and 414/1023). Eventually he became disillusioned with political life, withdrew to the country and dedicated himself to studying, teaching and writing. He died in 456/1064, having written hundreds of treatises.

Ibn Ḥazm belonged to the Ẓahirite school of jurisprudence – an extremely rigorous school that eventually merged with the Ḥanbalite school. The Qur'an, they argued, has a 'plain', *ẓahir*, meaning that must be taken and accepted as it is: either as indicative, *dalil*, or illustrative, *ishara*. Ibn Ḥazm accused philosophers, theologians and jurists of using rational arguments to justify their own preconceived ideas when they should have listened to the simple teaching of God's Word. To claim, he said, that the Qur'an has a 'hidden', *baṭin*, meaning, can lead only to arbitrary interpretations. His virulent attacks earned him the hostility of both theologians and rulers, and his books were publicly burnt in Seville.

Apart from the Qur'an, Ibn Ḥazm accepted the authority of only those of the Hadith's narratives that he deemed authentic. He gave little credit, if any, to the other two sources of Islamic law: *qiyas*, 'analogical deduction', and *ijma'*, 'consensus' (of the Muslim community). He considered that the use of reason in religion was legitimate only in the way it is used in the Qur'an – whose Arabic language is of primary importance. He accepted only those divine names that the Qur'an itself ascribes to God. Human reason, he argued, is incapable of discovering the truth by itself or of making moral judgments: its role is simply to help us gain a better understanding of what has already been revealed in the sacred text. The only union between God and man is that of *fahm*, understanding, which is achieved through the mediation of God's Word.

One of Ibn Ḥazm's early writings was *Ṭawq al-ḥamama*, a treatise on love and lovers, containing autobiographical information as well as moral and religious considerations. Another of his works, *Kitab al-Fiṣal*, represents a major contribution to the history of religious thought. Although it provides us with accurate and useful documentation, it is essentially a work of apologetics. The author's main objective in looking at different religions (especially Judaism and Christianity) and Islamic sects was to prove the truthfulness of what he saw as orthodox Islam. He makes no attempt to understand the underlying issues from perspectives other than his own. His approach remains on the surface of the relevant texts, a position, after all, in line with Zahirite teaching.

Abu Ḥamid al-Ghazali (450/1058 – 505/1111)

The acclaimed theologian and mystic, Ghazali (known in Europe as Algazel) was born and died in Ṭus (Iran).

His first teacher was Juwayni, who had a *madrasa* (school) in Nishapur. Following Juwayni's death (478/1085), Ghazali experienced a spiritual crisis. He moved to Baghdad, where he was appointed as a professor at the Niẓamiyya *madrasa* (484/1091). There he wrote a few controversial pamphlets against schismatic Muslims, but personally remained dissatisfied with himself. He began to look into philosophy, especially that of al-Farabi and Avicenna, but found no satisfactory answers. In *Tahafut al-falasifa*, 'The Inconsistency of the Philosophers', he criticized philosophical systems, especially Neoplatonism, which were based on intellectual speculation. Eventually he turned to Sufism and in 488/1095 experienced a personal and dramatic conversion. As a result he abandoned his post, left Baghdad and dedicated himself to asceticism, contemplation, travelling and pilgrimage. In 499/1105 he returned to Nishapur, where he resumed his teaching at its *madrasa* for the remainder of his life.

In *al-Munqiẓ min-al-ḍalal*, 'The Rescuer from Error', Ghazali gives an account of his mystical experience. His greatest work is *Iḥya' 'ulumi-l-din*, 'The Revival of Religious Sciences', some parts of which have been translated into European languages. Ghazali's major contribution to Islamic thought is his effort to reconcile theology with philosophy, Islamic orthodoxy with Sufism, and tradition with reason. In his treatise on God's Names, *al-Maqṣad*, he explains that the nearest to God, *al-muqarrabun* (the mystics), are above *al-'ulama'* (the scholars), in that they not only know and understand God's names but also share in God's attributes. Ghazali quotes the famous hadith, '*Takhallaqu bi-akhlaqi-llah*', 'Have the same character as God', but repudiates the doctrine of union, *ittiḥad*, between man and God, and that of the indwelling of God in man, *ḥulul*. In doing so he denounces as non-Islamic the ideal and ultimate objective held by many Sufis, and rejects the Christian doctrine of the incarnation.[3]

Fakhr-ul-Din al-Razi (543/1149 – 606/1209)

One of the greatest Muslim scholars, Razi was born at Rayy (near modern Teheran). He died in Ḥerat (in present-day Afghanistan), then the prestigious intellectual centre of Islamic Persia. His father was a jurist, preacher and theologian.

Razi studied philosophy as well as theology, and some of his early writings were devoted to a critical but appreciative study of Avicenna (428/1037). He became a popular preacher and an Ashʿarite theologian, spending many years travelling in central Asia refuting Muʿtazilite doctrines, in writing as well as in debates with their promoters. He eventually settled in Ḥerat, where he had a large following.

Razi's comprehensive theological work was *al-Muḥaṣṣal*, which (according to its full title) is a précis of ideas related to scholars, philosophers and theologians, ancient and modern. Many later Muslim thinkers wrote their own commentaries on this work. Razi also produced a renowned treatise on God's names, *Lawamiʿ al-bayyinat*, which was inspired by Ghazali's *Maqṣad*. His major work remains his encyclopaedic commentary on the Qur'an, *al-Tafsir al-kabir*, also known as *Mafatiḥ al-Ghayb*, 'The Keys of the Unseen' – which, according to the Qur'an, are possessed only by God (6:59). The commentary is based on strict exegetical rules and takes on board alternative readings of the Qur'anic text. It is concerned with theological and philosophical issues and has many references to the Hadith. Razi often concludes his exegesis with considerations of a spiritual and practical nature.

The *Tafsir* has been influential throughout the centuries and continues to be an inspiring source for Qur'anic exegesis. This does not mean, however, that Razi is unanimously acclaimed by Muslims; some scholars take issue with him. Ibn Taymiyya, for example, strongly criticized him for introducing philosophical concepts alien to Islamic doctrine.

Muhyi-l-Din b. al-ʿArabi (560/1165 – 638/1240)

Ibn ʿArabi (as he is known) was born at Murcia (south-east Spain) to an Arab home of Sufi tradition and died in Damascus. He is known to his followers as *al-Shaykh al-Akbar*, 'the Greatest Master'.

In 568/1172 he moved with his family to Seville, where he settled and later studied *fiqh* and the Hadith. He met with the spiritual leaders of Andalusia and with the renowned Arab philosopher Ibn Rushd, known in Europe as Averroës.

He travelled extensively in Spain and North Africa and in 598/1201 set out for the East, where he spent the rest of his life. This decision was probably motivated by a desire to escape the rigorous and oppressive regime of the Almohads, who were the rulers of Spain and part of North Africa. *En route* to Mecca he stayed in Cairo, where he was seen as heretical, *zindiq*, by some Muslims who tried unsuccessfully to assassinate him. He spent three years in Mecca, where he was the recipient of divine revelations, and for twenty years tirelessly visited the major cities of the Middle East before settling in Damascus in 620/1223.[4]

Ibn ʿArabi's greatest work is *al-Futuhat al-makkiyya*, 'The Illuminations of Mecca'. It is a complete system of mystic knowledge laid out in 560 chapters, of which the penultimate gives a summary of the whole. He is credited with hundreds of writings. In a work he wrote a year before he died, *Fuṣuṣ al-ḥikam*, he explains that God's multifaceted Wisdom is displayed in each of his prophets: for example, transcendence in Noah, love in Abraham, truth in Isaac, sublimeness in Ishmael, prophecy in Jesus, and unity in Muhammad.[5]

At the heart of Ibn ʿArabi's philosophical mysticism is monism, *wahdat al-wujud*, the oneness of existence, a doctrine derived from the Islamic understanding of *tawḥid* (monotheism): God is the Unique Being, therefore all other beings are like his shade, distinct from him only in their physical and deceptive appearance. Mystical experience comes from realizing the reality of this oneness. It implies a spiritual initiation and the abolition, *fana*, of the self. In Ibn ʿArabi's religious system Muhammad is the pre-existent principle of creation, the 'Primordial Muhammadan Reality', *al-ḥaqiqa al-muḥammadiyya*, being refracted in each of the prophets.

Ibn ʿArabi taught that there is only one religion, known only to the Gnostics, *al-ʿarifun*, and that all religions represent an aspect of this universal religion. God's mercy is seen as key to who God is and this rules out the very idea of eternal punishment. In other words, according to Ibn ʿArabi, hell is a temporary reality; eventually, all people (both Muslims and non-Muslims) will enjoy eternal bliss.

Taqi-l-Din Aḥmad b. Taymiyya (661/1263 – 728/1328)

Known as Ibn Taymiyya, this Ḥanbalite theologian and jurist was born in Ḥarran (south-east of modern Turkey). Before the Mongol invasion, his father, a well-known Ḥanbalite scholar, fled with his family and took refuge in Damascus in 667/1269.

Ibn Taymiyya was educated in the school where his father was director. When his father died in 682/1284 he succeeded him as professor of Ḥanbalite law, and in the following year began to give lectures in Qur'anic exegesis at the Umayyad mosque. In 695/1296 he was appointed to the *Ḥanbaliyya*, the Ḥanbalite *madrasa* in Damascus.

Ibn Taymiyya was not only a scholar. He preached *jihad*, 'holy war', against the Mongols and took part in several military expeditions against people whom he saw as deviant Muslims (e.g. Shi'is and Sufis). Because of his polemical style of writing and preaching he had many enemies inside the Muslim community. He strongly criticized Muslim philosophers (e.g. Avicenna and Ghazali), arguing that philosophy can lead only to unbelief and divisions among Muslims. He blamed Muslim theologians for relying on reason, *'aql*, more than on revelation, *naql*, and denounced Muslim leaders for their immoral lifestyles. Without condemning Sufism as such, he opposed unorthodox Sufis (e.g. Ibn 'Arabi) and their heretical teachings.

In 705/1306 Ibn Taymiyya was accused of anthropomorphism (comparing God to a human being). He was tried in Cairo and imprisoned. When released two years later he resumed his offensive teaching and was put under house arrest in Alexandria. A year later he was allowed to return to Cairo, where he spent three years before returning to Damascus in 712/1313.

He resumed his uncompromising teaching and renewed his criticisms of *bida'*, new ideas and practices that he deemed non-Islamic (e.g. intercession of saints, and pilgrimage to the tombs of saints and prophets). For fifteen years he taught and delivered *fatwas*, 'decrees', which often provoked opposition from religious and political leaders. In 726/1326 he was arrested again and put in prison, where he continued to write and propagate his ideas. He died in jail two years later, having produced a considerable number of writings.

Ibn Taymiyya adopted a literal approach to the Qur'an. He taught that if the Qur'anic text appears to contradict reason, one should not resort to an allegorical interpretation. Instead we must actively trust God and rely entirely on him, *tafwiḍ*. We must acknowledge his supremacy and submit unreservedly to him, *taslim*. The teaching of the early Muslims, *salaf*, played a key role in Ibn Taymiyya's religious thought. Thus the example and ideas of the Prophet's companions and their immediate successors far outweighed the doctrines of Muslim scholars, even the most celebrated ones. Ibn Taymiyya also advocated a close association between Islam and the State. The State, he argued, has the duty of ensuring that Islam is prevalent in society; and on the other hand, the implementation of Islamic law is to prevent the State from becoming merely a human institution or dictatorship. Thus the mission of the Islamic State is to promote justice and to establish a society committed to the worship of God. This vision leaves little room, if any, for non-Muslims living alongside the Muslim community. In fact, Ibn Taymiyya was opposed to the building of synagogues and churches in Islamic lands.

Today Ibn Taymiyya remains a controversial figure. While some Muslims consider him heretical, others have a great admiration for his personal godliness, his courage in enduring persecution, his understanding of Islam as an all-embracing religion, and, above all, for the commanding part played by the Qur'an and the Hadith in his teaching. It is no wonder that conservative Muslims – and often fundamentalist Muslims – see him as an inspiring example and champion of the Islamic faith.

Muḥammad 'Abduh (1265/1849 – 1323/1905)

Muḥammad 'Abduh was a celebrated Muslim theologian and reformer who played a leading role in the revival of Islamic thought during the nineteenth century. He was born to a peasant family in Egypt and in 1862 was sent to a theological school in Ṭanṭa, where he was more interested in Sufism. From 1866 to 1877 he studied at al-Azhar, the most prestigious academic institution in the Muslim world, yet was profoundly disappointed with the old-fashioned teaching he received.

In 1872 he met Jamal-ul-Din al-Afghani (1838–1897), a Muslim intellectual and revolutionary, and became one of his disciples. In 1878 he was appointed as a teacher at one of the al-Azhar colleges, and two years later became the editor of the official Egyptian gazette. In 1881 he was accused of taking part in the revolt against the regime and the British. He was exiled the following year, moving to Beirut and then to Paris, where, together with Afghani, he launched a paper to propagate their nationalistic ideology. In 1885 he returned to Beirut, where he stayed for three years, teaching at a theological school and writing his main theological work, *Risalat al-tawḥid*, 'The Epistle on Monotheism'.

Muḥammad 'Abduh was allowed to return to Egypt in 1888. He held various posts in the judiciary before being appointed to the newly created Executive Council of al-Azhar. He undertook an ambitious programme: reforming Islamic teaching, modernizing Arabic language and introducing the teaching of European languages. In 1893 he became *Grand*

Mufti of Egypt, which involved interpreting the Shari'a. He issued several *fatwas*, which seemed very courageous at the time. He declared lawful the lending of money with interest – despite the Qur'anic prohibition (2:276), and permitted the wearing of European clothes and the eating of meat from animals slaughtered by non-Muslims.

In his reforms 'Abduh sought to reconcile Islam with modernity, religion with science, and faith with reason. One of his slogans was that 'Islam is a rational and scientific religion', *al-islam din-ul-'aql wa-l-'ilm*. He believed that Muslims could benefit from the scientific and techno-logical progress achieved in Europe without renouncing any of their fun-damental beliefs. Muslims, he said, had to look critically at Islamic tradition and stick only to the Qur'an and authentic Sunna. On many theological issues he suggested a middle (and narrow) path between the Ash'arite and Mu'tazilite schools, often leaning towards the latter because of its emphasis on rational thinking, which seemed more in tune with modern civilization.

'Abduh was a pioneer in his attitude to other religions, possibly because he had many Christian friends. He taught that non-Muslims who follow their prophets and comply with rational religious standards will be saved on the Day of Judgment. His apologetic pamphlet against Christianity was a response to attacks on Islam by European authors (e.g. Ernest Renan) and Arab Christians. For him, Islam, being a rational religion, less idealistic and more concerned with the issues of this world, was superior to Christianity.

'Abduh's influence is still felt worldwide among Muslims, especially through his well-known commentary on the Qur'an, *Tafsir al-Manar*. This commentary, which he taught at al-Azhar (1890–1905), was initially published in the monthly *al-Manar* ('The Lighthouse'). By the time of his death only some portions had appeared. The full commentary was later collated by one of his disciples, Rachid Rida, who not only edited it but also added his own views. Although Rida was 'Abduh's most devout disciple, he was very different from his mentor: he did not have the same academic background and intellectual calibre, and his writings reflected a passionate, conservative and polemical approach to religion. Rida was the first to publish the *Gospel of Barnabas* in Arabic.

Notes

[1] Cf. L. Massignon, *Hallaj: Mystic and Martyr*.
[2] French edition by J. D. Luciani (Paris: Leroux, 1938).

3 Ghazali, *The Ninety-Nine Beautiful Names of God*, pp. 149–158.
4 See C. Addas, *Quest for the Red Sulphur: The Life of Ibn 'Arabi*.
5 See A. Culme-Seymour (tr.), *The Wisdom of the Prophets*.

Appendix B
Time-line of Christian–Muslim relations

570	Birth of Muhammad.
582	Muhammad makes his first journey to Syria with his uncle Abu Ṭalib. He meets a Nestorian Christian monk, Baḥira.
615	Some Muslims seek refuge in the Christian Kingdom of Abyssinia.
622	The *hijrah* or emigration. Year one in the Islamic calendar. With seventy companions Muhammad leaves his hometown and settles in Yathrib, which is renamed Medina.
623	Muhammad issues the 'Constitution of Medina', which gives equal status to all citizens in Medina regardless of their beliefs, provided they accept Islamic leadership.
624	The *qibla*, the direction of prayer for the Muslim community, is changed from Jerusalem to Mecca. Relations with the Jewish community deteriorate and result in the expulsion of all Jews from Medina.
628	Muhammad is said to have sent letters to the Byzantine and Persian emperors, to the Negus and to the Governor of Alexandria inviting them to convert to Islam.
629	Battle of Mu'ta (east of the River Jordan). The Muslims are defeated by the Byzantines.
630	A Christian delegation from Najran (south of Arabia) holds talks with Muhammad in Medina.
631	Battle of Tabuk with the Byzantine army. The outcome

	is inconclusive but many Arab tribes convert to Islam, as well as many Jews and Christians.
632	Death of Muhammad.
634	Fall of Jerusalem.
634–44	'Umar b. al-Khaṭṭab, the second caliph. He orders the expulsion of Jews and Christians from Arabia. His name is also associated with what is known as 'the Covenant of 'Umar', which regulates the relationship between the non-Muslim population and the Muslim rule in a conquered territory. Based on sura 9:29, this Covenant guarantees to Jews and Christians freedom of worship and protection of their lives and property. In return, they must pay a poll tax called *jizya* and submit to Islamic social and political order. Their status is that of *dhimmis*, a group of people protected by and subject to the Islamic regime. A Christian Persian slave assassinates 'Umar.
635	Fall of Damascus.
641	Conquest of Egypt. Since the Christians had been badly treated by the Byzantine rulers who saw them as heretics (due to their monophysite beliefs), they welcomed the Muslim conquerors.
661–750	The Umayyad Empire with Damascus as its capital.
675–752	St John of Damascus. A former high-ranking civil servant in the Umayyad administration, John is a monk, theologian, poet and musician. He sees Islam as a Christian heresy.
711	Muslim army crosses over Gibraltar into Spain.
718	Muslim army defeated by the Byzantine army near Constantinople.
732	Battle of Poitiers (France). The Muslim army is defeated by Charles Martel.
750–1258	The Abbasid Empire with Baghdad as its capital.
756–1031	Umayyad dynasty in Spain with Cordoba as its capital. Spain becomes *al-Andalus*, Andalusia.
780–855	Ibn Ḥanbal.
781	The third caliph, al-Mahdi, and the head of the Nestorian Church, the Catholicos Timothy, engage in Christian–Muslim dialogue.
800–1080	Christian scholars in Baghdad translate philosophical,

medical and scientific works from Greek and Syriac into Arabic. Syrian Christians (e.g. Ḥunayn Ibn Isḥaq) translate the Bible into Arabic for the first time, together with other Christian writings.

847–61   The Abbasid caliph, al-Mutawakkil. He issues discriminatory laws against Jews and Christians (850). They have to observe a dress code, *ghiyar*, to mark them out as non-Muslims.

850–60   The Spanish Martyrs' Movement. Muslim authorities execute some fifty Christians in response to public defamation of Muhammad and Islam by Spanish Christians.

858–922   Ḥallaj.

870–950   Farabi. This Muslim philosopher, known as 'the second Master' (the first being Aristotle), had Christian teachers in Baghdad.

873–935   Ashʿari.

909–1169   The Fatimid caliphate in Egypt. The caliph al-Ḥakim (1000–1021) persecutes Christians and destroys the Tomb of the Holy Sepulchre in Jerusalem (1009).

980–1037   Ibn Sina (Avicenna). His teacher in medicine was a Nestorian Christian, *al-Masiḥi*, 'The Christian'.

994–1064   Ibn Ḥazm.

1054   Split in the church resulting in two separate churches: the Latin or Roman Catholic Church and the Greek or Byzantine Orthodox Church.

1058–1111   Ghazali (Algazel).

1071   The Byzantine army is defeated by the Seljuk Turks (from Central Asia) at Mantzikert (Turkey). As a result, the Seljuks (who had invaded Baghdad in 1055) expand their empire into most of Asia Minor, a former Byzantine territory. The Byzantine emperor appeals to the pope for help.

1086–1147   A Berber dynasty, al-Murabiṭun (Almoravids), rules in Spain and part of North Africa. They undertake the re-Islamization of the Muslim population and deport Arabic-speaking Christians from Spain to Morocco (1127). Al-Murabiṭun are replaced by another Berber dynasty, al-Muwaḥḥidun (Almohads), who carry out a radical Islamic reform (1147–1269). Synagogues are destroyed in Morocco, and Jews are summoned to choose between conversion to Islam and death. Many flee, including Cordoba-born Jewish philosopher Ibn Maymun (Maimonides), who leaves Fez and settles in Cairo (1165). Five Franciscan missionaries, who came to Marrakesh (1220), and seven others, who came to Ceuta (1227), are executed.

1092–1156	Peter the Venerable writes two apologetical works on Islam. He is the initiator of the first Latin translation of the Qur'an, completed in 1143 in Toledo.
1096	Capture of Jerusalem by the Crusaders, who slaughter the Jewish and Muslim populations of the city. The Dome of the Rock is turned into a church.
1100–1250	Jewish and Christian scholars in Andalusia (especially in Toledo) translate Greek works and Muslim commentaries on them from Arabic into Latin.
1126–96	Ibn Rushd (Averroës).
1149–1209	Razi.
1165–1240	Ibn 'Arabi.
1187	Ṣalaḥ al-Din (Saladin) recaptures Jerusalem. His attitude towards Christians is exemplary. He guarantees their safety and gives them back the control of the holy sites.
1219	Francis of Assisi meets the Sultan of Egypt, al-Malik al-Kamil. His loving attitude towards Muslims stands in sharp contrast to the attitudes of other Christian leaders in the crusading movement (e.g. Peter the Hermit, Bernard of Clairvaux).
1225–74	Thomas Aquinas. His writings show that both Avicenna and Averroës (whom he quotes) have exerted a significant influence on his thought.
1235–1316	Ramon Lull (born in Majorca). He learns Arabic and becomes (at the age of sixty) a missionary to Tunisia and Algeria, where he dies.
1250–1382	The Baḥri Mameluke Sultanate of Egypt and Syria. Under this dynasty of a Turkish background, Jews and Christians often suffer persecution. Churches and synagogues are destroyed and people are forced to convert to Islam.
1263–1328	Ibn Taymiyya.
1270	Louis IX (St Louis), King of France, dies (from illness)

in Carthage (Tunisia) during the Eighth Crusade. He had led the Seventh Crusade to Egypt, where he was made prisoner and was ransomed with a huge sum paid in gold.

1281–1918   The Ottoman Empire.

1332–1406   Ibn Khaldun (a great historian and sociologist).

1354   The Ottoman army crosses over into Europe. As a result of the battle of Kosovo (1389) the Ottomans conquer the Balkans in the subsequent decades.

1453   Fall of Constantinople. Mehmed II conquers the capital of the Byzantine Empire. The city, given the new name of Istanbul, becomes the capital of the Ottoman Empire. Santa Sophia is turned into a mosque.

1492   Fall of Granada. End of Muslim rule in Spain.

1529   Unsuccessful siege of Vienna by the Ottoman army.

1683   Ottoman attack on Vienna repulsed.

1849–1905   Muḥammad ʿAbduh.

1855   The status of *dhimmis* is abolished in Egypt. Other Muslim countries will follow suit.

1918   Collapse of the Ottoman Empire in the aftermath of World War I.

1920   The League of Nations establishes British mandate over Iraq and Palestine. France is given mandate over Syria and Lebanon.

1924   Kemal Ataturk founds the secular Republic of Turkey and abolishes the caliphate.

1948   The State of Israel is created in Palestine. First war between Israel and Arab countries.

1979   Foundation of the Islamic Republic of Iran.

Bibliography

'Abduh, Muḥammad *Tafsir al-Manar*, 12 vols. (Cairo: Dar al-manar, 4th edn, 1954).

Abu Dawud, *Sunan*, 3 vols., tr. Ahmad Hasan (1984; Lahore: Ashraf Publishers, repr. 1988).

Abu El-Assal, Riah, *Caught in Between: The Story of an Arab Palestinian Christian Israeli* (London: SPCK, 1999).

Addas, C., *Quest for the Red Sulphur: The Life of Ibn 'Arabi* (Cambridge: Islamic Texts Society, 1993).

'Ali, 'Abdullah Yusuf, *The Holy Qur'an: Translation and Commentary* (Beltsville, MD: Amana Corporation, 6th edn, 1989).

Anderson, Norman, *Islam in the Modern World: A Christian Perspective* (Leicester: Apollos, 1990).

'Ata ur-Rahim, Muḥammad, *Jesus, a Prophet of Islam* (London: MWH Publishers, 2nd edn, 1979).

Ateek, Naim, *Justice, Only Justice: A Palestinian Theology of Liberation* (Maryknoll, NY: Orbis, 1989).

Ayoub, M., 'Towards an Islamic Christology: An Image of Jesus in Early Shi'i Muslim Literature', *Muslim World*, vol. 66, no. 3 (July 1976), pp. 163–188.

Badawi, Jamal, *Muhammad in the Bible* (Halifax, NS: Islamic Information Foundation; repr. from *al-Ittihad* (January–March 1992).

Baqillani, Abu Bakr Muḥammad, *Kitab al-Tamhid*, ed. R. McCarthy (Beirut: Librairie Orientale, 1957).

Bennis, P., and K. Mansour, '"Praise God and Pass the Ammunition!" The Changing Nature of Israel's US Backers', *Middle East Report*, no.

208 (fall 1998), pp. 16–18, 43.

Blomberg, Craig, *The Historical Reliability of the Gospels* (Leicester: Inter-Varsity Press, 1987).

Borrmans, Maurice, *Jésus et les musulmans d'aujourd'hui* (Paris: Desclée, coll. 'Jésus et Jésus-Christ', no. 69, 1996).

Bucaille, Maurice, *The Bible, the Qur'an and the Science: The Holy Scriptures Examined in the Light of Modern Knowledge* (Indianapolis, IN: American Trust Publications, 1979).

Bukhari, *Ṣaḥīḥ*, 9 vols., tr. Muḥammad Muḥsen Khan (Beirut: Dar al-arabia, Arabic–English edn, 1985).

Campbell, William, *The Qur'an and the Bible in the Light of History and Science* (Marseilles: Middle East Resources, n.d.).

Chacour, Elias, *Blood Brothers* (Eastbourne: Kingsway, 1984).

Chapman, Colin, *Whose Promised Land? Israel or Palestine?* (Oxford: Lion, 1983).

—————— *Islam and the West: Conflict, Co-existence or Conversion?* (Carlisle: Paternoster, 1998).

Chodkiewicz, Michel, *The Seal of the Saints: Prophethood and Sainthood in the Doctrine of Ibn 'Arabi* (Cambridge: Islamic Text Society, 1986).

Cirillo, Luigi, and Michel Frémaux (eds.), *Evangile de Barnabé, Recherches sur la composition et l'origine; texte et traduction* (Paris: Beauchesne, 1977).

Cragg, Kenneth, *Jesus and the Muslim: An Exploration* (London: George Allen & Unwin, 1985).

—————— *Readings in the Qur'an* (London: Collins, 1988).

—————— *Palestine: The Prize and Price of Zion* (London: Cassell, 1997).

Culme-Seymour, A. (tr.), *The Wisdom of the Prophets* (Aldsworth, UK: Beshara, 1975).

Deedat, Ahmed, *What the Bible Says about Muhammad* (Birmingham: Islamic Vision, n.d.).

—————— *Crucifixion or Cruci-fiction?* (Durban: Islamic Propagation Centre International, 1984).

Encyclopaedia of the Hadith (*Mawsu'at al-Hadith al-sharif*) (Cairo: Sakhr Software, 1995).

Faruqi, Isma'il, *Islam and Other Faiths*, ed. A. Siddiqui (Leicester: Islamic Foundation, 1998).

—————— *et al. Christian Mission and Islamic Da'wah* (Leicester: Islamic Foundation, 1982).

Gaudeul, Jean-Marie, *Encounters and Clashes: Islam and Christianity in History*, vol. 1: Survey; vol. 2: Texts (Rome: PISAI, 1984).

Ghazali, Abu Ḥamid, *al-Radd al-jamil li-ilahiyyat ʿIsa bi-ṣariḥi l-Injil*, ed. and tr. R. Chidiac, with Introduction, Notes and Commentary, as *Réfutation excellente de la divinité de Jésus-Christ d'après les évangiles* (Paris: Presses Universitaires de France, Arabic–French edn, 1939).

——— *The Ninety-Nine Beautiful Names of God*, tr. D. Burrell and N. Dahar (Cambridge: Islamic Texts Society, 1995).

Gimaret, Daniel, *Les Noms divins en Islam* (Paris: Cerf, coll. 'Patrimoines', 1988).

——— *La Doctrine d'al-Ashʿari* (Paris: Cerf, coll. 'Patrimoines', 1990).

——— *Dieu à l'image de l'homme* (Paris: Cerf, coll. 'Patrimoines', 1997).

Goddard, Hugh, *Muslim Perceptions of Christianity* (London: Grey Seal, 1996).

——— *A History of Christian–Muslim Relations* (Edinburgh: Edinburgh University Press, 2000).

Guillaume, Alfred (ed.), *The Life of Muhammad: A Translation of Ibn Ishaq's Sirat rasul Allah* (Oxford: Oxford University Press, 1955).

Ḥamidullah, Muḥammad, *Le Saint Coran* (Brentwood, MD: Amana, 1989).

Ibn ʿArabi, Muḥyi l-Din, *al-Futuḥat al-makkiyya*, 4 vols. (1911; Beirut: Dar Sader, repr. 1980).

Ibn Ḥazm, A. M., *Kitab al-Fiṣal fi l-milal wa l-ahwaʾ wa l-niḥal*, 3 vols. (1400 Le Caire: Dar al-fikr, repr. 1980).

Ibn Majah Sunan, tr. M. T. Ansari, 5 vols. (New Delhi: Kitab Bhavan, Arabic–English edn, 1994).

Ibn Taymiyya, Taqi-l-Din Aḥmad, *al-Jawab al-ṣaḥiḥ liman baddala dina l-Masiḥ*, tr. T. David, with Introduction, Notes and Commentary, as *A Muslim Theologian's Response to Christianity* (Delmar, NY: Caravan, 1984).

Juwayni, Abu l-Maʿali, *Shifaʾ al-ghalil fi bayan ma waqaʿa fi l-Tawrat wa-l-Injil min al-tabdil*, ed. M. Allard, with Notes and Commentary, in *Textes apologétiques de Guwayni* (Beirut: Dar al-mashriq, Arabic–French edn, 1968).

Kerr, David, ' "He walked in the Path of the Prophets": Toward Christian Theological Recognition of the Prophethood of Muhammad', in Y. Ḥaddad and W. Z. Ḥaddad (eds.), *Christian–Muslim Encounters* (Gainesville, FL: University Press of Florida, 1995).

Khawwam, Mounir, *al-Masiḥ fi l-fikri l-islami l-ḥadith wa fi l-masiḥiyya* (Beirut: Khalifa, 1983).

Masood, Steven, *Jesus and the Indian Messiah* (Oldham: Word of Life, 1994).

Massignon, Louis, *Hallaj: Mystic and Martyr*, ed. and tr. H. Mason (Princeton, NJ: Princeton University Press, abridged edn, 1994).

——— *Opera Minora*, 3 vols., ed. Youakim Moubarac (Beirut: Dar al-ma'aref, 1963).

Morey, Robert, *Islam Unveiled: The True Desert Storm* (Shermans Dale, PA: Scholars, 1991).

Moshay, G. J. O., *Who Is This Allah?* (Ibadan, Nigeria: Fireliners International, 1990).

Muslim Christian Research Group, *The Challenge of Scriptures: The Bible and the Qur'an* (Maryknoll, NY: Orbis, 1989).

Muslim, *Sahih*, 4 vols., tr. Abdul Hamid Siddiqi (1977; New Delhi: Kitab Bhavan, repr. 1982).

Neuner, J., and J. Dupuis (eds.), *The Christian Faith in the Documents of the Catholic Church* (London: HarperCollins, 5th edn, 1992).

Newbigin, Lesslie, L. Sanneh and J. Taylor, *Faith and Power: Christianity and Islam in 'Secular' Britain.* (London: SPCK, 1998).

Nielsen, Jorgen, *Muslims in Western Europe* (Edinburgh: Edinburgh University Press, 1992).

O'Mahony, Anthony (ed.), *Palestinian Christians: Religion, Politics and Society in the Holy Land* (London: Melisende, 1999).

Pacini, Andrea (ed.), *Christian Communities in the Arab East: The Challenge of the Future* (Oxford: Clarendon, 1998).

Ragg, Londsale, and Laura Ragg (tr.), *The Gospel of Barnabas* (Oxford: Clarendon, 1907; repr. Rome: Islamic European Cultural Centre, 1986).

Rantisi, Audeh, *Blessed Are the Peacemakers: The Story of a Palestinian Christian* (Guildford: Eagle, 1990).

Razi, Fakhr-ul-Din, *al-Tafsir al-kabir*, 16 vols (1411; Beirut: Dar al-kutub al-'ilmiyya, 1990.

——— *Munazara fi l-radd 'ala l-Nasara* (Beirut: Dar al-gharb al-islami, 1986).

Shahrastani, Muhammad. *Kitab al-Milal wa l-nihal*, tr. D. Gimaret and G. Monnot, with Introduction, Notes and Commentary (Paris: Peeters/ Unesco, 1986).

Shahrur, Muhammad, *al-Kitab wa-l-Qur'an. Qira'a mu'asira* (Damascus: Dar al-ahali, 5th edn, 1992).

Siddiqui, Ataullah, *Christian–Muslim Dialogue in the Twentieth Century* (Basingstoke: Macmillan, 1997).

Slomp, J., 'The Gospel in Dispute', *Islamochristiana*, vol. 4 (1978), pp. 67–111.

Sox, David, *The Gospel of Barnabas* (London: George Allen & Unwin, 1984).

Tabari, Abu Ja'far Muḥammad, *Jami 'l-bayan 'an ta'wili l-Qur'an* (1388; Cairo: Ḥalabi, repr. 1968–1976).

Walker, Peter, *Jesus and the Holy City: New Testament Perspectives on Jerusalem* (Grand Rapids, MI, Cambridge: Eerdmans, 1996).

——— (ed.), *Jerusalem: Past and Present in the Purposes of God* (Cambridge: Tyndale House, 1992).

Weber, T., 'How Evangelicals Became the Best Friends of Israel', *Christianity Today*, vol. 42, no. 11 (5 October 1998), pp. 38–49.

Whiston, William (tr.), *The Works of Flavius Josephus* (London: Ward, Lock & Bowden, n.d.).

Wright, Christopher, *Deuteronomy* (Peabody, MA: Hendrickson, 1996).

Zebiri, Kate, *Muslims and Christians Face to Face* (Oxford: Oneworld, 1997).

General index

Index of Qur'anic references

Index of biblical references